Contents

Identifying more able mathematicians

Giftedness and higher ability in Key Stage 1

Many feel that children in this age group are too young to be labelled as 'gifted'. However, there are certainly children who are more able. There are particular difficulties with identifying more able children in Key Stage 1. For example: children's performance in tests and assessed activities may be highly influenced by the classroom environment and by other factors such as home background; there can be a pronounced difference between children's cognitive and physical development; high levels of mathematical understanding may be masked by poor basic numeracy or literacy skills; children's potential ability will manifest at different rates; and it is more likely at Key Stage 1 than at Key Stage 2 that you will find children who display high ability in one area of maths but not another.

What characteristics might more able mathematicians display?

More able mathematicians are likely to have good powers of logic, reasoning and deduction, and will be able to hypothesise, experiment and categorise. This list of questions may be useful in establishing mathematical ability:

- Do they enjoy number puzzles?
- Do they show a good awareness of patterns and sequences?
- Do they ask interesting mathematical questions?
- Do they give explanations you may not have thought of?
- Are they good at solving problems?
- Are they good at applying knowledge in unfamiliar contexts?
- Do they like to choose their own methods?

This list is by no means exhaustive; there are many more characteristics that may be observed in more able mathematicians, and many able children will display only some of these qualities. For example, a child who you believe to be a high achiever may not show advanced problem-solving skills. This may be because they don't yet know how to set about solving a problem, because they haven't learned the strategies required.

What about children who don't show any of these traits?

There may be highly able mathematicians in your class who do not display any of these characteristics. This could be due to one or more of these factors:

- lack of confidence
- unwillingness to stand out from their peers
- the desire to avoid 'extra' work
- an insufficiently stimulating learning environment
- lack of challenging activities
- lack of familiarity with basic number facts and skills
- language barriers
- problems with reading and/or writing.

What can be done to identify more able mathematicians?

Here are a few suggestions of practical steps that can be taken:

- Ask parents and carers to supply information about any mathematical abilities they have noticed at home. In the early years of schooling, it is especially important to involve parents or carers as early on as possible. They are likely to have observed unusual strengths in their children and this information can be key in identifying the more able early on.
- Conduct a brief interview with children at the beginning of the school year to find out about their interests and anything they think they are especially good at.
- Keep a good record of what you observe children doing and saying in practical maths activities.
- Keep a portfolio of particularly good work completed either at home or in school. This will help to assess progress and spot patterns.
- Testing can provide evidence of high ability, but it is important to remember that, especially at Key Stage 1, some very able children may not perform well in tests, and many factors can affect children's performance in a test environment.

The identification–provision cycle

A two-way process of identification and provision is needed. You will not be able to observe exceptional abilities in children unless they are given the opportunity to demonstrate them. Activities must be provided that challenge children and allow them the scope to show what they can do. In this way, appropriate provision leads to identification, which in turn allows you to make better provision.

We recommend that at the beginning of each topic you include the whole class in an activity that gives opportunities for children to take the work as far as they can. This will allow you to identify the children who are more able in that area of maths. (See the assessment activities on pages 18–27.)

Providing for more able mathematicians

How can a stimulating learning environment be created?

It is important to create an atmosphere in which children feel they are able to ask questions, and have access to resources to find the answers. One practical thing you can do is to create interactive displays, or perhaps a 'Challenge corner': an area of the classroom where you can set out maths resources, puzzles, problem-solving scenarios, prompts and questions for children to explore. This should be accessible by all children in the class, giving everyone the opportunity to challenge themselves. If you have a 'role play' corner, this can provide lots of opportunities for children to use and apply mathematics in real-life contexts.

How can questions be used?

More able children should be asked probing and open-ended questions. These will allow you to assess and extend their understanding, get them to think more deeply, and lead them to continue their explorations. Here are some examples of the types of question you might ask:

- What do you think will happen if …?
- How many different ways can you …?
- Is it always true that …?
- Why?
- What patterns can you see?
- Why did you choose to work it out like that?
- Why do you think this happens?
- How do you know that?
- Can you make up a rule?

Children should be encouraged to ask these sorts of question themselves.

What are 'challenge' activities?

'Challenging' work can be defined as something difficult that requires the learner to learn something new. For children to enjoy a challenging activity there must be something about it that motivates them. For example, it could be about a subject that they are particularly interested in, or it could be placed in a meaningful context, with a goal that has nothing to do with completing a page of calculations. The level of challenge must be just right – it must stretch them without being so difficult that children are demotivated and want to give up. The best challenge activities will allow different levels of outcome, so that a wide range of children can succeed at them.

More able children need to be given opportunities to:

- be creative
- exercise their curiosity and explore new ideas
- choose their own ways of working and representing their results
- ask questions and find the answers
- make conjectures and test them out
- discuss their ideas with adults and other children
- reflect on their own work.

More able mathematicians are likely to acquire new skills more quickly than their peers. If they are then asked to practise these skills for too long, they may lose interest. More able mathematicians are also likely to be able to spot quicker or more efficient ways to work things out, and they should be encouraged to explore their chosen methods.

How should children record their work?

Where possible, give children the opportunity to choose how they record their workings and answers: in writing; in pictures; in diagrams; using ICT; taking photographs; or using physical objects such as cubes. As often as possible, leave a variety of equipment on the table when children are taking part in activities, and make it clear that they can choose anything they wish to record their thinking.

What thinking skills should more able children be using?

More able children need to be given opportunities to access their higher-order thinking skills. Bloom's Taxonomy identifies six levels of thinking:

- knowledge – the acquisition and recall of facts
- comprehension – the ability to describe what you know in your own words
- application – the application of what you have learned in context
- analysis – for example, categorising things and identifying patterns
- synthesis – the creation of new ideas or products
- evaluation – the evaluation of ideas, processes and products.

The first three are generally thought of as lower-order skills, although application requires a deeper level of thinking than the first two. If you can plan activities that incorporate the three higher-order thinking skills, children will be challenged.

Introducing *Abacus Evolve Challenge*

What is *Abacus Evolve Challenge*?

Abacus Evolve Challenge is designed to stretch and motivate more able mathematicians. The activities are creative and engaging, and offer opportunities for written, verbal and practical work. Using & Applying skills are practised throughout, with plenty of open-ended investigations and problem solving. Speaking & Listening skills are promoted through the high proportion of paired and group work.

Which children is *Challenge* for?

Challenge is not just for those children who would be classed as 'gifted' or highly able. The activities have been written with the whole of the 'top table' in mind. Differentiation by outcome is often possible because of the open-ended nature of the activities, and the teacher notes accompanying the activities usually suggest ways to differentiate further.

What types of enrichment and extension are provided?

Breadth – allows children to experience additional material outside of the core offering, rehearse ideas in different contexts, and make connections between areas of maths.

Depth – is achieved by asking children to delve deeper into the concepts. It is about thinking intellectually.

Pace – refers to speed in covering the curriculum and can result in achievement at a level exceptional for the age range.

What types of activity are provided?

Adult-led – these activities allow children to work with an adult. There are two adult-led activities per two-week block.

Game – these activities allow children to use what they have learned with the rest of the class by playing a game in pairs or groups.

Problem – these activities allow children to apply their mathematical understanding to solve problems.

Investigate – these activities allow children to explore a concept freely, asking questions, looking for patterns and drawing conclusions.

When should the *Challenge* activities be used?

There are 90 activities per Year; six for every two-week block. They are intended to be used by small groups of children in the part of the maths lesson when the class is split into groups for differentiated work. This allows the more able children to be included in the whole-class parts of the lesson.

What level of adult support is needed?

The *Challenge* resources have been designed with effective classroom management in mind. Four of the activities in each two-week block can be carried out by children without adult support, allowing you to focus on the other groups. Some of these will require a couple of minutes to get the group started on the activity, but after this children should be able to continue unaided.

Two of the activities in each two-week block require adult support, so that your more able children have the benefits of adult input.

How does *Challenge* fit alongside the *Abacus Evolve* maths scheme?

The *Challenge* activities are organised using the same blocked structure as *Abacus Evolve*. You can use the *Abacus Evolve* weekly plans, and fit the *Challenge* activities into these. *Abacus Evolve* objectives are referenced for each activity, and these will help you to decide which core activities to run them alongside. If you also have the *Challenge* Module of I-Planner Online, you will be able to see the *Challenge* activities allocated to suitable days in the weekly plans.

It is intended that the more able children join in with the whole-class parts of the lesson: the mental oral starter, the main teaching activity, and the plenary. When the class is split up into 1-dot, 2-dot and 3-dot groups to do Textbook activities or practical activities, you can give your top group a *Challenge* activity that fits in well with what the rest of the class are doing.

Can I use *Challenge* with another maths scheme or my own planning?

Although the *Challenge* activities complement *Abacus Evolve* activities, they are not specifically linked to them, so there is no dependence on any part of the *Abacus Evolve* scheme. The *Challenge* activities can be used to accompany any other maths scheme or your own planning. You can search for *Challenge* activities that fit your teaching by looking at the Renewed Framework objectives in this Teacher Guide. All of the Renewed Framework objectives are covered by the *Challenge* activities.

Using the *Challenge* resources

What resources are in the *Challenge* range?

Each Year includes:

- a Teacher Guide
- a Workbook or Textbook
- an I-Planner Online Module.

Teacher Guide

The Teacher Guide contains detailed notes to accompany each activity. The information provided includes:

- suggested group size and adult support
- resources required (Workbook pages, Photocopy Masters and other resources)
- *Abacus Evolve* objectives
- Renewed Framework objectives
- a description of the activity
- 'Extra help': ideas for differentiating at a lower level
- 'Further extension': ideas for differentiating at a higher level
- 'If you have time': ideas for continuing the activity
- background maths information for the non-specialist teacher
- 'Be aware': things to watch out for, such as common misconceptions
- outcomes for the activity, given in child-friendly language
- ideas for other resources to support the activity, such as useful websites or stories.

Textbook

Roughly half of the Year 2 *Challenge* activities are accompanied by a Textbook page. The pages are colourful and engaging, and they include the following features:

- speech bubbles to indicate opportunities for discussion
- an Extra activity at the bottom of each page for children who finish early.

The Textbook pages are not just intended for children to use individually. They are usually suitable for paired or group work.

I-Planner Online

The *Abacus Evolve* I-Planner is a powerful online tool that provides ready-to-use weekly, medium-term and yearly plans that are completely flexible. It can save hours of planning time, but allows you to adapt the plans to meet the exact needs of your class. The *Challenge* module of I-Planner for each Year includes an extra column in the weekly plans in which you can see all the *Challenge* activities allocated to suitable days. This allows you to plan the *Challenge* activities seamlessly into your maths lessons.

What support is provided for assessing the children?

The adult-led activities are ideal for day-to-day observational assessment, as they provide plenty of opportunities to work closely with the children and ask probing questions to ascertain their level of understanding.

The charts on pages 10–13 of this book show the Assessment Foci from the Assessing Pupils' Progress guidelines, and the *Challenge* activities that can be used to provide evidence towards this type of periodic assessment.

On pages 18–27 of this book you will find six assessment activities. These will help you to assess prior learning and identify children's potential in each strand of maths.

Icon guide

Group size

Children working individually, without an adult

Children working in pairs, without an adult

Children working in groups, without an adult

Children working in groups, with an adult

Type of resource

Textbook

Photocopy Master

Additional resources

Type of enrichment/extension

Breadth

Depth

Pace

Type of activity

Adult-led

Game

Problem

Investigate

Support for Assessing Pupil's Progress

If you are using Assessing Pupil's Progress to assess children, you may find this chart helpful when deciding which of the *Challenge* activities could be used to provide evidence towards each Assessment Focus.

We do not recommend that you use every activity to make an assessment. It is also important to recognise that a full assessment cannot be made on the basis of the *Challenge* activities alone; you will need to draw on other sources of information as well. We would advise that in each block of work you use this chart as guidance towards choosing one activity to assess against APP criteria, to complement other day-to-day or periodic assessments.

The Year 2 *Challenge* activities should give children the opportunity to work at a high Level 2, and in many cases at a low or secure Level 3.

	Ma1 Using and applying mathematics		
	Problem solving	**Communicating**	**Reasoning**
Level 3	• A1.5 Digits • C1.3 Measure me! • D2.3 Packaging • A3.6 Difference • B3.1 Carpet tiles • C3.3 Water lines • D3.5 Waiting for hours • E3.3 Totals with 2p and 5p coins • E3.5 Shape fractions	• D2.2 The shape sorter • D2.3 Packaging • E2.6 Remainder game • A3.1 HTU game • A3.2 Number chains • C3.4 Subtraction towers • C3.6 Raffle ticket table • E3.1 Multiplying then dividing • E3.4 Near doubles	• A1.5 Digits • A2.2 Odd and even dominoes • A2.3 Walk the plank! • D2.3 Packaging • B3.4 Clothes problems • C3.4 Subtraction towers • E3.2 Multiplication and division arrays • E3.5 Shape fractions
Level 2	• A1.3 How many? • B1.1 Fame and fortune	• A1.4 Moving the zero • A1.6 Star numbers • C1.4 My day • D1.1 Pass it on! • A2.4 Order puzzles • B2.5 Ice-skating • D2.1 In my basket	• B1.2 Doughnuts • B1.3 Chasing 21 • B1.4 To and fro • B1.5 Punctuation maths • D1.5 Last can! • E1.2 Function machines • E1.4 Two coins investigation

Ma2 Number

	Numbers and the number system	Fractions and decimals	Operations, relationships between them
Level 3	• A1.5 Digits • A2.1 Number cascades • A2.5 Number puzzles • A2.6 Greater than, less than • A3.1 HTU game • A3.2 Number chains • A3.3 5 up, 50 up	• E3.6 Chomp the chocolate	• E1.5 Which three toys? • E1.6 Snack shop • B2.3 Darts • D2.6 Question swap • E2.1 Exploring multiples • E2.2 Multiplication race • E2.4 Multiplication monsters • E2.5 Plates of fruit • A3.6 Difference • B3.4 Clothes problems • B3.6 Spokes and wheels • D3.3 Misprints • E3.1 Multiplying then dividing • E3.2 Multiplication and division arrays
Level 2	• A1.1 Number strips • A1.2 Target 100 • A1.3 How many? • A1.4 Moving the zero • A1.6 Star numbers • B1.4 To and fro	• B3.2 Halving shapes • B3.3 Queuing at the supermarket • E3.5 Shape fractions	• B1.5 Punctuation maths

Ma2 Number			
	Mental methods	**Solving numerical problems**	**Written methods**
Level 3	• E1.2 Function machines • E1.3 Three in a row • D2.5 How much change? • D2.6 Question swap • E2.1 Exploring multiples • E2.2 Multiplication race • E2.3 Known multiplication facts • B3.5 Matching outfits • C3.5 Digit tree • D3.1 The cruise 1 • D3.2 The cruise 2 • D3.3 Misprints • E3.3 Totals with 2p and 5p coins • E3.4 Near doubles	• D1.4 Word problems • E1.5 Which three toys? • E1.6 Snack shop • D2.4 Egg boxes • E2.3 Known multiplication facts • E2.5 Plates of fruit • E2.6 Remainder game • A3.4 Frog additions • A3.5 Kangaroo additions • B3.3 Queuing at the supermarket • B3.5 Matching outfits • B3.6 Spokes and wheels • C3.2 Fruit cocktail • D3.1 The cruise 1 • D3.2 The cruise 2 • D3.4 It's ready!	
Level 2	• B1.1 Fame and fortune • B1.2 Doughnuts • B1.3 Chasing 21 • D1.6 Crocodile teeth • E1.1 Half a length • B2.1 Building monsters • B2.2 Making squares	• B1.6 Missing coins • C1.6 30 days hath September • E1.4 Two coins investigation	• D1.5 Last can! • D1.6 Crocodile teeth • E2.4 Multiplication monsters • E2.6 Remainder game • E3.2 Multiplication and division arrays

Ma3 Shape, space and measures			
	Properties of shape	**Properties of position and movement**	**Measures**
Level 3	• D2.2 The shape sorter • D2.3 Packaging • B3.2 Halving shapes	• B2.4 Square corners • B2.5 Ice-skating • B2.6 Getting to the wedding	• C1.1 Strip book • C1.3 Measure me! • C2.1 How heavy? • C2.2 More or less? • C2.3 Changing times • C3.1 Litre line • C3.2 Fruit cocktail • C3.3 Water lines • D3.4 It's ready! • D3.5 Waiting for hours • D3.6 The clock shop
Level 2	• D1.1 Pass it on! • D2.1 In my basket • B3.1 Carpet tiles	• D1.2 What's missing? • D1.3 What is the shape? • A2.4 Order puzzles	• C1.2 Duck dinner time • C1.4 My day • C1.5 Units of time game • C1.6 30 days hath September • E1.1 Half a length • B2.6 Getting to the wedding

Ma4 Handling data		
	Processing and representing data	**Interpreting data**
Level 3	• C2.5 Tom's drinks • C2.6 Fun in the snow	• C2.5 Tom's drinks • C2.6 Fun in the snow
Level 2	• C2.4 Names in our class • C3.6 Raffle ticket table	• C2.4 Names in our class • C3.6 Raffle ticket table

Talk Maths Extra pupil software

Abacus Evolve *Talk Maths Extra* will reinforce key maths skills and get children talking about maths.

1 Addition and subtraction

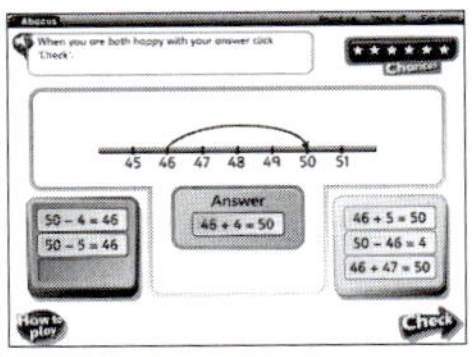

Find the sentence that matches an addition or subtraction shown on a number line.

2 Addition facts

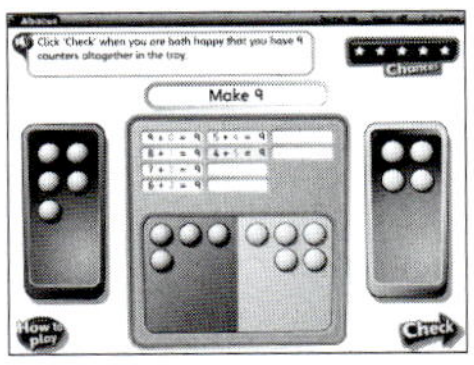

Partition a small number in different ways by placing blue and green counters in a tray.

3 Symmetry

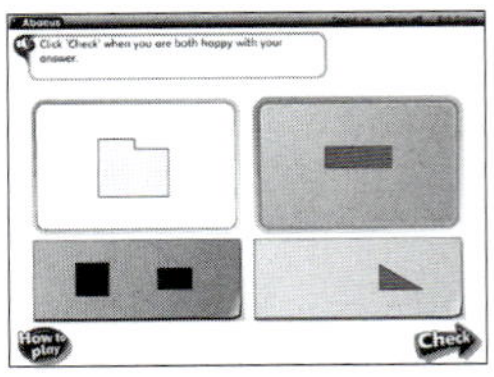

Work out what shape has been cut out of the centre of a piece of paper folded twice.

4 Subtraction

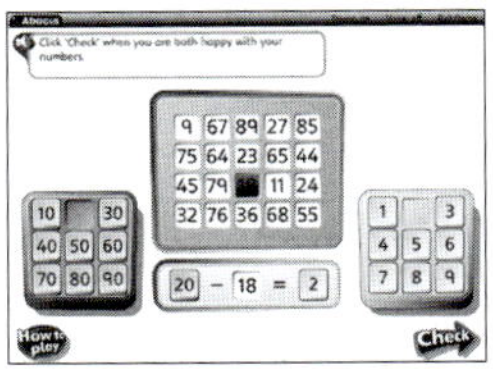

Make 1-digit target numbers by subtracting 2-digit numbers from multiples of 10.

5 Money problems

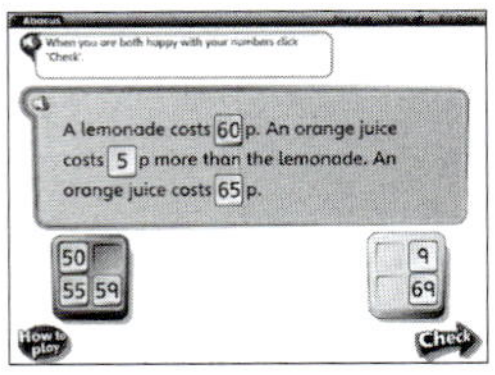

Fill in numbers in a word problem to make a correct addition or subtraction.

6 Number puzzle

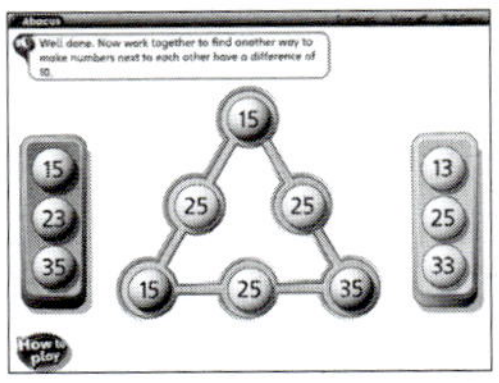

Place numbers so that each pair of adjacent numbers has a difference of 10.

7 Ordering numbers

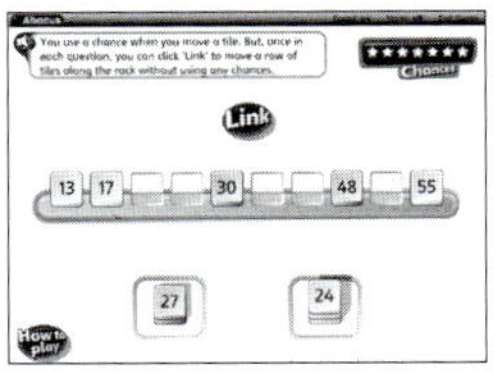

Place non-consecutive numbers onto a rack, aiming to end up with the numbers in order.

8 Printing shapes

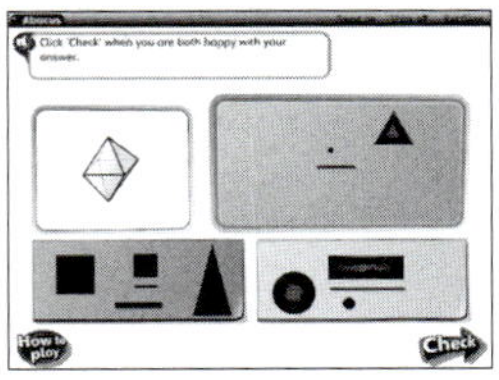

Work out which prints could be made using faces, edges and corners of 3D shapes.

9 Addition and subtraction

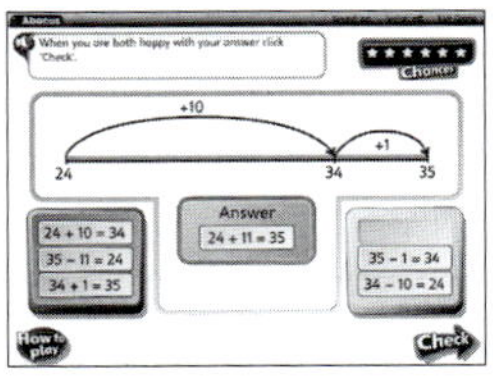

Find the sentence that matches an addition or subtraction shown on a number line.

10 Counting in 2s, 5s and 10s

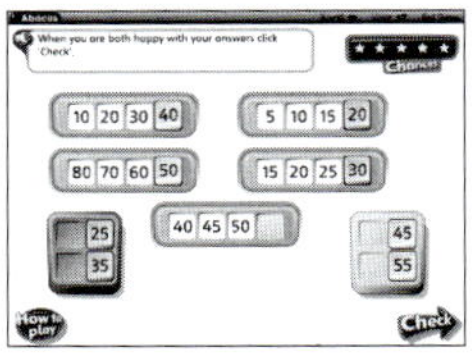

Complete number sequences counting on and back in 2s, 5s and 10s.

11 Making amounts

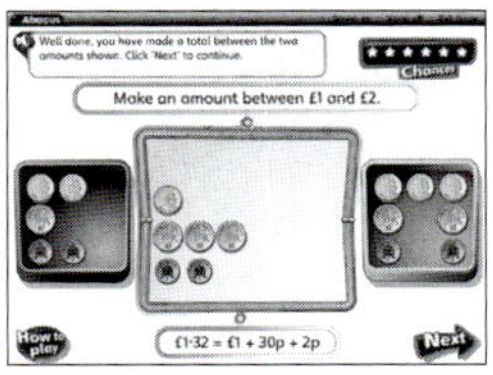

Make amounts in a given range with 1p, 10p and £1 coins.

12 Number puzzle

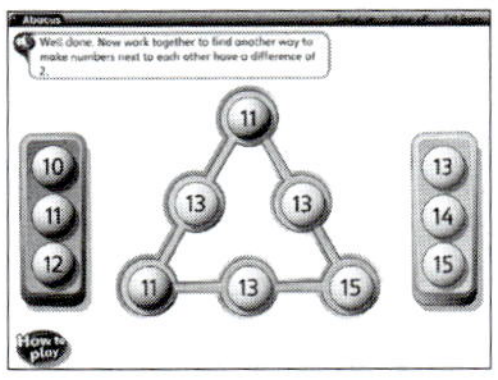

Place numbers so that each pair of adjacent numbers has a difference of 2.

13 Addition facts

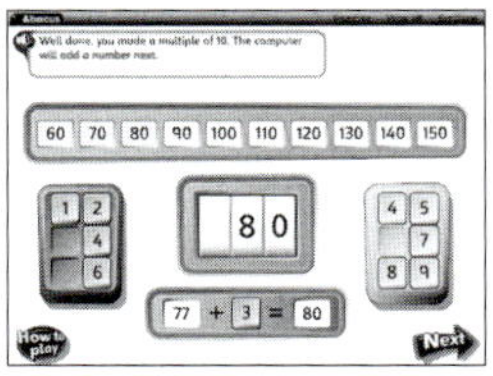

Add to a 2-digit number to make the next multiple of 10.

14 Ordering clocks

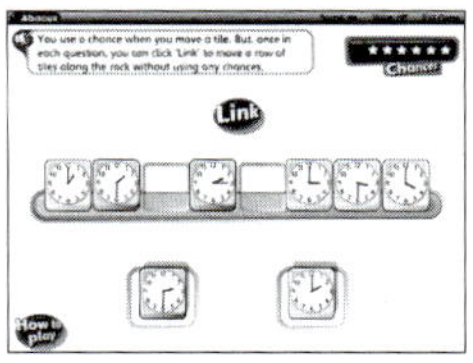

Place non-consecutive o'clock, half past and quarter past times in order.

15 Number detective

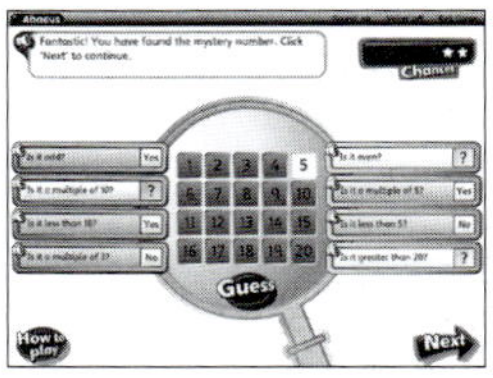

Find a mystery number by eliminating numbers based on clues.

16 Estimating quantities

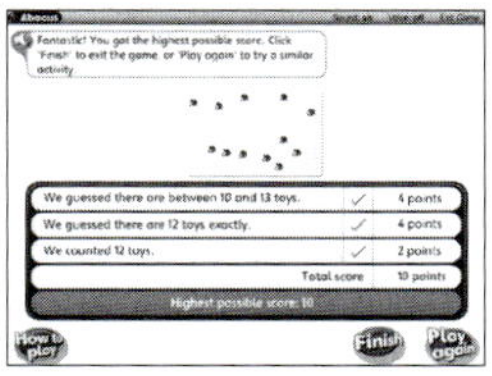

Estimate a number of objects, then count them.

17 Sorting 2D shapes

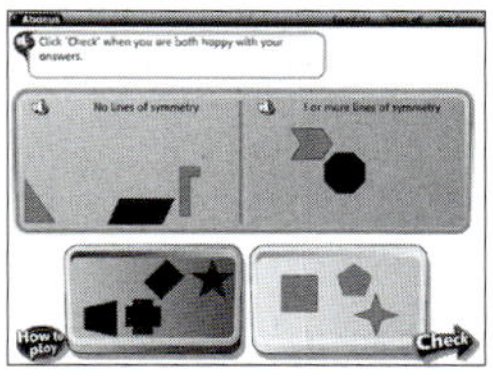

Sort 2D shapes into two sets according to their properties.

18 Toy shelves

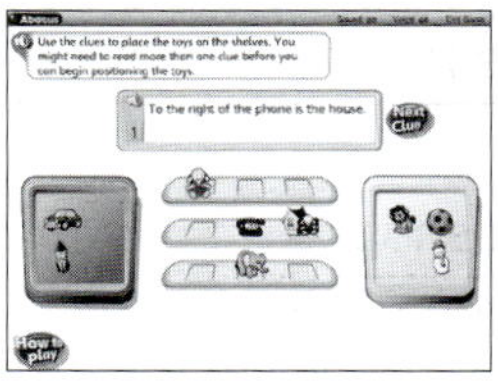

Follow clues to position toys on a shelf.

This chart shows which *Talk Maths Extra* activities could be used to extend some of the *Challenge* activities. The 4-dot version of each *Talk Maths Extra* activity is likely to be the most suitable for your children.

***Challenge* activity**	**Related *Talk Maths Extra* activities**
A1.2 Target 100	6 Number puzzle
A1.3 How many?	16 Estimating quantities
A1.5 Digits	11 Making amounts
A1.6 Star numbers	7 Ordering numbers
B1.1 Fame and fortune	1 Addition and subtraction, 13 Addition facts
B1.4 To and fro	2 Addition facts
B1.5 Punctuation maths	1 Addition and subtraction, 4 Subtraction
B1.6 Missing coins	5 Money problems
D1.1 Pass it on!	17 Sorting 2D shapes
D1.2 What's missing?	3 Symmetry
D1.4 Word problems	1 Addition and subtraction
D1.6 Crocodile teeth	1 Addition and subtraction, 4 Subtraction
E1.5 Which three toys?	5 Money problems
E1.6 Snack shop	4 Subtraction, 5 Money problems
A2.1 Number cascades	6 Number puzzle
A2.2 Odd and even dominoes	2 Addition facts
A2.5 Number puzzles	7 Ordering numbers
A2.6 Greater than, less than	7 Ordering numbers
B2.1 Building monsters	2 Addition facts
B2.2 Making squares	1 Addition and subtraction
B2.3 Darts	1 Addition and subtraction, 2 Addition facts
B2.4 Square corners	3 Symmetry
B2.6 Getting to the wedding	18 Toy shelves
C2.3 Changing times	14 Ordering clocks
D2.2 The shape sorter	8 Printing shapes, 17 Sorting 2D shapes
D2.3 Packaging	8 Printing shapes
D2.5 How much change?	9 Addition and subtraction
D2.6 Question swap	9 Addition and subtraction
E2.1 Exploring multiples	10 Counting in 2s, 5s and 10s
E2.2 Multiplication race	10 Counting in 2s, 5s and 10s
A3.1 HTU game	11 Making amounts
A3.2 Number chains	11 Making amounts
A3.5 Kangaroo additions	13 Addition facts
A3.6 Difference	12 Number puzzle
B3.1 Carpet tiles	17 Sorting 2D shapes
B3.6 Spokes and wheels	2 Addition facts, 13 Addition facts
C3.4 Subtraction towers	11 Making amounts, 13 Addition facts
C3.6 Raffle ticket table	7 Ordering numbers, 15 Number detective
D3.1 The cruise 1	13 Addition facts
D3.2 The cruise 2	4 Subtraction, 13 Addition facts
D3.3 Misprints	4 Subtraction, 13 Addition facts
D3.6 The clock shop	14 Ordering clocks
E3.3 Totals with 2p and 5p coins	15 Number detective
E3.4 Near doubles	13 Addition facts

Solve the Problem pupil software

Abacus Evolve *Solve the Problem* will challenge children with rich, open-ended problems that draw on a range of mathematical strategies.

Acorn Run

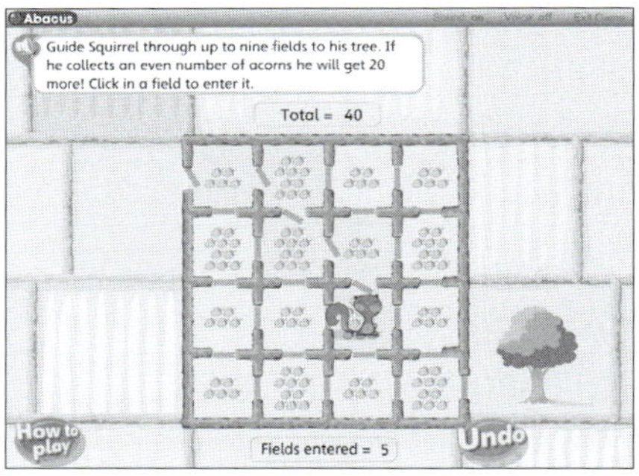

There are sixteen fields, each containing 5 or 10 acorns. The aim is for Squirrel to find a route back to his tree, collecting acorns but visiting no more than nine adjacent fields. If he finishes with an even number of acorns, he will earn 20 bonus acorns.

Nature Reserve

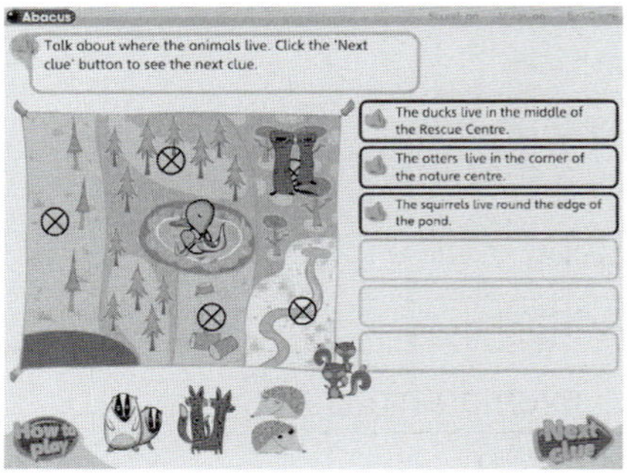

Six pairs of animals need to be given new homes in six different environments. Children are given clues to help them decide which animals should live in which areas. The children can play the game twice; the second time they will receive a different set of clues.

Perfect Day

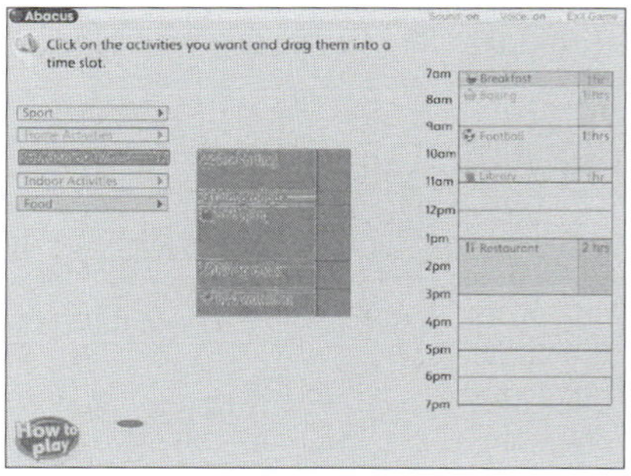

Children select activities and organise them into a timetable for their 'perfect' day. The duration of each activity is a multiple of 30 minutes. Activities can be arranged in any order, although challenges can be set by adding constraints.

Underwater Olympics

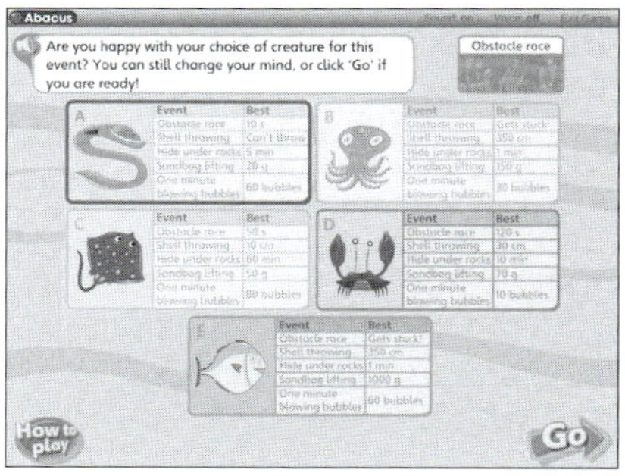

Underwater Olympics competitions are being staged across three kingdoms. There are three events in each competition. Children select a sea creature to enter for each event, using the creatures' personal best data to help them. The aim is to win each competition.

River Crossing

Kangaroo, Rabbit and Frog each need to cross a river via a rope bridge. Kangaroo can jump five steps at a time, Rabbit can jump two, and Frog can jump one. The aim is to get all three animals across the river in as few dice rolls as possible.

Design a Page

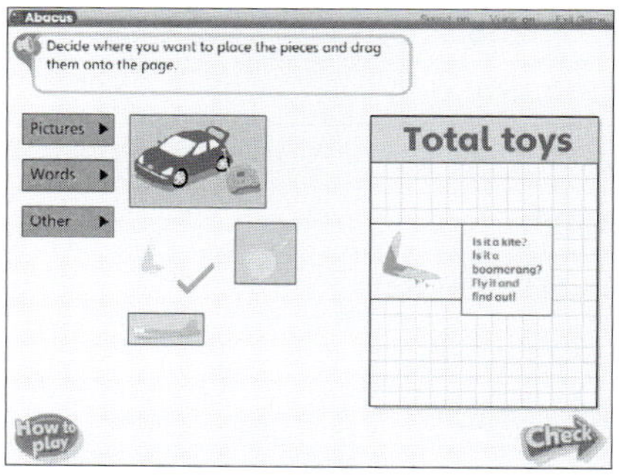

Children design the front page of a magazine by dragging 'tiles' containing the various page elements (title, pictures, articles, etc.) onto a grid. The challenge is to use all the elements and fill the page completely, leaving no spaces.

This chart shows which *Solve the Problem* activities could be used to extend some of the *Challenge* activities. The *Solve the Problem* activities are suitable for all ability levels, as children can set their own problems.

***Challenge* activity**	**Related *Solve the Problem* activities**
A1.3 How many?	Acorn Run
A1.6 Star numbers	Underwater Olympics
B1.4 To and fro	River Crossing
C1.4 My day	Perfect Day
C1.5 Units of time game	Perfect Day
D1.1 Pass it on!	Design a Page
E1.1 Half a length	Underwater Olympics
E1.2 Function machines	Acorn Run, River Crossing
A2.2 Odd and even dominoes	Acorn Run
A2.3 Walk the plank!	Acorn Run
A2.5 Number puzzles	Underwater Olympics
A2.6 Greater than, less than	Underwater Olympics
B2.1 Building monsters	River Crossing
B2.3 Darts	River Crossing
B2.6 Getting to the wedding	Nature Reserve
C2.1 How heavy?	Underwater Olympics
C2.2 More or less?	Underwater Olympics
C2.3 Changing times	Perfect Day
E2.1 Exploring multiples	Acorn Run, River Crossing
E2.2 Multiplication race	Acorn Run, River Crossing
E2.3 Known multiplication facts	Acorn Run, River Crossing
B3.1 Carpet tiles	Design a Page
B3.6 Spokes and wheels	River Crossing
C3.6 Raffle ticket table	Underwater Olympics
D3.4 It's ready!	Underwater Olympics
D3.5 Waiting for hours	Perfect Day, Underwater Olympics
D3.6 The clock shop	Perfect Day
E3.3 Totals with 2p and 5p coins	Acorn Run, River Crossing

Year 2 Assessment Activities

What do the six assessment activities cover?

In Key Stage 1, some children may perform very well in some areas of maths, and not so well in others. This is why we have provided six assessment activities, one for each strand of maths. These activities are intended to help you to assess children's prior learning and identify children with the potential to perform at a high level in maths. The activities allow for a mixture of ways to suit the needs of the children and to enable them to express their mathematical understanding appropriately. The outcomes of these activities may help you to decide which children should be in your 'Challenge' group for each strand.

Why is there no assessment activity for Using & Applying?

There is no separate assessment activity for the Using and applying mathematics strand. Instead, Using & Applying is embedded in the six activities, and some guidance is given below about what to look out for when trying to identify exceptional Using & Applying skills. Sometimes, gifted or more able mathematicians may have poor basic numeracy skills, so their ability may not be evident. Focusing on these children's Using & Applying skills can be a good way to identify their potential.

Which children should take part in the assessment activities?

The assessment activities are designed to be accessible for every child in the class. They are intended to give all children the chance to demonstrate their mathematical understanding, and thereby help you to identify those children who have the potential to perform at a high level.

When should the assessment activities be used?

The timing of the assessment activities is up to you. Here are some examples of when and how you might choose to use them.

- Carry out each activity at the beginning of a related block of work. The table below shows when each strand is covered throughout the year.
- Carry out one or two activities per term, spreading the six activities across the whole year.
- Carry out all six activities several times throughout the year, for example at the beginning of each term. This may help you to monitor children's progress from term to term.

This table shows the *Abacus Evolve* blocks in which each strand is covered in Year 2.

Strand	***Abacus Evolve* blocks**		
	Autumn	**Spring**	**Summer**
Using and applying mathematics	Embedded throughout		
Counting and understanding number	A1	A2, E2	A3, B3, E3
Knowing and using number facts	B1, E1	B2	B3, E3
Calculating	B1, D1	B2, D2, E2	A3, B3, C3, D3, E3
Understanding shape	D1	B2, D2	B3
Measuring	C1	C2	C3, D3
Handling data		C2	C3

How are the assessment activities structured?

There are two parts to each activity: a core activity and an extension activity. It is intended that the core activity is carried out by all the children. This part of the activity should allow you to identify those children who are ready for something a bit more challenging. Those children can be moved on to the extension activity, while the rest of the class continue with the core activity. The extension activity should help you to see which children have exceptional mathematical understanding, and therefore may benefit from the *Challenge* activities in this book.

What guidance is given for the assessment activities?

Within the core activity, suggestions are given for questions that could be asked or things that might be observed that may indicate which children have a higher level of understanding. These assessment points should aid you in deciding which children to move on to the extension activity.

For the extension activity, suggestions are provided for things that you might observe and things that children might say that could indicate that they have the potential to perform at a high level in that area of maths. Some of these assessment points are specific to that strand, and some are related to Using & Applying.

Some guidance is given as to the National Curriculum levels children may be working at, based on Assessment Foci from Assessing Pupils' Progress (APP). However, as noted below, the principle purpose of these activities is not to assign levels to children.

How should the activities be observed?

The activities are intended to be carried out in small groups, with an adult moving from group to group. Giving children an opportunity to try out activities in small groups can offer opportunities to observe their ability to collaborate, the extent to which they understand key words and their ability to communicate with others. It can also reveal their ability to concentrate and understand the task. Recording what children say and do is an essential part of any assessment, particularly of younger children. Recording children working together using sound or video can greatly ease the burden of recording.

How can the assessment activities be used to promote Speaking & Listening?

The idea of these activities is that within a structured play environment the focus can be firmly set within Speaking & Listening. The assessment therefore is based on the spoken interactions which demonstrate problem-solving skills through dialogue with peers. This ensures that every child has the opportunity to participate in the activities.

Should the assessment activities involve mark making?

During the activities it may be helpful to allow children to record their ideas, perhaps in a blank book so that they are not restricted by squares or lines. Giving children opportunities to select and record their work in the most appropriate way is an important part of any maths activity. Being able to link their words and their number sentences to diagrams and pictures is a crucial step in their development. Using this to assess over a period of time through a careful analysis of their work can be revealing and help to identify those children who like to record in different ways.

Are there any *Challenge* assessment tests?

Young children's high ability in maths is not always evident via testing. Their ability can be masked by factors such as poor numeracy or literacy skills, and children's performance can be greatly affected by particular circumstances on the day of testing. Therefore these children will not always perform well in a test environment, or against National Curriculum level descriptors in less formal assessments. Children with latent abilities in maths may exhibit a range of skills that relate to Using & Applying, such as thinking skills, creativity, and the ability to explain their ideas, which are best assessed through observation.

Can I use the assessment activities to assign National Curriculum levels?

The main purpose of these assessment activities is to give all children – those who may not perform well against the National Curriculum level descriptors as well as those that do – an opportunity to display their skills in collaborative problem solving, Speaking & Listening and personal learning and thinking skills as areas that might identify them as more able. It may be inappropriate to assign National Curriculum levels to these activities, although they could be used to support APP if required.

How can I assess the progress of children in the 'Challenge' group?

The *Challenge* activities on pages 28–117 of this book can be used to provide evidence of children's ongoing progress. The adult-led activities will be particularly useful for this purpose. If your school is using APP for periodic assessment, you may find the charts on pages 10–13 of this book helpful. These charts show you which of the *Challenge* activities could be used to provide evidence towards each of the Assessment Foci, with an indication of the levels that could be achieved by children taking part in the activities.

While there are no assessment tests included in the *Challenge* resources, there are plenty of assessment materials readily available that can be used alongside the *Challenge* activities. For example, within the core *Abacus Evolve* scheme you will find:

- Review Tasks: these can be used to assess children's prior learning at the start of a week, topic or block.
- Assessment Tasks: these can be used with groups to determine children's understanding from observation and questioning, and they are linked to APP.
- Assessment Tests: these are mental and written tests that allow you to track progress more formally.

Using and applying mathematics

Using and applying mathematics is the strand that is likely to offer the most useful opportunities for identifying gifted and able children.

All of the assessment activities incorporate aspects of Using & Applying and therefore all of the activities have guidance at the end of the activity, with suggestions for the types of learning that might be needed to successfully use and apply mathematics within the task.

The extension activity which is embedded in each task offers particular opportunities for children to extend their learning and enrich their experiences into areas which are perhaps less familiar to them.

Look out for children who:

- grasp what the problem is
- know how to get started
- develop systems
- can describe their strategies clearly
- record in ways that help them to explain their ideas
- use a range of mathematical vocabulary within the context
- predict an outcome and then test it
- are interested in other ways of working
- see patterns in numbers and shapes
- see relationships between the work at the beginning of the activity and the work at the end
- use their earlier experiences to tackle more challenging activities
- are good leaders within the group (although some able children prefer to work alone)
- listen and respond to the ideas of others in the group
- are not afraid to try things out and then modify or change their ideas.

Children demonstrate many of the aspects of Using & Applying at Level 3 if they can:

- select the mathematics they use in a wider range of classroom activities
- try different approaches
- find ways of overcoming difficulties that arise when solving problems
- begin to organise their work
- begin to check their results
- discuss their mathematical work
- begin to explain their thinking
- understand a general statement by finding examples that match it
- review their work and reasoning.

Children demonstrate many of the aspects of Using & Applying at Level 2 if they can:

- select the mathematics they use in the activity
- discuss their work using mathematical language
- represent their work using symbols and simple diagrams
- predict what comes next
- explain why an answer is correct
- give reasons for their opinions.

Counting and understanding numbers

Resources
Five skipping ropes; coloured tape; number cards 0–100; 100 pegs; five envelopes

Preparation
On each rope, measure an equal length (for example, 1 metre), using coloured tape to mark the two ends of the length. Select seven cards from each set of 20 (for example, for 1–20 you might choose 4, 7, 10, 11, 15, 18, 19). Make sure you include the numbers 10, 30, 50, 70 and 90. Shuffle each set of seven cards and place them in an envelope labelled with the relevant set of 20 (for example, *1–20*). Shuffle the rest of the number cards and put them somewhere out of sight of the children.

Core activity
Organise children into five groups. *I want you to make a really big number line!* Give each group a skipping rope, an envelope of cards, and seven pegs. Tell them which set of 20 each group will be working on. *I couldn't find all of the number cards! The ones I found are in the envelopes.* Ask children to peg their cards along their rope in order. *When I find the rest of the cards, it would be really good if I could add them without moving any numbers.* As children create their sections of the number line, listen out for children who are talking about the order of the numbers, and where they need to leave spaces. Ask children to work together to tie each section together to make one long 1–100 number line.

Extension activity
Bring out the remaining cards and 65 pegs. *I've found the other numbers! Can some of you help me to add them to the number line?* Ask two children to hold each end of the line. Lay out the number cards on a table, and ask the children who performed well in the core activity to help you to put them on the number line. Leave the children to decide between them how they will organise themselves and who will deal with which numbers. After each number is placed, ask children to explain how they knew where to put it.

Look out for children who:

- immediately order their set of cards to see what they have
- identify the number card which starts or ends their section of the number line
- space the cards out before pegging them on the line
- use one of the cards as a spacer to help position the others
- check by counting along the number line, including the numbers that are not there
- suggest which rope needs to be attached next
- can see immediately where their card needs to go and can explain how they know
- discuss their ideas with others
- notice mistakes made by other children.

Look out for ideas such as:

- *We can't put this one right at the end. It's our biggest number card, but we need to leave room for the rest.*
- *The 30 card needs to go in the centre. Let's fold the rope in half to find the middle.*
- *The 66 card goes after the 62 card, but we need to leave spaces for 63, 64 and 65.*

This activity could provide evidence towards the following Assessment Foci from APP:

	Ma2 Number
	Numbers and the number system
Level 3	• Do children understand the place value in numbers up to 100? • Can children compare numbers using a number line?
Level 2	• Are children beginning to understand the place value of each digit? • Can children use their knowledge of place value to order numbers up to 100?

Knowing and using number facts

Resources
Coloured linking cubes; number bond to 10 cards

Core activity
Show a tower of four red cubes and six blue cubes. *What number bond does this represent?* (4 + 6 = 10) Turn the tower around. *What number bond does it represent now?* (6 + 4 = 10) Split the tower in two to give one tower of red cubes and one tower of blue cubes. Put the red cubes behind your back. *I've taken away the four red cubes. How many cubes are left? What number bond does this represent?* (10 − 4 = 6) *What about if I had taken the blue cubes away?* (10 − 6 = 4) Ask children to use cubes to explore other number bonds.

Extension activity
Arrange 12 cubes in an array with three rows and four columns. *What multiplication does this represent?* (3 × 4 = 12, or 4 × 3 = 12) *Does it also represent a division?* (12 ÷ 3 = 4, or 12 ÷ 4 = 3) Ask children to use cubes to explore other multiplications and divisions. Encourage pairs to make arrays and challenge other pairs to say four matching calculations.

Look out for children who:
- quickly choose two different colours to make their bond
- keep the cubes in two sets while exploring
- understand that, having found one calculation, there are three more in the same family
- can say the four multiplication/division facts without making an array
- can explain the link between an array and a set of facts
- want to work with larger numbers
- ask other children challenging questions
- think of other ways to represent calculations.

Look out for ideas such as:
- *3 × 4 = 12 is the same as 4 × 3 = 12.*
- *If I know that 5 × 6 = 30, I know that 6 × 5 = 30, 30 ÷ 5 = 6 and 30 ÷ 6 = 5.*
- *If I make an array with four rows and four columns, there are only two different facts.*

This activity could provide evidence towards the following Assessment Foci from APP:

	Ma2 Number	
	Operations, relationships between them	**Mental methods**
Level 3	• Can children derive division facts from multiplication facts? • Do children understand the role of the = sign?	• Do children recall the 2, 3, 4, 5 and 10 times tables? • Are children beginning to know multiplication facts for ×6, ×7, ×8 and ×9 tables?
Level 2	• Do children understand that subtraction is the inverse of addition? • Can they use this knowledge to make related addition and subtraction facts?	• Do they use mental recall of addition and subtraction facts to 10?

Calculating

Resources
Digit cards 1–6 (one set per group of three or four children); +, − and = cards

Core activity
Organise children into groups of three or four. Give each group a set of digit cards 1–6, and several + and = cards. One child should act as scribe for the group in addition to joining in with the discussion. The role of scribe could be rotated amongst the group. Ask each group to use all their digit cards and as many addition signs as they wish to make as many different number sentences with a total of around 50 as they can. All digits must be used each time, but they can be combined to make 2- or 3-digit numbers. The scribe must record every number sentence made. Look out for children who take the lead in deciding what number sentences to make, and for those children who are quick to find the answers.

Extension activity
Now give children several – cards. They repeat the activity, but this time they can use a mixture of addition and subtraction signs. Again, all digits must be used in each number sentence, and all number sentences must be recorded.

Look out for children who:
- adapt the current number sentence rather than starting again from scratch
- add or subtract using known facts rather than by counting on or back in 1s
- ask if they can use subtraction before the subtraction cards are given out
- are comfortable using a combination of addition and subtraction
- make a 3-digit number to subtract from
- ask if they can use multiplication and division signs
- suggest different combinations to try
- work systematically
- relate the problem to recent classroom activities and experiences
- ask each other questions.

Look out for ideas such as:
- *We can't use the 5 or the 6 card as a tens digit, because that would definitely take us over 50.*
- *65 − 24 + 13 = 54, so we have 4 too many. If we swapped the 5 and the 4 we would get a bit closer to 50 because we would be adding less and taking away more.*
- *421 − 356 = 65. That's not too far off. What could we change to get closer to 50?*

This activity could provide evidence towards the following Assessment Foci from APP:

	Ma2 Number		
	Numbers and the number system	**Mental methods**	**Written methods**
Level 3	• Do children understand place value? • Do children use place value to help them make approximations?	• Can children add and subtract 2-digit numbers mentally?	• Can children add and subtract 3-digit numbers using a written method?
Level 2	• Are children beginning to understand the place value of each digit?	• Do children use mental recall of addition and subtraction facts to 10?	• Can children record their work in writing?

Understanding shape

Resources

Thin card cut into 6 cm squares (six squares per pair, plus 10 more per pair for the extension activity); masking tape; large and small cubes and cuboids, including dice; felt-tipped pens or small circular stickers

Core activity

Organise children into pairs. On each table, put out a collection of cut-out squares, a few cubes, masking tape, scissors, and black felt-tipped pens or stickers. Show children a large cube. *I would like you to use some of the squares to make a cube. You are going to use your cube as a dice, so you will need to keep as much of the masking tape as possible on the inside of the cube!* When pairs have made their cube, they turn it into a dice using felt-tipped pens or stickers to mark the dots. Look out for children who know how many squares they will need, and who understands how to construct their cube.

Extension activity

Put out some more cut-out squares on the tables, enough for 10 per pair. Challenge pairs to use squares to make a cuboid. Place some cuboids on each table for support.

Look out for children who:

- join the squares at the edges
- explain to their partner why a square needs to be added in a particular position
- check that their construction is definitely a cube
- successfully turn their cube into a dice
- understand the difference between a cube and a cuboid
- express ideas about how to make a cuboid
- can design a net that will produce a cuboid
- recognise that several nets are possible
- understand that to make a cuboid net, sides of the same length must be joined
- work together with their partner.

Look out for ideas such as:

- *To make a cuboid, we could use four rectangles and two squares.*
- *We could make the rectangles by joining two squares together.*
- *I could make the same cuboid by joining the squares in a different way.*

This activity could provide evidence towards the following Assessment Foci from APP:

	Ma3 Shape, Space and Measures	
	Properties of shape	**Properties of position and movement**
Level 3	• Do children recognise cubes and cuboids? • Are children beginning to recognise nets of cubes and cuboids?	• Do children recognise shapes in different orientations?
Level 2	• Do children use mathematical names for squares, cubes and cuboids? • Do children refer to properties and features such as edge, face, corner? • Can children visualise cubes and cuboids?	• Do children recognise that a shape stays the same even when it is held up in different orientations?

Measuring

Resources
Weighing scales (one per group of four); spare jumpers from lost property if children are not wearing jumpers

Core activity
Organise children into groups of four. *Someone told me the other day that a jumper weighs more than a shoe. I don't know if it's true or not. What do you think?* Give children a chance to discuss in their groups, then ask a volunteer from each group to say whether the group thinks the statement is true or false, and why. *If you think it is true, do you think it is true for every single person, even if their jumpers and shoes are different?* Give groups the weighing scales and give them time to weigh their own jumpers and shoes. Ask groups to tell the rest of the class what they discovered. Discuss any differences of opinion.

Extension activity
Ask children to sort themselves into two groups: those whose shoe weighs more, and those whose jumper weighs more. Have a fashion parade for each group. Ask children to record what they notice about the shoes and jumpers of the group they observe. When both fashion parades are over, ask children to explain what they observed. *Why do you think these children's shoes weighed more than their jumpers?* Ask children to predict whether your shoe or jumper is heavier. Can they explain their prediction?

Look out for children who:

- check both shoes to see if they weigh the same
- swap items with another child to check that their measurements are correct
- offer an explanation for a differing result
- want to find out how much more or less the shoe or jumper weighs
- draw a conclusion as to why a particular shoe might be heavier than a particular jumper
- make a generalised statement about the situations in which a shoe might be heavier than a jumper, and vice versa
- offer a reasoned prediction for the relative weights of your shoe and jumper.

Look out for ideas such as:

- *My shoe weighs more than my jumper but yours won't because you're wearing trainers.*
- *My jumper weighs more than my shoe but you've got bigger feet than me so your shoe will be heavier.*
- *Our shoes weigh more than our jumpers. I wonder if all our jumpers weigh the same and all our shoes weigh the same?*

This activity could provide evidence towards the following Assessment Foci from APP:

	Ma3 Shape, Space and Measures
	Measures
Level 3	• Can children use standard metric units of mass? • Can children read a simple scale on a set of weighing scales?
Level 2	• Are children beginning to use standard units to measure mass? • Do children know what measuring tool to use to find how much an object weighs? • Can children read a scale to the nearest labelled division?

Handling data

Resources
Colouring pencils; squared paper; rulers

Core activity
Organise children into groups of four. Give each group a set of colouring pencils. *It's time to buy some new colouring pencils. We can either buy them in sets which have one of each colour, or we can buy them in boxes of 12 pencils in the same colour. I don't know which type to buy, or how many we need!* Ask each group to examine their container of pencils and decide what you should do. Tell them they will need to make some record of their thinking. When they have finished, ask each group to present their ideas to the rest of the class.

Extension activity
Pool all the information. *Could you present all of this information in a single way?* Ask children to work in pairs to collect all the data and choose a way to represent it. Ask each pair to use the collated data to predict how many pencils you should buy, and in what packs, to last the rest of the school year. Ask each pair to present their results to the others.

Look out for children who:
- quickly decide on a method of sorting
- decide what information is useful and what information is irrelevant to the problem
- pose questions effectively
- recognise that collecting data needs to be organised efficiently
- present the data in a clear and concise way
- make the link between the data from their group and the implications for the class
- choose an appropriate method of recording the collated data, such as a table or graph
- draw conclusions from the collated data
- discuss their ideas in a group and listen to other ideas
- build on the ideas of others to complete the task
- think of different options and consider several of them before starting the problem.

Look out for ideas such as:
- *How many pencils are there in total? Do we need the same number next year?*
- *How many of each colour are there? Which colours do we use the most/least?*
- *How much do the packs cost? That would help us to decide which packs to buy.*

This activity could provide evidence towards the following Assessment Foci from APP:

	Ma4 Handling data	
	Processing and representing data	**Interpreting data**
Level 3	• Can children decide on an appropriate way to gather the data? • Do children make appropriate choices for recording the data? • Can children construct bar charts and pictograms where the symbol represents a group of units?	• Can children extract and interpret information presented in simple tables, lists, bar charts and pictograms?
Level 2	• Do children understand vocabulary related to handling data? • Can children collect and sort data to test a simple hypothesis? • Can children record results in simple lists, tables, pictograms and block graphs?	• Can children communicate their findings?

Challenge Plan: Year 2

A1: counting in 1s or 10s; estimating and counting objects by grouping; partitioning numbers into T and U; ordering numbers up to 100

Summary

Y2 ☆ A1.1 — **Number strips**

Groups working independently

Year 2 Challenge PCM 1

Abacus Evolve objectives

- Count on and back in 1s or 10s from a 2-digit number
- Read and write numbers up to 100 in figures

Framework objectives

- Read and write 2-digit and 3-digit numbers in figures and words; describe and extend number sequences and recognise odd and even numbers
- Ensure everyone contributes, allocate tasks, consider alternatives and reach agreement

Teacher notes

Preparation
Photocopy PCM 1, three copies per group. Cut into number strips. Keep the sets separate.

Getting started
Put two of the sets of number strips to one side. Give each child a number strip from the first set. Ask them to count on in 1s from the start number, then in 10s. Give each child a chance to try both.
Explain how to play the game: *Everyone starts with a strip and decides for themselves whether to count on 1 or 10. Write the new number in the box underneath the top one. Pass the strip to the person on your left. Look at the new strip. If the child before counted on 1, you must count on 10. If the child before counted on 10, you must count on 1. Write the new number in the box below, and pass it on. Keep passing strips round until you reach the bottom of each strip.*

Activity
Groups play the game as described above, using the first set of number strips. Once they have finished, they play twice more using the other two sets of strips. For each game they should aim to get faster and faster.

Extra help
Give children a 1–100 number line or a 1–100 square to support counting on and back.

Further extension
Add a 9 in front of each starting digit: *95, 94, 97,* etc. Children can play the same game, but counting back in 10s or 1s.

If you have time
Ask children to place the strips in order according to the start number, then look at the final numbers. *Does the smallest start number produce the smallest final number? Is the order of the final numbers the same as the order of the start numbers? Why?*

Be aware

- Switching from counting in 1s to counting in 10s is challenging. There are likely to be several mistakes. Remind children to always check what the person before them did, and then do the other. If necessary use practical resources to demonstrate counting in 1s, then 10s.

Outcomes

- I can count on and back in 10s and 1s.

Challenge Plan: Year 2

A1: counting in 1s or 10s; estimating and counting objects by grouping; partitioning numbers into T and U; ordering numbers up to 100

Summary

Y2 ☆ A1.2 **Target 100**

Pairs working independently

Year 2 Challenge Textbook page 3

Dice with sides labelled + and −; dice with sides labelled 1, 10 and 20

Abacus Evolve objectives

- Count on and back in 1s or 10s from a 2-digit number
- Read and write numbers up to 100 in figures

Framework objectives

- Read and write 2-digit and 3-digit numbers in figures and words; describe and extend number sequences and recognise odd and even numbers
- Adopt appropriate roles in small or large groups and consider alternative courses of action

Teacher notes

Preparation
Collect the necessary dice, one of each per pair. If you do not have +/− or 1/10/20 dice, make them by covering the spots or numerals on an ordinary dice with stickers and writing on the stickers.

Getting started
Show children the two dice. *You will need to choose a start number between 25 and 40. Then roll the two dice and do what they say: + 10, − 10, + 20, − 20, + 1 or − 1. You take turns to do this, counting on or back from each other's number each time. The target to reach is 100. If you go over 100, your partner wins.*

Activity
Children work from Textbook page 3. They play the game in pairs. If a child reaches exactly 100, they win. If a child goes over 100, their partner wins.
If children have time, they can play the game again.

Extra help
Give children a 1–100 number line or 1–100 square to support counting on and back.

If you have time
Ask children to discuss these questions as a group: *Is it easy or hard to get to 100? Why? Does it matter what number you start from? What would make it easier?*

Be aware

- Switching between counting on and back in 1s, 10s and 20s is challenging, so it is useful to play a game such as this one to practise it in a fun setting.

Outcomes

- I can count on and back in 1s, 10s and 20s.

Challenge Plan: Year 2

A1: counting in 1s or 10s; estimating and counting objects by grouping; partitioning numbers into T and U; ordering numbers up to 100

Summary

Y2 ☆ A1.3 — **How many?**

A small group working with an adult

Year 2 Challenge PCMs 2, 3, 4 and 5 (optional)

Small stamps or stickers (optional)

Abacus Evolve objectives

- Begin to count up to 100 objects by grouping in 5s or 10s
- Estimate a number of objects up to 50

Framework objectives

- *Count up to 100 objects by grouping them and counting in 10s, 5s or 2s; explain what each digit in a 2-digit number represents, including numbers where 0 is a place holder; partition 2-digit numbers in different ways, including into multiples of 10 and 1*
- Estimate a number of objects; round 2-digit numbers to the nearest 10
- Listen to a talk by an adult, remember some specific points and identify what they have learned

Teacher notes

Preparation

Photocopy PCMs 2, 3 and 4, one copy of each per pair. If possible, enlarge a copy of PCM 2.

Activity

- Show children the enlarged copy of PCM 2. Ask each pair to estimate how many caterpillars there are. Give them a few seconds to think, then ask pairs for their estimates.
- Show children how to draw around a few groups of five caterpillars. Explain that counting by grouping in 5s is quicker than counting in 1s.
- Give each pair a copy of PCM 2. Ask each pair to choose how they would like to group the caterpillars: in 2s, 5s or 10s. Encourage pairs to make and record an estimate of the total number of caterpillars. They then group the caterpillars in 2s, 5s or 10s. Support children in counting in groups, then in counting on in 1s for any caterpillars left over.
- Ask the group to compare their work to ensure everyone has reached the same total.
- Repeat with PCM 3 (cats) and PCM 4 (handprints). Explain that each pair must have a go at grouping in 2s, 5s and 10s, so they must choose a different way to group for each PCM.

Extra help

If children get confused when grouping their objects, give them a coloured pencil so they can start again on the same sheet. Have a spare copy of each PCM available in case children become muddled and their copy is too messy to continue working from.

Further extension

Give each child a copy of PCM 5 and ask them to make up a counting problem for another pair by drawing a set of objects, or using stamps or stickers. Children swap problems and estimate, then count each other's pictures, stamps or stickers, grouping in their choice of 2s, 5s or 10s.

If you have time

Share the story *The King's Commissioners* together to rehearse grouping and counting in 2s, 5s and 10s.

Be aware

- You may need to remind children what to count in, and how to count the few that cannot be grouped.

Outcomes

- I can count up to 100 objects by grouping them in 2s, 5s and 10s.

Supporting resources

- Read a story about grouping, such as *The King's Commissioners* by Aileen Friedman, ISBN 978 0 590489 89 8 (published by Scholastic).

Challenge Plan: Year 2

A1: counting in 1s or 10s; estimating and counting objects by grouping; partitioning numbers into T and U; ordering numbers up to 100

Summary

Y2 ☆ A1.4 **Moving the zero**

A small group working with an adult

Year 2 Challenge Textbook page 4

Year 2 Challenge PCM 6

Thin card; baskets or similar containers

Abacus Evolve objectives

- Know what each digit in a 2-digit number represents, including 0 as a place holder
- Partition 2-digit numbers into T and U
- Begin to partition 3-digit numbers into H, T and U

Framework objectives

- *Count up to 100 objects by grouping them and counting in 10s, 5s or 2s; explain what each digit in a 2-digit number represents, including numbers where 0 is a place holder; partition 2-digit numbers in different ways, including into multiples of 10 and 1*
- Use language and gesture to support the use of models, diagrams or displays when explaining

Teacher notes

Preparation
Photocopy PCM 6 onto thin card. Cut out the digit cards.

Activity
- Put each set of digit cards 1–9 into a basket. Give each child or pair a basket of numbers.
- Children follow the instructions on Textbook page 4. Each child or pair picks two digits from their basket. They choose which way around to place the cards to make a 2-digit number.
- Give each child or pair a 0 card. Ask them to explore which 3-digit numbers they can make by putting the 0 card in different places in the 2-digit number.
- Underline one digit in each number. Children write the value of each underlined digit.
- Children repeat, starting with two new digit cards.

Further extension
Extend to taking three digit cards and positioning a 0 card in various places. Read the numbers together and ask children to say what a particular digit represents.
Alternatively, you could give children a second 0 to explore with. For example, using two 0s with 35 could produce 0035, 0305, 0350, 3005, 3050 and 3500.

If you have time
Children are often fascinated by large numbers and may well want to explore using several 0s. You could do this together at the end of the session. Challenge children to work together to make the largest number they can, using two digits 1–9 and any number of 0s. You will probably have to read it to them!

Be aware

- Children may not understand that placing a 0 in front of the number has no effect. Explain that you could place any number of 0s in front of the number and the number would still remain unchanged. A 0 in any other position pushes the other digits into new positions.

Outcomes

- I can make different numbers using the same two digit cards and a 0 card.
- I can say what each digit in a 2- or 3-digit number is worth.

Supporting resources

- Read *A Place for Zero, A Math Adventure* by Angeline Sparagna LoPresti, ISBN 978 1 570911 96 5.

Challenge Plan: Year 2

A1: counting in 1s or 10s; estimating and counting objects by grouping; partitioning numbers into T and U; ordering numbers up to 100

Summary

Y2 ☆ A1.5 — **Digits**

Pairs working independently

Year 2 Challenge Textbook page 5

Year 2 Challenge PCM 6

Thin card

Abacus Evolve objectives

- **Y3** Know what each digit in a 3-digit number represents, including 0 as a place holder
- **Y3** Partition 3-digit numbers into H, T and U
- **Y3** Compare two 3-digit numbers
- **Y3** Order numbers up to at least 1000

Framework objectives

- **Y3** *Partition 3-digit numbers into multiples of 100, 10 and 1 in different ways*
- **Y3** Read, write and order whole numbers to at least 1000 and position them on a number line; count on from and back to zero in single-digit steps or multiples of 10
- **Y3** Follow a line of enquiry by deciding what information is important; make and use lists, tables and graphs to organise and interpret the information
- **Y3** Sustain conversation, explaining or giving reasons for their views or choices

Teacher notes

Preparation
Photocopy PCM 6 onto thin card. Cut out the digit cards. The 0 cards are not needed for this activity.

Gettng started
Shuffle each set of digit cards 1–9 and give a set to each pair of children. Ask them to choose three cards at random. Show children how to use their three digit cards to make different numbers. Explain that each number can have one, two or three digits, so each number does not have to contain all three digits. Each digit card can only be used once in each of the numbers.

Activity
Children work from Textbook page 5. Pairs use their three digit cards to make as many different 1-, 2- and 3-digit numbers as they can. They record each number as they find it. Pairs should discuss whether they are sure they have found all the possibilities. They then write their numbers in order, from smallest to largest.

Extra help
Once children have found a few different numbers, prompt them to think about a system they could use to work through the possibilities methodically. This will make it much easier for them to find all possibilities, and to be sure that they have found them all.

Further extension
Ask children to repeat the investigation, but this time using four digit cards.

Be aware

- Children may get frustrated if they struggle to find all the possibilities. Showing them how to use a system to work through the possibilities methodically will help them to see a clear route through the problem.

Outcomes

- I can find all the possible numbers that can be made using three digits.
- I can put a set of 1-, 2- and 3-digit numbers in order.

A1: counting in 1s or 10s; estimating and counting objects by grouping; partitioning numbers into T and U; ordering numbers up to 100

Summary

Y2 ☆ A1.6 **Star numbers**

Individuals, pairs or groups working independently

Year 2 Challenge Textbook page 6

Rulers; 0–100 number line (optional)

Abacus Evolve objectives

- Order numbers up to at least 100 and position them on a 100-square
- Say a number lying between two numbers, up to at least 100
- Know what each digit in a 2-digit number represents, including 0 as a place holder
- Partition 2-digit numbers into T and U
- Begin to partition 3-digit numbers into H, T and U

Framework objectives

- Order 2-digit numbers and position them on a number line; use the greater than (>), less than (<) signs
- *Count up to 100 objects by grouping them and counting in 10s, 5s or 2s; explain what each digit in a 2-digit number represents, including numbers where 0 is a place holder; partition 2-digit numbers in different ways, including into multiples of 10 and 1*

Teacher notes

Getting started
Look at the first star on Textbook page 6 together and talk about how to put the numbers in order. Explain that they should check for single-digit numbers first, then look for the smallest number of tens, and so on.

Activity
Children work from Textbook page 6. They order the numbers on each star, from smallest to largest. They then draw a number line and place all the numbers in order on the line.

Extra help
Provide a 0–100 number line if children are not confident drawing their own.

Further extension
Introduce the < and > signs to children. Ask them to compare pairs of 2- or 3-digit numbers, and write them with the correct sign in between.

Be aware

- Children may find it hard to get the spacing correct when placing numbers on a 0–100 or 0–1000 number line. Give them support if necessary.

Outcomes

- I can put sets of five numbers in order from smallest to largest.
- I can position a large set of numbers on a 0–100 number line.

B1: adding by counting on in 1s; adding three numbers; addition and subtraction facts up to 9; missing-number additions and subtractions

Summary

Y2 ☆ B1.1 **Fame and fortune**

A small group working with an adult

Year 2 Challenge Textbook page 7

Year 2 Challenge PCM 7

Abacus Evolve objectives

- Add by counting on in 1s from the larger number, crossing a multiple of 10
- Recognise addition as counting on
- Add a 1-digit number to a 2-digit number, bridging a multiple of 10 without crossing 100
- Add two 2-digit numbers using an appropriate strategy
- Partition additions into T and U, then recombine

Framework objectives

- *Add or subtract mentally a one-digit number or a multiple of 10 to or from any 2-digit number; use practical and informal written methods to add and subtract 2-digit numbers*
- Listen to others in class, ask relevant questions and follow instructions

Teacher notes

Preparation
Photocopy PCM 7, one copy per pair.

Activity
- *Start with 19 and count on 6.* Make sure children start from 19 and count on in 1s until they reach 25.
- *Start with 22 and count on 14.* Emphasise the fact that children don't have to count on 14 in 1s. Model splitting the 14 into tens and units, then counting on the tens first, and then the units.
- *Start with 122 and count on 14.* Make sure children realise that the method is exactly the same.
- Look at Textbook page 7 together. *Mr Moneybags and Miss Bigbank are celebrities. They are always arguing over who has more money.*
- *On Monday, Mr Moneybags has £550 in his wallet, and Miss Bigbank has £500. During the week, they each put more money into their wallets. Who do you think has more money at the end of Friday?*
- Children work from Textbook page 7, and look at the amount of money each celebrity gains each day. They use PCM 7 to help them with their counting on, and to record their answers to question 1.
- Bring the group back together to discuss children's answers. *Did you all come up with the same amounts?* If there are any discrepancies, ask children to explain how they reached their results, and give other children the opportunity to explain where they went wrong.
- *Who had more money at the end of the week – Mr Moneybags or Miss Bigbank?*

Further extension
Discuss millionaires. *What are they? How much money do they have?*

If you have time
Find out about large numbers. *What are the names given to numbers bigger than millions?*

Be aware

- Some children may struggle with the processes of splitting the number to be added into tens and units, and then adding each part to the original number. If necessary, use resources such as base 10 equipment to help children envisage the steps and keep the numbers in their heads.

Outcomes

- I can add a 1-digit number to a 2-digit number by counting on in 1s.
- I can add a 2-digit number to a 3-digit number by counting on in 10s and 1s.

B1: adding by counting on in 1s; adding three numbers; addition and subtraction facts up to 9; missing-number additions and subtractions

Summary

Y2 ☆ B1.2 **Doughnuts**

Pairs working independently

Year 2 Challenge PCMs 8 and 9

Abacus Evolve objectives

- Add three numbers by putting the largest number first
- Recognise that addition can be done in any order
- Begin to add three 1-digit numbers mentally
- Know by heart addition and subtraction facts for pairs of numbers that total 20

Framework objectives

- *Add or subtract mentally a one-digit number or a multiple of 10 to or from any 2-digit number; use practical and informal written methods to add and subtract 2-digit numbers*
- *Derive and recall all addition and subtraction facts for each number to at least 10, all pairs with totals to 20 and all pairs of multiples of 10 with totals up to 100*
- Solve problems involving addition, subtraction, multiplication or division in contexts of numbers, measures or pounds and pence

Teacher notes

Preparation
Photocopy PCMs 8 and 9, one copy of each per child.

Getting started
Remind children of some strategies for adding three numbers. Explain that this activity is about 'doughnuts' – squares of numbers with a hole in the middle. *In a doughnut each column and each row add up to the same number. No number can be used more than once.*

Activity
Children work from PCM 8. They look at two completed doughnuts and discuss them in pairs. They should notice that each row and column adds to 20.
Children complete more '20' doughnuts, then investigate how many different '20' doughnuts they can make on PCM 9.
They then make a '21' and a '19' doughnut and note down what they notice. Children will notice that it is more difficult to find the corner numbers as they are part of a column and a row. They can use the '20' doughnuts to make '21' and '19' doughnuts, by adding/ subtracting 1 to/from each of the centre numbers.

Extra help
Allow children to practise first on doughnuts with a row/column total of 10 or less.

Further extension
Ask children to show you their systematic way of checking they have found all the possible '20' doughnuts. For example, they may choose to make a list of all possible combinations of three numbers that add to give a total of 20. Ask them to find all the possible ways to make a '21' doughnut. What do they notice?

If you have time
Introduce the concept of magic squares, in which all the columns, rows and diagonals add up to the same number. For example, this magic square has a magic total of 15.

8	1	6
3	5	7
4	9	2

Be aware

- This activity encourages developing systems to look for similar examples. Children may adopt a variety of different methods, so discussion is important.

Outcomes

- I can add three small numbers together to find totals.

Supporting resources

Children can try some magic square puzzles at:
- http://nrich.maths.org/public/viewer.php?obj_id=1819

Challenge Plan: Year 2

B1: adding by counting on in 1s; adding three numbers; addition and subtraction facts up to 9; missing-number additions and subtractions

Summary

Y2 ☆ B1.3 **Chasing 21**

A small group working with an adult

Year 2 Challenge PCM 10

Two 1–6 dice per pair; one 0, 10, 20 dice per pair

Abacus Evolve objectives

- Add three numbers by putting the largest number first
- Recognise that addition can be done in any order
- Use the +, − and = signs to record addition and subtraction sentences
- Begin to add three 1-digit numbers mentally

Framework objectives

- *Add or subtract mentally a one-digit number or a multiple of 10 to or from any 2-digit number; use practical and informal written methods to add and subtract 2-digit numbers*
- *Use the symbols +, −, ×, ÷ and = to record and interpret number sentences involving all four operations; calculate the value of an unknown in a number sentence (e.g. 30 − □ = 24, □ ÷ 2 = 6)*

Teacher notes

Preparation
Photocopy PCM 10, one copy per pair.
Provide two 1–6 dice and one 0, 10, 20 dice for each pair. To make a 0, 10, 20 dice, put stickers on a standard 1–6 dice and write 0 on two of the faces, 10 on two of the faces and 20 on two of the faces.

Activity
Give each pair a copy of PCM 10. They can read the rules of the game as you explain them.

- Player A throws the three dice and finds the total. For example, he throws 6, 5, 0, and the total is 11.
- *How close is this to 21?* If Player A is happy with his total, he writes it in the table, and records how far it is from 21. For example, *10 from 21*.
- If Player A is not happy with his total, he can throw one, two or all three of the dice again. For example, he keeps the 6 and throws the other two dice again. He throws a 6 and a 10, giving him 6, 6, 10, and a total of 22. Player A cannot choose to throw the dice again, so he must keep this score. He writes it in the table, and records how far it is from 21. For example, *1 from 21*.
- Player B then has her turn. The children continue for five turns each, recording their scores on PCM 10.
- At the end of the game, they each add up their five scores. The player whose score is closest to 0 wins.

Children play the game in pairs. *Is this a game of chance? Do you have any strategies for winning the game?*

Extra help
Make the activity simpler by using three 1–6 dice and aiming for a total of 12.

Further extension
How can you decide what your chances are of throwing exactly 21? Can you make better decisions about when to re-throw the dice if you work out your chances each time?

If you have time
Use three dice and have four turns to get nearer to 21. *What happens to your chances of getting exactly 21 now? Will you change your strategies?*

Be aware

- Winning is more likely if children know the chances of throwing particular numbers. Children are unlikely to know the chances, but this is a good opportunity to discuss why children may decide to re-throw.

Outcomes

- I can record addition and subtraction calculations using +, − and =.

Supporting resources

Children can practise addition with this 'Safari Units' game:

- http://www.bbc.co.uk/schools/ks1bitesize/numeracy/units/index.shtml/

B1: adding by counting on in 1s; adding three numbers; addition and subtraction facts up to 9; missing-number additions and subtractions

Summary

Y2 ☆ B1.4 — **To and fro**

Groups working independently

Year 2 Challenge PCM 11

6-sided dice

Abacus Evolve objectives

- Rehearse addition and subtraction facts for pairs of numbers that total up to 9
- Use patterns of similar calculations

Framework objectives

- *Derive and recall all addition and subtraction facts for each number to at least 10, all pairs with totals to 20 and all pairs of multiples of 10 with totals up to 100*
- Describe patterns and relationships involving numbers or shapes, make predictions and test these with examples
- Listen to others in class, ask relevant questions and follow instructions

Teacher notes

Preparation
Photocopy PCM 11, one copy per pair.

Getting started
Organise children into pairs. Give the group a 1–6 dice. Give children PCM 11. Explain how to play the game:

- One child in the group throws the dice, for example: 5.
- Pair 1 takes this as their start number. The first child in the pair adds 2: *5 + 2 = 7*. The second child subtracts 1: *7 − 1 = 6*. They write the start number (5) and the final answer (6) in the table on PCM 11.
- Pair 2 then takes the answer as their start number, and they add 2 and subtract 1.
- Play continues until each pair has had a turn.

Activity
Children work from PCM 11. They play the game, recording the start numbers and answers on the PCM. Children look at the sequence of numbers as a group and try to explain why it occurs. They repeat the game, using the rule add 3, subtract 2. Again, they look at the sequence of numbers and try to explain why it occurs.
Each pair then finds another two-step operation that gives the same sequence of answers.

Extra help
Children could start by using one-step operations such as + 1 or − 2 and explain the pattern together.

Further extension
Repeat the activity but add a smaller number and subtract a larger number, e.g. + 2 then − 3. This takes the answers into negative numbers.

If you have time
Ask children to think of a two-step rule that will give a sequence of answers that go up in 2s.

Information
The purpose of this activity is to understand the cumulative effect of consistently applying rules. Two-step operations have a combined overall impact on the answer. For example, with + 5 then − 2, the answer is + 3 so the sequence of answers will be + 3 each time.

Be aware

- It is important for children to use the words *add* and *subtract*, then move to formal recording with the + and − symbols when they are ready.

Outcomes

- I can play a game using addition and subtraction rules.

Supporting resources

Children can practise looking at sequences involving dominoes here:

- http://nrich.maths.org/public/viewer.php?obj_id=241

Summary

Y2 ☆ B1.5 **Punctuation maths**

A small group working with an adult

Year 2 Challenge PCM 12

Abacus Evolve objectives

- Recognise the use of a symbol to stand for an unknown number
- Relate addition and subtraction facts to missing number sentences
- Use the +, − and = signs to record addition and subtraction sentences

Framework objectives

- *Use the symbols +, −, ×, ÷ and = to record and interpret number sentences involving all four operations; calculate the value of an unknown in a number sentence (e.g. 30 − □ = 24, □ ÷ 2 = 6)*
- Present solutions to puzzles and problems in an organised way; explain decisions, methods and results in pictorial, spoken or written form, using mathematical language and number sentences
- Use language and gesture to support the use of models, diagrams or displays when explaining

Teacher notes

Preparation
Photocopy PCM 12, one copy per child.

Activity
Mrs Barton has written some calculations on the board for the class but she has pressed the wrong keys on the keyboard! Can you work out what the right digits should be?
Children work from PCM 12. They find the answers to the calculations in order to find the digits that have been replaced by the # symbol and the ! symbol. They then use what they have found to find answers to calculations where Mrs Barton has used both # and ! in the same calculation.
Ask children to make up their own similar problems for a partner to solve.

Extra help
Remind children that # only represents one digit and ! only represents one digit.

Further extension
Use * to represent any digit in a calculation so that there are many possible answers, e.g. 3* + 2* = 60.
This problem has nine possible answers: 39 + 21 = 60, 38 + 22 = 60, 37 + 23 = 60, 36 + 24 = 60, 35 + 25 = 60, 34 + 26 = 60, 33 + 27 = 60, 32 + 28 = 60 or 31 + 29 = 60.

If you have time
Make up other codes using letters instead of numbers. See if your partner can crack the code!
For example: if A = 1, B = 2 and C = 3, what is the answer to A + B + C = ?

Information
represents 6 and ! represents 5.

Be aware

- It is important to distinguish between using a symbol as a particular missing number and using symbols to represent any number. In this example the symbols represent a particular number and the number is always the same. This is a code. When a symbol is used to represent the general case for any number this is algebra.

Outcomes

- I can solve addition and subtraction puzzles that use symbols.

Supporting resources

This is a helpful article about using symbols in maths:
- http://nrich.maths.org/public/viewer.php?obj_id=2549

B1: adding by counting on in 1s; adding three numbers; addition and subtraction facts up to 9; missing-number additions and subtractions

Summary

Y2 ☆ B1.6 — **Missing coins**

Individuals or pairs working independently

Year 2 Challenge Textbook page 8

1p, 2p and 5p coins (real, if possible); items for the play shop (optional); labels (optional)

Abacus Evolve objectives

- Relate addition and subtraction facts to missing number sentences
- Use the +, − and = signs to record addition and subtraction sentences
- Find totals of sets of coins: relate to adding three or more numbers
- Solve 'real-life' problems involving money (paying an exact sum)

Framework objectives

- *Use the symbols +, −, ×, ÷ and = to record and interpret number sentences involving all four operations; calculate the value of an unknown in a number sentence (e.g. 30 − □ = 24, □ ÷ 2 = 6)*
- Solve problems involving addition, subtraction, multiplication or division in contexts of numbers, measures or pounds and pence
- Listen to others in class, ask relevant questions and follow instructions

Teacher notes

Getting started
Give children 1p, 2p and 5p coins to look at.
Explain to them that they will work on their own or in pairs from Textbook page 8. At the end, they should check their answers as a group.

Activity
Children work from Textbook page 8. Asha's purse is meant to have 12p in it, but each time she looks some coins have gone missing. Children work out which coins are missing from Asha's purse each time, then write the corresponding number sentences.

Extra help
Children can practise finding sets of coins that make total amounts of 10p or less.

Further extension
Evan has a travel card for the London Underground. He buys £2 worth of credit.
This is where he goes: Journey 1: 3 stops = 50p
Journey 2: 1 stop = 20p
Journey 3: 2 stops = 35p
How much credit does he have left on his travel card?
Ask children to make up some similar problems for a partner to solve.

If you have time
Set up a play shop. Add price labels to items and put them in the shop. Supply real or plastic money for children to practise paying for items and giving change.

Be aware

- There will be more than one answer for each purse. Decide if you would like children to find all the possible combinations or just one combination per purse.
- Some children may find it difficult to be systematic. If necessary encourage the group to work together, using a large piece of paper, to reach answers together and make sure they have found all the possibilities.

Outcomes

- I can work out which coins are missing when I know the total amount.

Summary

Y2 ☆ C1.1	**Strip book**
	Individuals or pairs working independently
	Year 2 Challenge Textbook page 9
	Assorted coloured A3 paper; 30 cm rulers; scissors; staplers

Abacus Evolve objectives

- Estimate, measure and compare lengths using standard units: centimetres
- **Y3** Use a ruler to draw and measure lines to the nearest half centimetre

Framework objectives

- Estimate, compare and measure lengths, weights and capacities, choosing and using standard units (m, cm, kg, litre) and suitable measuring instruments
- **Y3** *Read, to the nearest division and half-division, scales that are numbered or partially numbered; use the information to measure and draw to a suitable degree of accuracy*

Teacher notes

Preparation
Cut coloured A3 paper into 2 cm wide strips. Each child or pair will need two or three strips.
Prepare a strip book using different lengths to those used in the Textbook. Label each strip with its length.

Getting started
Remind children how to use a ruler for measuring to the nearest centimetre, including marking the correct length and cutting straight across the paper strip. Then show them how to measure and cut to the nearest half centimetre. Show children Textbook page 9 and your prepared strip book. Check that they understand the instructions.

Activity
Children work from Textbook page 9. They cut strips of paper to given lengths (whole and half centimetres), measuring and marking them carefully using a ruler. They label each strip with its length. Each child or pair then puts all their strips together in a stack, with the ends aligned. The strips should be in order of length, from the longest on the bottom to the shortest on the top. Children staple the strips together at one end to make a strip book. Children then compare their strip book with someone else's to make sure they are the same.

Extra help
Children can use your prepared strip book for support. This will help them to understand that they need to cut a different strip for each length, not simply mark one strip with the values.

If you have time
When children compare their strip books with another child or pair, they can work out which strips do not match, and trim or replace the incorrect strips.

Be aware

- Children often find it difficult to cut straight across a strip of paper. If necessary, show children how to fold the strip first, matching the sides to ensure that the fold is straight.

Outcomes

- I can measure lengths in centimetres using a ruler.
- I can measure lengths to the nearest half centimetre.

Supporting resources

- Have a range of different rulers and tape measures available for measuring with.
- Read this story about imperial and metric measures: *Millions to Measure* by David M Schwartz, ISBN 978 0 688129 16 3.

Challenge Plan: Year 2

C1: lengths in centimetres; lengths in metres; units of time: hours and days; units of time: months and seasons

Summary

Y2 ☆ C1.2 — **Duck dinner time**

Groups working independently

Year 2 Challenge PCM 13

String; scissors; 30 cm rulers; a 1–3 dice; counters; a metre stick (optional)

Abacus Evolve objectives

- Use a ruler to draw and measure lines to the nearest centimetre
- Recognise the relationship between metres and centimetres
- **Y3** Measure and compare lengths using standard units: metres, centimetres
- **Y3** Know the relationship between kilometres and metres, metres and centimetres

Framework objectives

- Read the numbered divisions on a scale, and interpret the divisions between them, (e.g. on a scale from 0 to 25 with intervals of 1 shown but only the divisions 0, 5, 10, 15 and 20 numbered); use a ruler to draw and measure lines to the nearest centimetre
- Estimate, compare and measure lengths, weights and capacities, choosing and using standard units (m, cm, kg, litre) and suitable measuring instruments
- **Y3** Know the relationships between kilometres and metres, metres and centimetres, kilograms and grams, litres and millilitres; choose and use appropriate units to estimate, measure and record measurements

Teacher notes

Preparation
Photocopy PCM 13, one copy per group, preferably enlarging it to A3. If you do not have a 1–3 dice, make one by covering 4, 5 and 6 on an ordinary dice with small sticky labels. Write 1, 2 or 3 on each label as appropriate.
Make sure the string is thin enough for children to cut. Dampen the string to make it easier to straighten.

Getting started
Explain how to play the game. *How many 10 cm worms would you need to collect to feed the duck for a day?*
Using some of the left over string, cut several different lengths of string (one per child). Hold them in your hand with a bit of each string poking out. Ask each child to pull out a piece of string. When they all have a piece of string, they compare the lengths. The child with the longest piece will go first, the child with the next longest piece will go second, and so on.

Activity
Children work from PCM 13. They start by cutting lots of 10 cm lengths of string, and putting them in the 'worm bank'. Children must measure carefully using a ruler to make sure each length of string is exactly 10 cm.
All the players place their counters on 'start'. Player 1 rolls the dice and moves their counter that number of spaces. They can choose which direction they go in. If they land on a worm, they take a 10 cm piece of string from the worm bank. Players take turns to move their counters, collecting pieces of string every time they land on a worm. The winner is the first player to collect 1 metre of worms.

Extra help
Have a metre stick available for checking cumulative lengths.

Further extension
Ask each player to lay their worms end to end to see how much they have collected. *Who has collected the least? Can you say how long your collected worms are without measuring?*

If you have time
Put all the worms collected by the group together. *How many days' food do you have for the duck?*
If each duck ate only 50 cm of worms a day, how many ducks could you feed for a day?

Be aware

- Make sure children count each worm as 10 cm, even if a worm has not been cut to exactly the correct length.

Outcomes

- I can measure length in centimetres.

Challenge Plan: Year 2

C1: lengths in centimetres; lengths in metres; units of time: hours and days; units of time: months and seasons

Summary

Y2 ☆ C1.3 **Measure me!**

A small group working with an adult

Year 2 Challenge Textbook page 10

Tape measures

Abacus Evolve objectives

- **Y3** Measure and compare lengths using standard units: metres, centimetres
- **Y3** Know the relationship between kilometres and metres, metres and centimetres

Framework objectives

- **Y3** Know the relationships between kilometres and metres, metres and centimetres, kilograms and grams, litres and millilitres; choose and use appropriate units to estimate, measure and record measurements
- **Y3** Use talk to organise roles and actions

Teacher notes

Activity

- Ask children to open their Textbooks at page 10. Point to each of the labels, explaining which part of the body each one relates to.
- Give each child a couple of minutes to draw a simple picture of themselves, and to add labels around their picture to match the Textbook page.
- *How tall do you think you are? How long do you think your foot is?* Encourage children to estimate verbally.
- *Now you are going to measure each other!* Explain how to measure each part of the body using a tape measure. Allow each pair to measure your wrist to practise.
- Support children as they measure each other. Make sure each child is measuring the same body part so that comparisons may be made. For example, everyone should measure their left wrist and hand span, and their right foot. Before taking each measurement, children should write an estimate.
- After taking each measurement, children should compare their measurement with their estimate. Talk about how close they were and encourage them to use this to make better estimates as the activity progresses. To support this, you could ask questions such as *Is your head bigger than your wrist? How much bigger?*
- Make sure children label their measurements with the units. *Did you use metres or centimetres?* When children measure each other's height, help them to convert the tape measure reading from centimetres into metres and centimetres.

If you have time

Ask children to order their six measurements from smallest to largest, then compare their order with other children's. *Is the order always the same?*

Be aware

- Children often read tape measures by the number rather than the mark. When you talk through how to measure parts of the body with a tape measure, focus on how the beginning of the tape measure overlaps with the rest of the tape and how to read the measurement correctly.
- Be careful when comparing waist measurements not to imply that a particular child is overweight. Leave that comparison out if it is likely to be a problem.

Outcomes

- I can measure parts of the body in centimetres and metres.

Summary

Y2 ☆ C1.4 **My day**

Individuals or pairs working independently

Year 2 Challenge PCM 14

Colouring pencils; cardboard analogue clock (optional)

Abacus Evolve objectives

- Use units of time and know the relationship between them: hours in a day, days in a week

Framework objectives

- *Use units of time (seconds, minutes, hours, days) and know the relationships between them; read the time to the quarter hour; identify time intervals, including those that cross the hour*
- Present solutions to puzzles and problems in an organised way; explain decisions, methods and results in pictorial, spoken or written form, using mathematical language and number sentences

Teacher notes

Preparation
Photocopy PCM 14 , one copy per child.

Getting started
Show children PCM 14. Explain how the two clock faces can be used to show what they do in a normal day. Look together at the key. Ask the group to suggest two items to add to the key. *You are going to build up a picture of what you do in one whole weekday by showing what you do in each hour.* Ask each child to pick a weekday and write it at the top of the PCM. Explain how to complete the key and colour in the clock faces. Children may halve some one-hour segments if they feel that is more representative of their day.

Activity
Each child completes their key, filling in the two blank labels and assigning a colour to each label. They then begin with midnight, colouring each one-hour segment of the first clock face according to the key to show what they are usually doing at that time.

Extra help
Children can use the analogue clock to help talk themselves through their day.

Further extension
Ask children how much time they spend each day doing each of the things detailed in the key. Ask them to count up the hours and write the total next to each item in the key. *Compare with a partner. Do you both spend the same amount of time on each thing?*

If you have time
Carry out the same activity for a day at the weekend. *How are the days the same? How are they different?*

Be aware

- Children may wish to record their day in more detail. However it is best to limit them to half-hour slots or the diagram becomes too complicated.

Outcomes

- I can record what I do in 24 hours.
- I know there are 24 hours in a day.

Supporting resources

- Read the time story *Cluck O'Clock* by Kes Gray, ISBN 978 0 340866 05 4.
- Have some diaries and calendars available for the children to explore.

Summary

Y2 ☆ C1.5 — **Units of time game**

Groups working independently

Year 2 Challenge PCMs 15 and 16

Thin card; a cloth bag

Abacus Evolve objectives

- Use units of time and know the relationship between them: hours in a day, days in a week
- Use units of time and know the relationship between them: months in a year, seasons in a year
- Use units of time and know the relationship between them: hours, minutes, seconds

Framework objectives

- *Use units of time (seconds, minutes, hours, days) and know the relationships between them; read the time to the quarter hour; identify time intervals, including those that cross the hour*
- Ensure everyone contributes, allocate tasks, consider alternatives and reach agreement

Teacher notes

Preparation
Photocopy PCM 15 onto white or coloured paper, one copy per child. Photocopy PCM 16 onto thin card, and cut out the cards. Put the cards in a bag.
If you have more than one group playing, photocopy each set of game cards onto a different colour to prevent the sets getting mixed up.

Getting started
Show children the game board on PCM 15. Make sure they can read each of the words: *months, hours, minutes, weeks, seconds, days*. Show one of the game cards, for example, *have a shower. How long does it take to have a shower? Months? Weeks?* Agree that having a shower would take minutes. Repeat for a couple more game cards to check that children can say which period of time each card represents.

Activity
Each child has a copy of PCM 15 in front of them. The bag of game cards is passed around the group. Each child removes one card and places it on the matching square on their game board. If that square already has a card on it, they must return the card to the bag and miss a turn. The winner is the first person to place a game card on each of the six squares on the game board.

Extra help
If a child is unsure of which is the appropriate unit of time for the event on the game card, they should talk to the rest of the group until they are happy they understand.

Further extension
Collect all the game cards together and sort them onto one game board. *Which game cards are 'missing'?* Write a list of additional cards for each time unit. They could also discuss where the seasons should feature.

Be aware

- Not all the days of the week or months of the year are included in the game cards. Children may briefly say which ones they think are missing, but should be reassured that this does not affect the playing of the game.

Outcomes

- I can sort events according to how much time they take.

Challenge Plan: Year 2

C1: lengths in centimetres; lengths in metres; units of time: hours and days; units of time: months and seasons

Summary

Y2 ☆ C1.6 — **30 days hath September**

A small group working with an adult

Year 2 Challenge Textbook page 11

A list of children's birthdays; 0–100 number lines (optional)

Abacus Evolve objectives

- Use units of time and know the relationship between them: months in a year, seasons in a year
- Order the months of the year
- Organise information in a table

Framework objectives

- *Use units of time (seconds, minutes, hours, days) and know the relationships between them; read the time to the quarter hour; identify time intervals, including those that cross the hour*
- Answer a question by collecting and recording data in lists and tables; represent the data as block graphs or pictograms to show results; use ICT to organise and present data

Teacher notes

Preparation
Obtain a list of children's birthdays from the school office.

Activity
- Children work from Textbook page 11. Read the poem together and discuss what it means.
- Ask each child to draw a table with two columns and 12 rows. Ask them to write the months of the year in the first column, in order from January to December.
- Support using the poem to write the number of days in each month in the second column of their table.
- Children then use their tables to work out the number of days in each season. Give each child a chance to explain to the group how they worked it out. If children have come up with different answers, encourage them to discuss why this might have been, and work as a group to find the correct answers.
- *Which of these answers would change in a leap year? Why?*

Extra help
When children have written their list of months, encourage them to colour the three months of each season in a different colour, for example, they might use yellow for the summer months of June, July and August. This should make it easier for children to work out which months to add.
Provide a number line to support addition if necessary.
Use the birthday list to support those children who reach the Extra activity and cannot remember which month their birthday is in.

If you have time
Share this information with children. A year is the amount of time it takes the Earth to travel around the Sun and is actually $365\frac{1}{4}$ days. Leap years happen every four years though there are some exceptions. Years that are exactly divisible by 100 are *not* leap years, unless they are also exactly divisible by 400. *Why do you think we need leap years? What would happen if we didn't have them?*

Information
The commonly accepted seasons are Spring: March, April, May; Summer: June, July, August; Autumn: September, October, November; Winter: December, January, February.

Be aware

- Make it clear to children that they are thinking of a common year not a leap year.

Outcomes

- I can answer questions about the number of days in a month and a season.

Supporting resources

Sing about number of days in each month with '31 Days in January' from the *Number Fun Song Resource Pack 1* by Dave Godfrey:
- http://www.numberfun.co.uk/resource/song_resource_pack_1.htm.
- Have some calendars available for the children to explore.

Challenge Plan: Year 2

D1: sorting and describing 2D shapes; line symmetry; counting back in 1s, not crossing a ten; counting back in 1s, crossing a ten

Summary

Y2 ☆ D1.1 — **Pass it on!**

A small group working with an adult

Year 2 Challenge PCMs 17 and 18

Coloured card; thin white card; a 6-sided dice; blank stickers; four bags

Abacus Evolve objectives

- Use the names of common 2D shapes, including: pentagon, hexagon, octagon
- Sort 2D shapes and describe their features: number of sides and corners

Framework objectives

- *Visualise common 2D shapes and 3D solids; identify shapes from pictures of them in different positions and orientations; sort, make and describe shapes, referring to their properties*
- Listen to others in class, ask relevant questions and follow instructions

Teacher notes

Preparation

Photocopy PCMs 17 and 18 onto different coloured card. Cut out the shapes. Put blank stickers on each face of a dice and draw shapes on four of the faces: pentagon, hexagon, quadrilateral, octagon. Leave two faces blank.

Activity

- If there are more than four children in the group, pair some children up or introduce other shapes.
- *You are each going to collect a set of shapes and then play a game with them.* Explain that it is important that children talk to each other about their shapes.
- Children sort the shapes from PCMs 17 and 18 into sets according to type of shape (pentagon, hexagon, quadrilateral or octagon). Ask them to explain their groupings, using the names of the shapes. Each child then chooses one set and places them in their bag. Each child must choose a different set.
- Play the game. The aim is for children to keep as many of their original shapes in their collection as possible. Children take turns to throw the dice. If the dice lands on another child's shapes set, that child gives one shape from their collection.
- For example: a child with the quadrilaterals throws the dice. It lands on hexagon. The child with hexagons gives a hexagon. If a child throws a blank, they pass any shape in their collection to any other player.
- Children keep track of their collections by drawing each shape.
- At the end of the game, ask each child to draw the shapes in their bag from memory. Children reveal their shapes and describe their collection to the group. *How can you group them?*

Extra help

Make a collection of regular shapes in different colours and then play the game as above.

Further extension

Give each child a piece of card and ask them to make their own collections of shapes before playing the game.

If you have time

Children take turns to throw two dice and add the numbers together. This is the number of sides their shape has. Give each child elastic bands and a geo-board. Ask them to create different shapes with that number of sides. Ask them to record all the different shapes using paper and pencil before throwing the dice again.

Be aware

- Children may think the shapes have to be regular for them to be part of their collection. Understanding how different shapes can look given the same properties is an important aspect of this activity.

Outcomes

- I can use the names of 2D shapes and describe them to others.
- I can listen to others in the class and follow instructions.

Supporting resources

Children can make 2D shapes and explore their properties on this interactive pinboard:

- http://www.crickweb.co.uk/assets/resources/flash.php&file=vpinboard4#scene_1

D1: sorting and describing 2D shapes; line symmetry; counting back in 1s, not crossing a ten; counting back in 1s, crossing a ten

Summary

Y2 ☆ D1.2 **What's missing?**

Individuals or pairs working independently

Year 2 Challenge Textbook page 12

Tracing paper; small mirrors; crayons (red, blue, green); digital camera (optional); scissors (optional); kaleidoscope (optional)

Abacus Evolve objectives

- Begin to recognise line symmetry
- Make symmetrical patterns by folding and cutting
- Begin to sketch the reflection of a simple shape in a mirror line

Framework objectives

- Identify reflective symmetry in patterns and 2D shapes and draw lines of symmetry in shapes
- Describe patterns and relationships involving numbers or shapes, make predictions and test these with examples
- Listen to others in class, ask relevant questions and follow instructions

Teacher notes

Preparation
Provide one small mirror per pair.

Getting started
Show Textbook page 12. Explain that the shapes are all symmetrical, but they have been cut in half by mistake. Make sure children understand what this means. *How could you find out what is missing?*

Activity
Children work from Textbook page 12. They trace the half pictures, then try to complete them. They compare their pictures with a partner, and talk about what methods they used. They check their pictures by holding a small mirror along the line of symmetry.

Extra help
Photocopy Textbook page 12 so that children can just complete the pictures, without having to copy them first.

Further extension
Give children a digital camera and ask them to take some photos of symmetrical objects. Print the pictures and then cut them in half. Children give one half to a partner to complete then check by sticking the picture back together.

If you have time
Ask children to investigate a kaleidoscope. *How are they made?*

Be aware

- Deciding on the line of symmetry is important and children need to realise that this has been pre-determined by where the pictures have been cut.

Outcomes

- I can recognise line symmetry.
- I can make symmetrical patterns by folding and cutting.

Supporting resources

Children can look at patterns and symmetry in car wheels in 'Watch those wheels':
- http://nrich.maths.org/public/viewer.php?obj_id=2815

Challenge Plan: Year 2

D1: sorting and describing 2D shapes; line symmetry; counting back in 1s, not crossing a ten; counting back in 1s, crossing a ten

Summary

Y2 ☆ D1.3 — **What is the shape?**

Individuals or pairs working independently

Year 2 Challenge Textbook page 13

Small mirrors

Abacus Evolve objectives

- **Y3** Sketch the reflection of a simple shape in a mirror line along one edge

Framework objectives

- **Y3** *Draw and complete shapes with reflective symmetry; and draw the reflection of a shape in a mirror line along one side*
- **Y3** Identify patterns and relationships involving numbers or shapes, and use these to solve problems

Teacher notes

Preparation
Provide one small mirror per pair.

Getting started
Show children Textbook page 13. Point to the four 'upside-down' words at the top of the page. *These are mirror images of four shape names. You are going to be detectives and find out the secret words!* Explain that children are going to reflect each word in a horizontal mirror line to find out what it is, then draw a shape to match each word, and reflect each of those shapes in a mirror line.

Activity
Children copy the 'upside-down' words, then draw their reflections to find out what the shape names are. Using a small mirror to help, they draw a shape to match each word. They then draw a mirror line along one side of each shape (they can choose where to draw the mirror line) and reflect the shapes in the mirror lines. They should talk to a partner about how the shapes have changed.

Extra help
Give children simpler shapes to reflect first, such as circle, rectangle, square and triangle.

Further extension
Children can make a repeating pattern using shapes drawn and check for lines of symmetry using a small mirror.

If you have time
Draw an imaginary mirror line down the centre of the room. Ask pupils to pair up; one is A, one is B. As stand on one side of the imaginary mirror line. Bs are their reflections. Bs find their partner and stand where they think the mirror image would be.

Be aware

- Drawing the image of a reflection is difficult and requires an understanding of reflection. Encourage pupils to experiment with a mirror image and think carefully about the principles of reflected shapes.
- Children need to know that when a shape is reflected the name of the shape doesn't change. The properties of the shape are the same but the position is different. Reflective symmetry is a transformation like rotation and translation.

Outcomes

- I can draw the reflection of a simple shape.

Supporting resources

Children can explore the symmetry of a square here:
- http://nrich.maths.org/public/viewer.php?obj_id=1873

Challenge Plan: Year 2

D1: sorting and describing 2D shapes; line symmetry; counting back in 1s, not crossing a ten; counting back in 1s, crossing a ten

Summary

Y2 ☆ D1.4 — **Word problems**

Groups working independently

Year 2 Challenge PCMs 19 and 20

Abacus Evolve objectives

- Count back in 1s, not crossing a multiple of 10
- Extend understanding of subtraction as taking away
- Count back in 1s, crossing a multiple of 10, beginning to partition

Framework objectives

- *Add or subtract mentally a one-digit number or a multiple of 10 to or from any two-digit number; use practical and informal written methods to add and subtract two-digit numbers*
- Solve problems involving addition, subtraction, multiplication or division in contexts of numbers, measures or pounds and pence
- Ensure everyone contributes, allocate tasks, consider alternatives and reach agreement

Teacher notes

Preparation
Photocopy PCM 19 and cut into four sections. Photocopy PCM 20, one copy per pair.

Getting started
Organise children into four pairs or groups. Give each pair one section of PCM 19 and explain what they should do. Give each pair a copy of PCM 20.

Activity
Each pair or group reads their part of the story. They work together to solve the word problem and write a number sentence to represent it. Each pair reads their word problem aloud and explains how they worked out the answer.
Children then work from PCM 20. They make up their own stories to fit the three subtractions. Each child reads their story and explains their choices. For each story, children discuss whether the words make sense of the numbers.

Extra help
Ask children to underline each time a number of bulbs is given in each word problem, and show them how to turn these numbers into a number sentence.

Further extension
Ask children to make up their own word problem stories to cut into four parts and repeat the activity using their story.

If you have time
Children can make up number stories for younger children. *What would make it interesting for them?*

Be aware

- Identifying subtraction as taking away in a range of different contexts requires children to understand that it is the same as counting backwards.
- Asking children to explain the context of a calculation to a group requires them to understand which operation is appropriate and therefore which symbol is appropriate in the number sentences.

Outcomes

- I can understand subtraction as taking away.
- I can describe subtractions in different contexts.

Challenge Plan: Year 2

D1: sorting and describing 2D shapes; line symmetry; counting back in 1s, not crossing a ten; counting back in 1s, crossing a ten

Summary

Y2 ☆ D1.5	**Last can!**
	Pairs working independently
	Year 2 Challenge PCM 21
	Tins or cans; dice (optional)

Abacus Evolve objectives

- Count back in 1s, crossing a multiple of 10, beginning to partition

Framework objectives

- *Add or subtract mentally a one-digit number or a multiple of 10 to or from any two-digit number; use practical and informal written methods to add and subtract two-digit numbers*
- Solve problems involving addition, subtraction, multiplication or division in contexts of numbers, measures or pounds and pence

Teacher notes

Preparation
Make a collection of tins or cans.

Getting started
Set up a play shop. Ask children to stack the cans in the shop in different ways in the play corner.
Show children PCM 21. *This shop has set up a display of 50 cans in a pyramid on the floor. You are going to play a game where you knock them down!* Run through the rules.

Activity
Children work from PCM 21. Player 1 chooses a number from 1–5. They 'knock down' the corresponding number of cans, by crossing them off on the picture, starting from 50. They write a number sentence to show how many cans are left in the stack, for example, *50 − 3 = 47*. Children take turns to do this, recording their number sentence each time. The winner is the child to knock down the last can. Children should think about and discuss what strategies they can use to increase their chances of winning.

Extra help
Children can play the game using a dice to dictate the number of cans they knock down each time. This will allow them to concentrate on the subtractions, rather than strategies for winning.

Further extension
If the total number of cans is 50 and you can choose any number from 1–6 to knock down each time, then if you get to a multiple of 7 you are always going to be able to win the game. Why is this?

If you have time
Change the total number of cans and the number of cans that you can take each time. *What difference does this make to your strategy?*

Be aware

- This game builds on children's understanding of subtraction and can develop pattern-making skills to spot links between the number of cans removed and the chances of winning the game.

Outcomes

- I can count backwards to subtract.
- I can play a game with a partner.

Supporting resources

Children can practise addition and subtraction here:
- http://www.bbc.co.uk/schools/ks1bitesize/numeracy/numbers/index.shtml/

Challenge Plan: Year 2

D1: sorting and describing 2D shapes; line symmetry; counting back in 1s, not crossing a ten; counting back in 1s, crossing a ten

Summary

Y2 ☆ D1.6 — **Crocodile teeth**

A small group working with an adult

Year 2 Challenge Textbook page 14

Year 2 Challenge PCM 22

A 1–6 dice; number line

Abacus Evolve objectives

- Count back in 1s, crossing a multiple of 10, beginning to partition
- Subtract one 2-digit number from another using an appropriate strategy

Framework objectives

- *Add or subtract mentally a one-digit number or a multiple of 10 to or from any 2-digit number; use practical and informal written methods to add and subtract 2-digit numbers*
- Solve problems involving addition, subtraction, multiplication or division in contexts of numbers, measures or pounds and pence
- Listen to others in class, ask relevant questions and follow instructions

Teacher notes

Preparation
Photocopy PCM 22, two copies per pair. Cut out the cards. Each pair should have 50 fish cards.

Getting started
Look at Textbook page 14. Make sure children understand the significance of the yellow teeth (multiples of 10).

Activity
- *How many teeth does Baby Croc have?* (50) *Each time he eats a fish one tooth falls out! You are going to play a game where you feed fish to Baby Croc. I want to know how many teeth are left after each meal.*
- Ask a child to roll the dice, and 'feed' that number of fish to the crocodile. *How will you work out how many teeth Baby Croc has left after this meal?* Discuss methods. Encourage children to think about taking away from 50 to find the number left. Use a number line to help. Once agreed, ask: *How do you want to record this?* (On a number line or with a number sentence.)
- Give each child a chance to start from 50, roll the dice, feed fish to Baby Croc, and work out how many teeth are left.
- *Now we're going to make it harder!* Two children take turns, recording subsequent subtractions as number sentences, for example, *50 − 6 = 44*, then *44 − 5 = 39*. Gather their fish. *What would have happened if we had fed all of these to Baby Croc at once?* (11 teeth would have fallen out at once.) Children work out and record the subtraction (50 − 11 = 39). *Is this the same as taking away 6, then 5? Why?*
- In pairs, children play the game, taking turns to generate and record a subtraction each, then putting the two subtractions together. Play until Baby Croc has lost all his teeth.

Extra help
Use a dice with only numbers 1–3 on the faces. Use a number line with all the numbers from 0–50 shown on it.

Further extension
Instead of dice, children choose a number of fish between 1 and 6, aiming to get to the next yellow tooth. For example, player 1 feeds Baby Croc 4 fish and writes the subtraction 50 − 4 = 46. Player 2 feeds Baby Croc 6 fish, and writes the subtraction *46 − 6 = 40*. Play until no teeth are left. *What patterns can you see?*

Be aware

- The link between fish and teeth removes a direct link between the dice and the subtraction calculation.

Outcomes

- I can count backwards to work out how many teeth are left.

Supporting resources

This crocodile activity allows children to practise more than and less than:
- http://www.innovationslearning.co.uk/subjects/maths/activities/year4/greater_than/start.htm

Summary

Y2 ☆ E1.1 **Half a length**

Pairs working independently

Large sheet of paper; strips of paper at least 30 cm long; rulers; scissors

Abacus Evolve objectives

- Recognise halving as the inverse of doubling
- Know by heart doubles for numbers up to at least 15 and the corresponding halves
- Estimate, measure and compare lengths using standard units: centimetres
- Use a ruler to draw and measure lines to the nearest centimetre

Framework objectives

- Understand that halving is the inverse of doubling and derive and recall doubles of all numbers to 20, and the corresponding halves
- Estimate, compare and measure lengths, weights and capacities, choosing and using standard units (m, cm, kg, litre) and suitable measuring instruments
- Read the numbered divisions on a scale, and interpret the divisions between them, e.g. on a scale from 0 to 25 with intervals of 1 shown but only the divisions 0, 5, 10, 15 and 20 numbered; use a ruler to draw and measure lines to the nearest centimetre

Teacher notes

Preparation
Write the following lengths on the board or on a large sheet of paper placed where children can see it: *8 cm*, *20 cm*, *16 cm*, *12 cm*, *18 cm*, and in a different colour *26 cm*, *22 cm*, *30 cm*.
Cut strips of paper at least 30 cm long. You will need about five strips per child.

Getting started
You are going to cut strips of paper to these lengths, then calculate how long half of each strip will be. Use one pair to model the activity, explaining each step. Ask children to work in pairs in the same way. Explain that the three lengths written in a different colour will be more challenging.

Activity
Children work in pairs. Each child chooses a length. They use a ruler to measure along a strip of paper, mark it, and cut it to length. On one side of the strip they write its length. On the other, they write how long half of the strip will be. They swap strips and each child folds their partner's strip in half carefully and measures to check. If any calculations are not accurate, pairs should talk about why this might have been. Children then choose new lengths and repeat.

Extra help
What is half of 20? How could you use this to help you find half of 24?

Further extension
Challenge children to find half of strips that are an odd number of centimetres long.

If you have time
Choose your own lengths to halve.

Information
The strips produced by children can be used with the whole class to rehearse doubling and halving in future mental oral starters, either by showing a strip folded and asking children for the double, or by showing the full length and asking children for the half.

Be aware

- Watch for children who cannot place a ruler correctly.

Outcomes

- I can recall half of numbers up to 20.
- I can measure lengths in cm using a ruler.

Challenge Plan: Year 2

E1: doubling numbers up to 15; doubling multiples of 5; finding totals of coins; paying exact sums using smaller coins

Summary

Y2 ☆ E1.2 — **Function machines**

Pairs working independently

Year 2 Challenge Textbook page 15

Year 2 Challenge PCM 23 (optional)

Digit cards 0–9; 5p and 10p coins (optional)

Abacus Evolve objectives

- Begin to derive doubles of multiples of 5 up to 100 and the corresponding halves
- Know by heart the multiplication facts for 2, 5 and 10 times tables
- Use patterns of similar calculations

Framework objectives

- Understand that halving is the inverse of doubling and derive and recall doubles of all numbers to 20, and the corresponding halves
- Derive and recall multiplication facts for the 2, 5 and 10 times tables and the related division facts; recognise multiples of 2, 5 and 10
- Describe patterns and relationships involving numbers or shapes, make predictions and test these with examples

Teacher notes

Preparation
Photocopy PCM 23 for children who you expect to reach the Extra activity. Children are likely to need two or three copies each.

Getting started
Give each pair a set of digit cards 0–9. Ask them to shuffle the cards and place them face down on the table. Read the instructions on the Textbook page together. Complete one example together, then encourage children to carry on individually.

Activity
Children work from Textbook page 15. They look at the function machine and its operations: × 5 and double. They pick a digit card 0–9 and put the number through the function machine. They fill in the results in the table. They repeat for the other numbers 0–9. Children look at the start, middle and end numbers and describe any patterns that they notice.

Extra help
Give children 5p and 10p coins. They could work out the × 5 part of the calculation by taking the appropriate number of 5p coins. They could then swap each 5p coin for a 10p coin to find the double.

Further extension
Children could use start numbers between 10 and 15 and use coins to support their calculation.

If you have time
What do you think would happen if we put the two parts of the function machine the other way round? So you would double first, and then multiply by 5. Ask children to test out their ideas using start numbers between 0 and 5, recording their work.

Information
When a number is multiplied by 5 and the answer is doubled, this is equivalent to multiplying the number by 10. This links to strategies such as doubling and doubling again to multiply by 4.

Be aware

- Children may say that the end number is the start number with 0 on the end. If so, draw out that this means it is the start number multiplied by 10.
- Children may need to explain the pattern verbally to a partner before attempting to write it down.

Outcomes

- I can multiply small numbers by 5.
- I can double multiples of 5 up to 50.
- I can describe a pattern.

Challenge Plan: Year 2

E1: doubling numbers up to 15; doubling multiples of 5; finding totals of coins; paying exact sums using smaller coins

Summary

Y2 ☆ E1.3 **Three in a row**

A small group working with an adult

Year 2 Challenge PCM 24

Individual whiteboards and pens; a 6-sided dice; counters in two colours

Abacus Evolve objectives

- **Y4** Double or halve 2-digit numbers by doubling or halving the tens first
- **Y4** Derive doubles of integers up to 50 and the corresponding halves
- Partition 2-digit numbers into T and U

Framework objectives

- **Y4** Identify the doubles of 2-digit numbers; use to calculate doubles of multiples of 10 and 100 and derive the corresponding halves
- *Count up to 100 objects by grouping them and counting in 10s, 5s or 2s; explain what each digit in a 2-digit number represents, including numbers where 0 is a place holder; partition 2-digit numbers in different ways, including into multiples of 10 and 1*
- Use language and gesture to support the use of models, diagrams or displays when explaining

Teacher notes

Preparation
Photocopy PCM 24. In each cell of the grid, write a 2-digit number less than 50. Only include numbers whose units digit is 5 or less.

Activity
- Ask children to think about how they would double 35 and record their method on individual whiteboards. When all children have done this, ask them to compare their method with a partner.
- As a group, discuss different methods used. Draw out that it is often helpful to partition 2-digit numbers in order to double them.
- Explain that you are going to use similar methods to double other 2-digit numbers. If necessary work through one or two other examples, such as double 24 or double 41, modelling how to record a partitioning method.
- Divide the group into two teams and show them the game board on PCM 24.
- Roll a dice to see which team starts.
- Team members agree on a number from the grid.
- All children from both teams then double this number on their whiteboards.
- The playing team have to agree on the answer, nominating one child to explain their method. The opposing team members listen and compare the solution to their own. They can challenge if they do not agree. If correct, the playing team places a counter in their colour over the number and they have 'won' this square. If incorrect, the number is left in play. Play alternates between the two teams.
- If a team wins three squares in a row, they win the game.
- As play continues, watch for any child who is finding it difficult to double a number or to record their method. Ask questions such as: *What did you do first? How could you record that?*
- Ensure all children have opportunities to explain methods. Support them towards giving clear explanations.

Further extension
Include some 2-digit numbers with units digits of 6, 7, 8 or 9. Alternatively, play a similar halving game.

Information
Although doubling any 2-digit number is a Year 4 objective, it is within the capabilities of able Year 2 children to double numbers such as 34 and 21 where the units digit is 5 or below.

Be aware

- Some children may forget to double both parts of a number, for example, giving the answer 62 to double 32.

Outcomes

- I can double numbers using partitioning.
- I can explain my choices and methods.

Challenge Plan: Year 2

E1: doubling numbers up to 15; doubling multiples of 5; finding totals of coins; paying exact sums using smaller coins

Summary

Y2 ☆ E1.4 **Two coins investigation**

A small group working with an adult

1p, 2p, 5p, 10p, 20p, 50p and £1 coins; individual whiteboards and pens; £2 coin (optional)

Abacus Evolve objectives

- Recognise all coins and begin to use £·p notation for money
- Find totals of sets of coins: relate to adding three or more numbers

Framework objectives

- Solve problems involving addition, subtraction, multiplication or division in contexts of numbers, measures or pounds and pence
- Present solutions to puzzles and problems in an organised way; explain decisions, methods and results in pictorial, spoken or written form, using mathematical language and number sentences
- Listen to others in class, ask relevant questions and follow instructions

Teacher notes

Activity

- Put one of each of these coins in the middle of the table: 1p, 2p, 5p, 10p, 20p, 50p, £1.
- *Owl and Pussy-Cat have taken these coins with them on their journey. Owl picks up two coins. Your challenge is to work out all of the different possible amounts that Owl could have.*
- Ask each pair to think of two coins that Owl could have chosen and write the total on their whiteboard.
- Choose one example. Ask the group if they agree that this amount could be made with two coins and ask them to identify the two coins that would make that amount.
- Look together at the different amounts that are written on the whiteboards. Ask children to check that each of these amounts could be made from two coins.
- *We've found lots of possible totals, but there are others. Working in pairs, try to write down all the possible totals.* Allow pairs to work independently for a few minutes. Observe them, identifying the pairs that start to work methodically.
- After a few minutes, bring the group together. *Often when you want to find all possible ways to do something, it is helpful to find examples in a particular order.* Choose a pair who has started to work methodically and ask them to describe their order and explain why they chose to work this way. Encourage children to compare and discuss alternative strategies.
- Where possible, encourage children to continue the investigation using the order that they have chosen.
- At the end of the session, bring the group together again to compare their solutions. Ensure children appreciate that, for example, 1p + 2p = 3p and 2p + 1p = 3p give the same total.

Extra help

Model a way to structure the investigation. Start by considering all the possible totals where one coin is a 1p piece. Record as follows:
One coin is a 1p piece:
1p + 2p = 3p   1p + 5p = 6p   1p + 10p = 11p
Ask children to explain the order of the examples so far, then complete this section by continuing with this order. Once they have completed this section, agree the next heading and continue in a similar way.

Further extension

Give children the same coins, plus a £2 coin. Ask them to find all the possible totals if Owl picks up three coins.

Information

There are 21 possible totals with two coins: 3p, 6p, 11p, 21p, 51p, £1·01, 7p, 12p, 22p, 52p, £1·02, 15p, 25p, 55p, £1·05, 30p, 60p, £1·10, 70p, £1·20, £1·50

Be aware

- Check that children are using £·p notation accurately, for example writing £1·01 rather than £1·1.

Outcomes

- I can find the total of two coins.
- I can find all the possible answers to a problem.

Challenge Plan: Year 2

E1: doubling numbers up to 15; doubling multiples of 5; finding totals of coins; paying exact sums using smaller coins

Summary

Y2 ☆ E1.5	**Which three toys?**
	Individuals or pairs working independently
	Year 2 Challenge Textbook page 16
	1p, 2p, 5p, 10p, 20p, 50p, £1 and £2 coins (optional)

Abacus Evolve objectives

- Recognise all coins and begin to use £·p notation for money
- Find totals of sets of coins: relate to adding three or more numbers
- Solve 'real-life' problems involving money (paying an exact sum)
- Add three numbers by putting the largest number first
- Recognise that addition can be done in any order

Framework objectives

- *Add or subtract mentally a single-digit number or a multiple of 10 to or from any 2-digit number; use practical and informal written methods to add and subtract 2-digit numbers*
- Solve problems involving addition, subtraction, multiplication or division in contexts of numbers, measures or pounds and pence

Teacher notes

Getting started
Ask children to look at the toys and their prices on the Textbook page. *One week, Jenny went into the toy shop and bought three toys each day*. They are told the total amount she paid on each day and need to work out which three toys she would have bought to make that total. Ensure that children understand the term 'total'.

Activity
Children work from Textbook page 16. They see seven toys and their prices. They are told that Jenny bought three toys each day from Monday to Friday. They are shown one toy that Jenny bought on Monday and are asked to find the other two. Children are then given the total cost spent for each of the remaining days, and they must work out which three toys Jenny must have bought to make the totals.

Extra help
If children are not sure how to start, suggest they begin with the most expensive toy that Jenny could have bought. Children could use coins to help them test out totals.

Further extension
Give children totals that can be made if Jenny bought four toys, for example: £1·72, 77p, £2·65, £3·07, £1·32.
Ask them to identify which four toys together would make each given total.

Information
Encourage children to be efficient by using reasoning to identify the toys rather than simply trying three toys randomly. A useful clue is to consider the most expensive toy that Jenny might have bought and use this as a starting point. Children could then use the inverse operation (subtraction) to find how much more money Jenny needs to spend to make the given total. This will help them to identify the other two toys.

Be aware

- Make sure that children understand £·p notation, for example appreciating that £2·07 means two pounds and seven pence.

Outcomes

- I can add costs to find a total.
- I can find three amounts that add to a given total.
- I can solve problems involving money.

Supporting resources

- Some children may find it helpful to use number lines to add the costs of the toys.

Challenge Plan: Year 2

E1: doubling numbers up to 15; doubling multiples of 5; finding totals of coins; paying exact sums using smaller coins

Summary

Y2 ☆ E1.6 — **Snack shop**

Pairs working independently

Year 2 Challenge Textbook page 17

1p, 2p, 5p, 10p, 20p, 50p and £1 coins; 0–100 number lines

Abacus Evolve objectives

- Find totals of sets of coins: relate to adding three or more numbers
- Pay an exact sum using smaller coins up to £2
- Solve 'real-life' problems involving money (paying an exact sum)
- Add or subtract mentally a single-digit number or a multiple of 10 to or from any 2-digit number; use practical and informal written methods to add and subtract 2-digit numbers

Framework objectives

- Solve problems involving addition, subtraction, multiplication or division in contexts of numbers, measures or pounds and pence
- Identify and record the information or calculation needed to solve a puzzle or problem; carry out the steps or calculations and check the solution in the context of the problem
- Ensure everyone contributes, allocate tasks, consider alternatives and reach agreement

Teacher notes

Getting started
Look at the Textbook page. *This is a menu for a snack shop.* Check that children all understand what a menu is. *Three friends, Amy, Bilal and Callie, went to the snack shop together.* Read through the items on the menu together. Ask one child to read aloud the problem involving what Amy bought. Explain to children that they are going to work in pairs to solve the problem. *You will need to discuss your ideas with your partner and talk about the best way to solve the problem. Make a note of your working. Then you are going to write your own problem for another pair to solve.*
Make coins and number lines available for children to use if they wish.

Activity
Children work from Textbook page 17. Pairs use the prices on the menu to solve the given problem. This involves finding the total cost of the jam sandwich and the apple, then working out the change from £1.
Children then devise a problem with their partner, write this down and work out the answer. Pairs then swap problems, solve the problem they have been given and compare solutions.

Extra help
If pairs are not sure how to solve the problem, ask questions such as: *What information from the menu do you need to use? What do you need to work out first? What calculation will this involve? What do you need to do next? What calculation will this involve? What does this tell you?*

Further extension
Encourage children to write questions that involve at least two steps.

If you have time
Pairs can write more than one problem. You could display the menu with the questions and answers generated.

Be aware

- Children sometimes struggle to answer problems that involve more than one step. Structure their thinking using questions such as: *What have you found so far? What do you need to do next?*

Outcomes

- I can solve problems involving money.
- I can find the total of prices.
- I can work out what change needs to be given in a shopping problem.

Supporting resources

- It may be useful to display key vocabulary used in money problems, including: *cost*, *price*, *total*, *pay*, *buy*, *amount*, *altogether*, *coins*, *change*, *How much...?* and *How much more...?*

Summary

Y2 ☆ A2.1	**Number cascades**
	Individuals or pairs working independently
	Year 2 Challenge PCM 25
	0–100 number line (optional); base-10 equipment (optional)

Abacus Evolve objectives

- **Y3** Count on and back in 100s from any number
- **Y3** Say the number that is 1, 10 or 100 more or less than a given number
- **Y3** Partition 3-digit numbers into H, T and U
- **Y3** Extend use of patterns of similar calculations

Framework objectives

- **Y3** Read, write and order whole numbers to at least 1000 and position them on a number line; count on from and back to zero in single-digit steps or multiples of 10
- **Y3** Partition 3-digit numbers into multiples of 100, 10 and 1 in different ways
- **Y3** Identify patterns and relationships involving numbers or shapes, and use these to solve problems

Teacher notes

Preparation
Photocopy PCM 25, one copy per child.

Getting started
Show children the first number cascade on PCM 25. *How do you think it works? How would you complete it?* Talk through some strategies for adding 1, 10 and 100 to 68.
Point out the last part of the activity involves counting back.

Activity
Children work from PCM 25. They complete the number cascades, counting on in 1s, 10s and 100s. For the last part of the activity, they draw their own number cascades and count back in 1s, 10s and 100s. They will need to think about what numbers they could start from (numbers larger than 300, to avoid going into negative numbers).

Extra help
A 0–100 number line or base-10 equipment could be useful.

Further extension
Ask children to look at the difference between numbers on the same row in any one cascade. *How do these differences change as the cascade grows? Can you explain why?*

Information
The differences between numbers on the cascades are:

9	90
18	180
27	270

The combination of adding 1 and 10 results in a difference of 9, increasing by 9 as you move to the next row. The combination of adding 10 and 100 results in a difference of 90, increasing by 90 as you move to the next row.

Be aware

- Switching between counting in 1s, 10s and 100s can be difficult. Children may prefer to view the numbers as if they were in columns and focus on one column at a time.

Outcomes

- I can count on (and back) in 1s, 10s and 100s from any 2- or 3-digit number.

A2: counting on and back in 1s, 10s or 100s; recognising odd and even numbers; understanding ordinal numbers; comparing 2-digit numbers

Summary

Y2 ☆ A2.2 — **Odd and even dominoes**

A small group working with an adult

Year 2 Challenge Textbook page 18

Sets of dominoes; sticky notes (optional); 0–20 number line (optional)

Abacus Evolve objectives

- Begin to recognise odd and even numbers up to at least 50
- Know by heart addition and subtraction facts for pairs of numbers that total up to 10
- Use patterns of similar calculations

Framework objectives

- Read and write 2- and 3-digit numbers in figures and words; describe and extend number sequences and recognise odd and even numbers
- *Derive and recall all addition and subtraction facts for each number to at least 10, all pairs with totals to 20 and all pairs of multiples of 10 with totals up to 100*
- Describe patterns and relationships involving numbers or shapes, make predictions and test these with examples
- Use language and gesture to support the use of models, diagrams or displays when explaining

Teacher notes

Activity

- Give each pair of children a set of dominoes.
- Look at a few dominoes together. *How many dots are on this side? Is that an odd number or an even number? How do you know? What about the other side?*
- *We are going to sort the dominoes into three piles. To do this, we will need to decide whether each number is odd or even.*
- Look at Textbook page 18 together and discuss the piles children will need to sort their dominoes into. Make sure they understand that an even/odd domino goes in the same pile as an odd/even domino. *They are the same, but one is turned the other way round!*
- Ask children to work in pairs to sort their set of dominoes into the three piles. Support children as they decide where to place each domino. Children may find it useful to use a sticky note to label each pile.
- Children work from Textbook page 18. In pairs, they mark out three columns, and draw the three types of domino at the tops of the columns. Below each type, they record the dominoes from that pile as number sentences, for example, *4 + 4* would go in the even/even column. Pairs then find the total of each domino.
- They discuss the totals in each column, then complete the rules *odd + odd = even*, *even + even = even* and *even + odd = odd*.
- As a group, encourage children to discuss what they have found out.

Extra help

A 0–20 number line will support addition.

Information

For the Extra activity, if children understand that odd and even depends on the units digit, they should be able to convince themselves that the statements odd + odd = even, even + even = even and odd + even (or even + odd) = odd are always true.

Be aware

- If you only have a short period of time, use one set of dominoes between the whole group. After sorting the dominoes, each pair could focus on one pile. Children can then pool their information and ideas to reach a conclusion.

Outcomes

- I can recognise odd and even numbers.
- I can add odd and even numbers and find patterns in the totals.

Challenge Plan: Year 2

A2: counting on and back in 1s, 10s or 100s; recognising odd and even numbers; understanding ordinal numbers; comparing 2-digit numbers

Summary

Y2 ☆ A2.3	**Walk the plank!**
	Pairs working independently
	Year 2 Challenge PCM 26
	Sets of dominoes; bags; counters; 6-sided dice (optional)

Abacus Evolve objectives

- Begin to recognise odd and even numbers up to at least 50
- Know by heart addition and subtraction facts for pairs of numbers that total up to 10

Framework objectives

- Read and write 2- and 3-digit numbers in figures and words; describe and extend number sequences and recognise odd and even numbers
- *Derive and recall all addition and subtraction facts for each number to at least 10, all pairs with totals to 20 and all pairs of multiples of 10 with totals up to 100*
- Describe patterns and relationships involving numbers or shapes, make predictions and test these with examples
- Ensure everyone contributes, allocate tasks, consider alternatives and reach agreement

Teacher notes

Preparation
Photocopy PCM 26, one copy per pair.

Getting started
Give each pair a copy of the PCM, a full set of 28 dominoes in a bag, and a counter each. Quickly run through the rules of the game and make sure children understand what to do.

Activity
Children play the game on PCM 26. They both place their counter on Start. They take turns to take a domino from the bag, and add the two numbers. If the total is even, they move up the plank. If the total is odd, they move down. If they go beyond either end of the plank, they are out and their partner is the winner.
Pairs should play the game several times, looking out for patterns.

Further extension
Ask children to play the game using a 1 to 6 dice, moving up or down according to the odd or even numbers rolled. Ask children what is different about playing the game this way. (There are just as many odd as even numbers on a 1 to 6 dice, so there should be no particular pattern to winning or losing, unless the dice is weighted.)

Information
Out of a full set of 28 dominoes, there are 16 with an even total and 12 with an odd total. If children have already completed activity A2.2, they should be familiar with the rules odd + odd = even, even + even = even and odd + even (or even + odd) = odd. They should therefore be able to identify that an even total is more likely, and so they are more likely to go beyond the even end of the plank.

Be aware

- It may take several games for children to spot any patterns. Encourage recording of who won and which end the losing player 'walked off' to help recognition.

Outcomes

- I can recognise odd and even numbers.
- I can use my understanding of odd and even to spot patterns.

A2: counting on and back in 1s, 10s or 100s; recognising odd and even numbers; understanding ordinal numbers; comparing 2-digit numbers

Summary

Y2 ☆ A2.4 — **Order puzzles**

Individuals or pairs working independently

Year 2 Challenge Textbook page 19

Squared paper (optional)

Abacus Evolve objectives

- Understand and use ordinal numbers up to at least 100th

Framework objectives

- Order 2-digit numbers and position them on a number line; use the greater than (>), less than (<) signs
- Solve problems involving addition, subtraction, multiplication or division in contexts of numbers, measures or pounds and pence

Teacher notes

Getting started
Look at the Textbook page. Explain that children must follow the clues to identify the correct letters. They then rearrange the letters to make the name of a shape, and draw the shape.

Activity
Children work from Textbook page 19. They solve the two puzzles, finding the letters, rearranging them to make the name of a shape, and drawing the shape.

Extra help
If children have found all the correct letters but cannot work out the words, give them the starting letter for each word or tell them that the word spells out the name of a shape that they know very well.

If you have time
Ask children to draw up a table of ordinal numbers and words.

1	first	1st
2	second	2nd
3	third	3rd

How far can they go? They could use a computer to make a poster showing the ordinal numbers in words and figures, to be displayed on the wall for everyone to use.

Information
The solutions to the puzzles are *square* and *circle*.

Be aware

- Some children may find it hard to work out the words, even with extra clues. If so, you could give them small pieces of paper to write each letter on. They can then physically move and swap letters and should be able to solve the puzzle.

Outcomes

- I can use ordinal numbers.
- I can solve puzzles using ordinal numbers.

Supporting resources

Here are some ideas for other activities involving ordinal numbers:
- http://www.numberlinelane.co.uk/activity?number=2

Summary

Y2 ☆ A2.5 **Number puzzles**

A small group working with an adult

Year 2 Challenge PCMs 27 and 28

1–100 squares (optional)

Abacus Evolve objectives

- Compare two or more 2-digit numbers; introduce the greater than (>), less than (<) signs
- Begin to recognise odd and even numbers up to at least 100

Framework objectives

- Order 2-digit numbers and position them on a number line; use the greater than (>), less than (<) signs
- Read and write 2- and 3-digit numbers in figures and words; describe and extend number sequences and recognise odd and even numbers
- Identify and record the information or calculation needed to solve a puzzle or problem; carry out the steps or calculations and check the solution in the context of the problem
- Listen to a talk by an adult, remember some specific points and identify what they have learned

Teacher notes

Preparation

Photocopy PCMs 27 and 28, one copy of each per child.

Activity

- Write the numbers 8 and 3. *Which number is larger? Which number is smaller?*
- *We sometimes say that the larger number is 'greater than' the smaller number, and we say that the smaller number is 'less than' the larger number. There are two special signs that mean 'greater than' and 'less than'.* Draw the < and > signs. Explain that the 'open' end of the sign faces the larger number. *So which sign should be between 8 and 3?* Draw the > sign between the two numbers.
- Work as a group to write some number statements using the signs. Check that all children understand what they mean and how and when to use them.
- Give each child a copy of PCM 27. Read the statements for the first puzzle together and check that everyone understands what they mean. Work together to solve the first puzzle. Show children how to cross out the numbers eliminated by the clues.
- Ask children to work in pairs to solve the second puzzle.
- Give each child a copy of PCM 28. Ask children to work either individually or with a partner to make up two number puzzles. Remind children of any number rules or patterns they could use as clues. Encourage the use of the > and < signs. Children swap with another child or pair and solve each other's puzzles.
- As a group, discuss which puzzles were harder to solve and which were easier. *Were any impossible to solve? Why?*

Extra help

Provide some spare 1–100 squares for children who might need to start again on one of the puzzles.

Provide some spare copies of PCM 28. When making up their own puzzles, children may need to experiment with writing clues and crossing out numbers before making a best copy to pass on to others to solve.

Information

The solutions to the puzzles on PCM 27 are 75 and 16.

Be aware

- It can be difficult to keep track of which numbers are eliminated, particularly when the clue includes the word 'not'. Check understanding of the more difficult clues before children action them.

Outcomes

- I can use the > and < signs to show which number is larger and which is smaller.
- I can solve clues to find a mystery number.

Challenge Plan: Year 2

A2: counting on and back in 1s, 10s or 100s; recognising odd and even numbers; understanding ordinal numbers; comparing 2-digit numbers

Summary

Y2 ☆ A2.6 — **Greater than, less than**

Individuals or pairs working independently

Year 2 Challenge Textbook page 20

Abacus Evolve objectives

- Compare two or more 2-digit numbers; introduce the greater than (>), less than (<) signs
- Say a number lying between two numbers, up to at least 100

Framework objectives

- Order 2-digit numbers and position them on a number line; use the greater than (>), less than (<) signs

Teacher notes

Getting started
Look at the Textbook page. Quickly read through the instructions together. Make sure children remember how to use the greater than (>) and less than (<) signs.

Activity
Children work from Textbook page 20. They choose two numbers from the number line and write a number sentence using > or <. They create 10 sentences like this. They move on to writing sentences with more than one inequality in it, for example, 12 < 37 < 65. They then write sets of three numbers with boxes in between, for example, 61 □ 94 □ 46. They give these to a partner, who fills in the missing > and < signs.

Extra help
For children who are less confident in using the > and < signs, encourage them to ask other children in the group to check their number sentences.

Further extension
Draw a 0–500 number line and label 10 or more numbers. Ask children to do the activity on the Textbook page, but using your number line rather than the one shown.

Be aware

- Even if children find it straightforward to order numbers, they may find it much more difficult to place them appropriately on a number line. Practise with numbers to 10, then 100, before moving on to 500 and then 1000.

Outcomes

- I can write number sentences using greater than > or less than <.

Challenge Plan: Year 2

B2: addition and subtraction facts that total up to 10; adding three 1-digit numbers mentally; right angles; clockwise and anticlockwise turns

Summary

Y2 ☆ B2.1 — **Building monsters**

A small group working with an adult

Year 2 Challenge PCM 29

6-sided dice

Abacus Evolve objectives

- Rehearse addition and subtraction facts for pairs of numbers that total up to 10

Framework objectives

- *Derive and recall all addition and subtraction facts for each number to at least 10, all pairs with totals to 20 and all pairs of multiples of 10 with totals up to 100*
- Use language and gesture to support the use of models, diagrams or displays when explaining

Teacher notes

Preparation
Photocopy PCM 29, one copy per child.

Activity
- Give each child a copy of the PCM. *You are going to create your own monsters!* Give each pair of children two 6-sided dice.
- Demonstrate the game with one child. These are the rules:
- Player A throws the two dice and finds the total.
- Player A decides which monster body parts to 'buy' using their dice score. This is what they can buy using the following scores: finger = 2; head = 10; body = 7; arm = 5; toe = 1; hand = 4; leg = 6; foot = 3. Player A can choose any body parts up to the total value on the dice. For example, if they threw a total of 12, they could buy a head and a finger, or six fingers, or one body and one arm, and so on.
- Player A draws their chosen body parts. They then record their score in the table, and write what they bought.
- Player B now has their turn.
- Children take turns until they have had five turns each.
- Once all the children in the group have completed the game, ask each child to work out the total score of their monster.
- Swap children around so they are each with a different partner. They should keep their monsters concealed from each other. They take turns to describe their monster, and their partner draws what they think the monster looks like. They compare their drawings.
- Discuss what was difficult about this activity, and what was easy. *Did anyone have any quick ways to add up the two numbers on the dice?*

Extra help
Use one dice and fewer features to make the monsters.

Further extension
There are two monsters, and we know all the body parts they have between them, but we don't know which body parts belong to each monster. Write out a list of all the body parts: *10 fingers, 2 heads, 2 bodies, 2 arms, 20 toes, 4 hands. The total score for one of the monsters is 30. Can you work out which body parts might belong to each monster?*

Be aware

- Many children are keen to do beautiful drawings and decorate them. It may be necessary to remind them they are drawing a diagram showing body parts only; a detailed drawing is not needed.

Outcomes

- I can find the total of two dice numbers.
- I can work out what I can 'buy' with my dice score.

Challenge Plan: Year 2

B2: addition and subtraction facts that total up to 10; adding three 1-digit numbers mentally; right angles; clockwise and anticlockwise turns

Summary

Y2 ☆ B2.2 — **Making squares**

Pairs working independently

Year 2 Challenge PCM 30

Abacus Evolve objectives

- Begin to add three 1-digit numbers mentally
- Add by counting on in 1s from the larger number, crossing a multiple of 10
- Add three numbers by putting the largest number first
- Recognise that addition can be done in any order

Framework objectives

- *Add or subtract mentally a single-digit number or a multiple of 10 to or from any 2-digit number; use practical and informal written methods to add and subtract 2-digit numbers*
- Adopt appropriate roles in small or large groups and consider alternative courses of action

Teacher notes

Preparation
Photocopy PCM 30, one copy per child.

Getting started
Give each pair two copies of the PCM. Ask a child to read the instructions aloud. Make sure everyone understands the rules of the game. Explain that they will use one copy of the PCM to play the game once, then use their spare copy to play again.

Activity
Children work from PCM 30. The object of the game is to colour a square of numbers on the number grid, with three numbers along each side. These are the rules:

- Player A choose three numbers in a line (the line must be horizontal or vertical), for example 3, 3, 7. They find the total, for example 13.
- Player B must check whether they have found the correct total.
- If Player B agrees that the total is correct, Player A can colour the three chosen numbers.
- It is now Player B's turn.
- Players continue to take turns, trying to complete four sides of a square. They may try to stop each other from completing their squares, so this is a game of strategy.

6	4	4	4	2
3	3	3	7	9
7	4	1	8	0
1	5	5	5	1
1	5	7	6	9

Children play the game twice to give them more time to come up with strategies for winning.

Extra help
Play a non-competitive version of this game where pairs calculate answers and complete a square together.

Further extension
Make a new version of the number grid using 2-digit numbers. Ask children to record their working.

If you have time
Play this game in teams and discuss which strategies work well.

Be aware

- Encourage children to add by starting with the largest number, or by looking for 'easy' pairs such as those that add to a multiple of 10.

Outcomes

- I can add three 1-digit numbers mentally to play a game with my partner.

Summary

Y2 ☆ B2.3 **Darts**

Pairs working independently

Year 2 Challenge PCM 31

Counters

Abacus Evolve objectives

- Begin to add three 1-digit numbers mentally
- Add by counting on in 1s from the larger number, crossing a multiple of 10
- Add three numbers by putting the largest number first
- Recognise that addition can be done in any order
- Count back in 1s, crossing a multiple of 10, beginning to partition
- Rehearse addition and subtraction facts for pairs of numbers that total 10

Framework objectives

- *Add or subtract mentally a single-digit number or a multiple of 10 to or from any 2-digit number; use practical and informal written methods to add and subtract 2-digit numbers*
- *Derive and recall all addition and subtraction facts for each number to at least 10, all pairs with totals to 20 and all pairs of multiples of 10 with totals up to 100*
- Ensure everyone contributes, allocate tasks, consider alternatives and reach agreement

Teacher notes

Preparation
Photocopy PCM 31, one copy per child.

Getting started
Give each pair two copies of the PCM, and three counters. *You are going to play a game like darts.* Ask a child to read aloud the instructions on the PCM. Make sure everyone understands how to play the game. If necessary, quickly run through some good strategies for mentally adding and subtracting small numbers. Explain why pairs have two copies of the PCM: one is for playing the game with a target of 23, and the other is for them to play again with their own target number.

Activity
Children work from PCM 31. They play the following game:

- Both players start with a score of 0, and their target is 23.
- Player A chooses three numbers from the dartboard, for example, 8, 9 and 10. They place a counter on each number to show that they have chosen them.
- Player A then decides whether to add or subtract each number from their total. For example, they might start from 0 and add all the numbers to give a total of 27. (They should be planning ahead to their next move, when they might want to subtract some numbers.)
- They record their new total in the table.
- Player B then has a turn.
- The players have four turns each. The player whose score is closest to 23 at the end is the winner.

Children play the game once with a target of 23, then play again with their own target number.
Children who think strategically will be thinking ahead more than one turn.

Further extension
Create a new version of the dartboard with an extra ring around the outside. Explain to children that a dart in this outer ring is worth double the number in the inner ring.

If you have time
Children could play this as a game of chance by throwing three dice to choose which three numbers to land on.

Be aware

- If children know the game of darts they may be confused by the rules of this game as they can choose to add or subtract numbers. You may need to point out that this is a maths game, therefore the rules are different today!

Outcomes

- I can add or subtract three small numbers in my head.

Challenge Plan: Year 2

B2: addition and subtraction facts that total up to 10; adding three 1-digit numbers mentally; right angles; clockwise and anticlockwise turns

Summary

Y2 ☆ B2.4 — **Square corners**

Pairs working independently

Year 2 Challenge Textbook page 21

Blue and white squares of paper; scissors; glue; A4 paper; digital camera (optional)

Abacus Evolve objectives

- Recognise right angles in simple shapes
- Make symmetrical patterns by folding and cutting

Framework objectives

- Recognise and use whole, half and quarter turns, both clockwise and anti-clockwise; know that a right angle represents a quarter turn
- Identify reflective symmetry in patterns and 2D shapes and draw lines of symmetry in shapes
- Ensure everyone contributes, allocate tasks, consider alternatives and reach agreement

Teacher notes

Preparation
Cut out identical sized squares of blue and white paper. You will need between two and four of each per pair.

Getting started
Look at the Textbook page. Explain that children are going to work in pairs to fold and cut their squares of paper to make the pattern shown on the page. Show them how to make a right-angle tester by neatly folding an A4 piece of paper in half lengthways and then widthways. Explain that they can use this to check whether they have made exact right angles. Give each pair one blue and one white square of paper, a pair of scissors and some glue. Explain that these are for them to use to make the pattern shown in the Textbook. Put a pile of blue and white squares in the middle of the table, and explain that these are for children to make up their own patterns.

Activity
Children work from Textbook page 21. They follow the instructions to make a blue and white pattern of squares and right-angled triangles. They will need to be very careful when folding and cutting the paper, to make sure their right angles are accurate. They can check their right angles using their right-angle testers.
Children answer questions about the numbers of right angles they can see. They then make their own patterns using blue and white squares, and see how many right angles they can make.

Extra help
For children who struggle with cutting along a straight line, you could prepare their right-angled triangles for them beforehand.

Further extension
Set the challenge of making blue and white patterns with a specific number of right angles, for example, *How many patterns can you make with 12 right angles? Can you make a pattern with an odd number of right angles?*

If you have time
Ask children to research rangoli patterns and count the right angles.

Be aware

- Children will need to be aware of symmetry in order to successfully cut a right angle from half a square.

Outcomes

- I can create a pattern with right angles.
- I can see right angles in patterns.

Supporting resources

Read about rangoli patterns:
- http://nrich.maths.org/public/viewer.php?obj_id=5369

Children could try this Right Angle Challenge:
- http://nrich.maths.org/public/viewer.php?obj_id=2812

B2: addition and subtraction facts that total up to 10; adding three 1-digit numbers mentally; right angles; clockwise and anticlockwise turns

Summary

Y2 ☆ B2.5 **Ice-skating**

A small group working with an adult

Year 2 Challenge Textbook page 22

Year 2 Challenge PCM 32

Analogue clock; A1 paper; pens; tack

Abacus Evolve objectives

- Recognise clockwise and anticlockwise turns
- Recognise whole, half and quarter turns
- Know that a right angle is a measure of a quarter turn

Framework objectives

- Recognise and use whole, half and quarter turns, both clockwise and anti-clockwise; know that a right angle represents a quarter turn
- Use language and gesture to support the use of models, diagrams or displays when explaining

Teacher notes

Preparation
Photocopy PCM 32, one copy per pair. Cut out the cards.

Activity

- *This activity is about ice-skating.* Discuss what children know about this.
- Ask children to spin round a half turn. *How do you know when you have finished? Can you do a whole turn?* Discuss the fact that the direction that you end up facing is important.
- Look at the Textbook page. Discuss the two different jumps shown in the diagrams, and explain how the arrows on the diagrams show the direction of the turn.
- Show children an analogue clock. Remind them about the different hands and how they turn. Demonstrate turning the minute hand a full turn. *The hands on a clock always turn in a clockwise direction. In one hour, the minute hand turns one full turn clockwise.*
- Explain the link between whole, half and quarter turns and right angles.
- Give each pair a set of cards from PCM 32. Ask them to put together pairs of cards: one showing the direction of the turn (*clockwise* or *anticlockwise*), and one showing the amount of the turn (*whole turn*, *half turn* or *quarter turn*). They challenge their partner to perform the turn shown by the cards. Ask them to record each turn using a diagram. They can stand on a piece of A1 paper and mark the direction in which their feet turn with a pen. They can then stick the two cards used below the diagram using tack.
- Children work from Textbook page 22. They read about the turns that four skaters performed in a routine, and decide which diagram belongs to each skater.

Extra help
When children are using the cards, you could take out the *half turn* and *quarter turn* cards. Children could then specify the number of whole turns their partner must perform.

Further extension
Introduce the idea of degrees. Discuss the fact that there are 360 degrees in a whole turn. Explain that this is how we compare the size of a turn. *Can anyone work out how many degrees there are in a half turn?*

If you have time
Ask children to devise a dance routine using the cards from the PCM, then record what they have decided. They could teach their routine to a small group of children, to perform during your next PE lesson.

Be aware

- Some children may be sensitive to turning and become confused. It is important to discuss giddiness and show children how to avoid it.

Outcomes

- I can recognise and describe clockwise and anticlockwise turns.

Supporting resources

Read about Olympic figure-skating:

- http://www.olympic.org/uk/sports/programme/disciplines_uk.asp?DiscCode=FS

Challenge Plan: Year 2

B2: addition and subtraction facts that total up to 10; adding three 1-digit numbers mentally; right angles; clockwise and anticlockwise turns

Summary

Y2 ☆ B2.6 — **Getting to the wedding**

Groups working independently

Year 2 Challenge Textbook page 23

Toy telephones or plastic cups (optional); local map (optional)

Abacus Evolve objectives

- Give instructions for moving along a route in straight lines and round corners
- Recognise clockwise and anticlockwise turns
- Recognise whole, half and quarter turns
- Estimate, measure and compare lengths using standard units: centimetres

Framework objectives

- Follow and give instructions involving position, direction and movement
- Recognise and use whole, half and quarter turns, both clockwise and anti-clockwise; know that a right angle represents a quarter turn
- Estimate, compare and measure lengths, weights and capacities, choosing and using standard units (m, cm, kg, litre) and suitable measuring instruments
- Listen to others in class, ask relevant questions and follow instructions

Teacher notes

Getting started

Look at the Textbook page. *Mr Jordan is going to a wedding. He is trying to decide which route to take to get to the church. He asks three friends for the best route, but they all come up with a different way.* Ask a child to read aloud the instructions on the page. Make sure everyone understands what they need to do. Emphasise that they only need to give very rough estimates of the lengths of the lines – it is the descriptions of the turns that are the most important thing. If possible, give children toy telephones or plastic cups, so they can pretend to be on the phone to each other.

Activity

Children work from Textbook page 23. One child in the pair secretly chooses a route. They describe it to their partner using phrases such as: *Go forwards roughly two centimetres; turn a quarter turn clockwise.* Their partner draws the route on a sheet of paper, without looking at the Textbook page. When they have finished, the first child shows their chosen route on the Textbook page, and they compare it to what the second child has drawn. Children then swap roles.

Extra help

Children could work together to describe the routes on the Textbook page.
Alternatively, the first child could secretly choose a route on the Textbook page, and describe it to their partner. The second child looks at the Textbook page during the description, and works out which route is being described.

Further extension

Children could do the activity in threes: child A describes a route; child B records the description of the route; child C draws the route. They swap so that everyone has a chance to do each role.

Be aware

- This activity focuses on the most efficient way of describing a route so that another person can follow it. Encourage children to be as precise and clear as possible.

Outcomes

- I can describe a route with straight lines and corners.
- I can draw a route from someone else's description.

Supporting resources

Use The AA Route Planner to look at different ways of giving instructions:

- http://www.theaa.com/route-planner/classic/planner_main.jsp

C2: estimating, measuring and comparing weights in kg and g; reading analogue and digital time; block graphs; pictograms

Summary

Y2 ☆ C2.1 **How heavy?**

Pairs working independently

Year 2 Challenge PCM 33

A 415 g tin of beans; a 250 g packet of biscuits; a 300 g jar of peanut butter; a 200 g tin of tuna; a 500 g packet of pasta; a 25 g packet of crisps (all weights approximate); sticky labels; weights, for example, 1 g, 10 g, 100 g, 1 kg (optional); scales (optional)

Abacus Evolve objectives

- Estimate, measure and compare weights using standard units: kilograms, grams
- Begin to recognise the relationship between grams and kilograms

Framework objectives

- Estimate, compare and measure lengths, weights and capacities, choosing and using standard units (m, cm, kg, litre) and suitable measuring instruments
- Adopt appropriate roles in small or large groups and consider alternative courses of action

Teacher notes

Preparation
Photocopy PCM 33, one copy per pair.
Collect the products shown on the PCM and use a sticky label to cover up the weight on each product.

Getting started
Give each pair a copy of the PCM. Put the six products on the table.

Activity
Children work from PCM 33. They estimate the weight of each product, and colour the weight that they think is the closest.

Extra help
Encourage children to handle the products themselves to aid estimates. You could also give children a variety of weights for them to handle and compare to the products.

Further extension
Ask children to weigh the products, then number the items 1–6 on the PCM, with 1 being the lightest and 6 being the heaviest.

If you have time
Ask children to swap sheets with another pair. Ask children to weigh the products, then mark each other's estimates.

Be aware

- Warn children that some of the items are quite heavy, especially if dropped on a toe, so they should handle them over the table.

Outcomes

- I can make reasonable estimates of weights.
- I know when to use grams and when to use kilograms.

C2: estimating, measuring and comparing weights in kg and g; reading analogue and digital time; block graphs; pictograms

Summary

Y2 ☆ C2.2 **More or less?**

A small group working with an adult

Year 2 Challenge PCM 34

Balance scales; weights; one tin of food; one packet of food; one jar of food; matching or similar empty tin, packet and jar (optional)

Abacus Evolve objectives

- Estimate, measure and compare weights using standard units: kilograms, grams
- Find the difference between two numbers by counting on

Framework objectives

- Estimate, compare and measure lengths, weights and capacities, choosing and using standard units (m, cm, kg, litre) and suitable measuring instruments
- Understand that subtraction is the inverse of addition and vice versa and use this to derive and record related addition and subtraction number sentences
- Listen to others in class, ask relevant questions and follow instructions

Teacher notes

Preparation
Photocopy PCM 34, one copy per child.
Collect three products: one tin of food, for example, beans; one packet of food, for example, flour; and one jar of food, for example, sauce.
Collect three empty food containers: one tin, one packet and one jar. These are needed for the 'Further extension' activity. Do not show them to children until they are needed.

Activity

- Show children the three food products. Ask them to find the weight written on each label. *We are going to check that the makers have labelled these products correctly!*
- Give each child a copy of PCM 34. Ask them to draw the three items in the boxes on the left.
- Ask children to weigh each item. They should put a product in the first pan of the balance scales, then collect the appropriate weights to make the amount shown on the product and place them in the second pan. The scales should not balance. Ask children to add weights until the pans balance and then work out how much additional weight was needed to balance the product. *This is the difference between the weight on the product label and the actual weight.*
- Ask children to record what they have found out on the PCM, then work in pairs to answer the questions.
- Bring the group back together for a quick discussion about answers to the questions.

Extra help
If children have weighed each item but cannot make any further progress, ask what else they have in their hand as well as the beans: *Something you cannot eat*. With some gentle support, they should recognise that they are also holding a tin/packet/jar.

Further extension
Give children the empty containers and ask them to find their weights. *Do they match the differences you found earlier?*

If you have time
Discuss the *e* that is sometimes shown after the weight on food packaging. *What might it stand for? Why would manufacturers label products in this way?* (The symbol e is used to show that the weight complies with the EU requirement for weight under the average system, i.e. the average pack is at least the weight shown.)

Be aware

- All three products should weigh more than their labelled weight. However, it might be a good idea to quickly check beforehand.

Outcomes

- I can weigh items in grams.
- I can work out the difference between two weights.

Summary

Y2 ☆ C2.3 **Changing times**

Pairs or groups working independently

Year 2 Challenge PCM 35

Card clock faces (optional); digital clocks (optional); number name cards one–twelve (optional)

Abacus Evolve objectives

- Read the time to the hour and half hour on analogue and 12-hour digital clocks

Framework objectives

- *Use units of time (seconds, minutes, hours, days) and know the relationships between them; read the time to the quarter hour; identify time intervals, including those that cross the hour*
- Ensure everyone contributes, allocate tasks, consider alternatives and reach agreement

Teacher notes

Preparation
Photocopy PCM 35, one per child.

Getting started
Give each child a copy of the PCM. Talk through the times in words and check that children can read the words *earlier* and *later*.

Activity
Children work from PCM 35. They read the time in words and the instruction for changing that time, for example *Two hours later than seven o'clock*. They work out the new time together and then each child records it on the blank analogue and digital clocks.

Extra help
Have card clock faces and digital clocks available for children to use. A list of number words from one to twelve with the appropriate number next to the word might be useful.

Further extension
Give children some extra copies of PCM 35. Ask them to cross out the existing instructions, and write their own. They then swap sheets with a partner and draw clocks to match each other's instructions.

If you have time
Ask one child in each pair to specify a time and another to say how much later or earlier. Both children then pick up a card clock face and race to set it to the new time. Children score a point for showing the correct time first. When it is time to stop, the child with the most points wins.

Be aware

- Children may find it difficult to add or subtract times to and from half an hour. Remind them that two halves make one whole, so two half hours make one hour.

Outcomes

- I can read o'clock and half past times in words.
- I can work out earlier and later times using hours and half hours.

Supporting resources

Have a range of clocks and timers, including sand timers, for children to explore.

Children can find out more about time with this interactive clock:

- http://www.time-for-time.com/swf/myclox.swf

Challenge Plan: Year 2

C2: estimating, measuring and comparing weights in kg and g; reading analogue and digital time; block graphs; pictograms

Summary

Y2 ☆ C2.4 — **Names in our class**

Individuals, pairs or groups working independently

Year 2 Challenge PCM 36

A list of first names of everyone in the class

Abacus Evolve objectives

- Sort, organise and interpret information in a block graph

Framework objectives

- Answer a question by collecting and recording data in lists and tables; represent the data as block graphs or pictograms to show results; use ICT to organise and present data
- Follow a line of enquiry; answer questions by choosing and using suitable equipment and selecting, organising and presenting information in lists, tables and simple diagrams
- Present solutions to puzzles and problems in an organised way; explain decisions, methods and results in pictorial, spoken or written form, using mathematical language and number sentences

Teacher notes

Preparation
Photocopy PCM 36, one copy per child.
Prepare a list of the first name of every child in the class. Photocopy the names list, one copy per child.

Getting started
Show children the list of names and ask them what they are. *What is different about each name?* They are likely to notice that there are different letters in each name but may need support to recognise that there are a different number of letters in each name, particularly if the first few have the same number. Give each child a copy of the PCM.

Activity
Children work from PCM 36. They work their way down the list of names, colouring in a section of the graph in the appropriate column for each name. They must start at the bottom of each column on the graph. Some children may choose to work their way down the list, and some may choose to find all the three-letter names, then all the four-letter names, etc. Once they have completed the graph, they answer the questions on the PCM.

Extra help
Encourage those children who get in a muddle to tick each name as they record it. Provide some spare name lists in case they need to check how far they have got.

Further extension
Talk to a partner about your answers to the questions. Are your conclusions the same? If not, why not? Has someone made a mistake? Ask each other some more questions about the graph.

If you have time
Ask children to find out which letter of the alphabet is used most often in the names.

Be aware

- There may be three or four columns with the same number of squares coloured, as most names tend to be within a fairly limited range.

Outcomes

- I can complete a block graph and answer questions about it.

Supporting resources

- Display a range of graphs and charts to ask and answer questions about.

Summary

Y2 ☆ C2.5 **Tom's drinks**

A small group working with an adult

Year 2 Challenge Textbook page 24

Squared paper; rulers; other block graphs (optional)

Abacus Evolve objectives

- Sort, organise and interpret information in a block graph

Framework objectives

- Answer a question by collecting and recording data in lists and tables; represent the data as block graphs or pictograms to show results; use ICT to organise and present data
- *Use lists, tables and diagrams to sort objects; explain choices using appropriate language, including 'not'*
- Follow a line of enquiry; answer questions by choosing and using suitable equipment and selecting, organising and presenting information in lists, tables and simple diagrams
- Explain their views to others in a small group; decide how to report the group's views to the class

Teacher notes

Activity
- Look at the Textbook page. *What does this chart show?* Check that children understand the abbreviations for the days of the week. Talk through what each column and row tells you.
- Give each child a sheet of squared paper. Ask them to draw a block graph of the data. *How many squares will you use to represent one drink?* Encourage children to see that it would be sensible to use one square per drink for this graph.
- When children have completed their graphs, ask the group to compare what they have done. *Does anyone's graph look different?*
- Children work from Textbook page 24. They answer the questions using their graph.

Extra help
Show examples of completed block graphs to support children with the layout.

If you have time
Discuss which information is easier to obtain from the block graph and which is easier to obtain from the chart.
Information about drinks on a particular day is best obtained from the chart. This information is lost when the data is turned into a graph. The graph summarises the information about a particular drink or drinks for the week.

Be aware

- Children sometimes find it difficult to align their axes with the lines of the squared paper, leaving themselves with part squares for the spaces next to the axes. You may need to show them how to line up the ruler with the lines of the squared paper.

Outcomes

- I can draw a block graph from information in a chart.
- I can use my block graph to answer questions.

Supporting resources

- Display a range of graphs and charts to ask and answer questions about.

Challenge Plan: Year 2

C2: estimating, measuring and comparing weights in kg and g; reading analogue and digital time; block graphs; pictograms

Summary

Y2 ☆ C2.6	**Fun in the snow**
	Pairs or groups working independently
	Year 2 Challenge Textbook page 25
	2 cm squared paper; examples of pictograms in books or on wallcharts (optional)

Abacus Evolve objectives

- **Y3** Solve a given problem by organising and interpreting data in pictograms (symbol representing two units)

Framework objectives

- **Y3** Answer a question by collecting, organising and interpreting data; use tally charts, frequency tables, pictograms and bar charts to represent results and illustrate observations; use ICT to create a simple bar chart
- **Y3** Follow a line of enquiry by deciding what information is important; make and use lists, tables and graphs to organise and interpret the information
- **Y3** Sustain conversation, explaining or giving reasons for their views or choices

Teacher notes

Getting started
Look at the Textbook page and talk through the scenario.

Activity
Children work from Textbook page 25. They each draw a pictogram, using the information and symbols provided. They then answer the questions. They should realise that some questions do not have a definite answer. Children should discuss their answers in pairs or groups.

Extra help
Look at some pictograms in books or on wallcharts to see how they have used one symbol to mean two or more objects.

Further extension
Ask children to write a list of socks, gloves, wellies and jeans, making sure they give a few half-pairs. They give their list to a partner, who draws a pictogram from the data. The first child then asks the second child some questions about the pictogram.

If you have time
Discuss the answers to the questions. *Is there more than one possible answer?*

Be aware

- Some children find the move to using one symbol to stand for two or more objects problematic. Try explaining it as a quick, shorter way of showing information.

Outcomes

- I can draw a pictogram, using one symbol for two items.

Supporting resources

- Display other examples of pictograms with a scale of 2 and using half a symbol for one item.

Summary

Y2 ☆ D2.1 **In my basket**

Groups working independently

Year 2 Challenge PCM 37

Everyday objects shaped like cubes, cuboids, cylinders, spheres and cones; basket

Abacus Evolve objectives

- Use the names of common 3D shapes, including: cube, cuboid, cylinder, sphere, cone
- Relate solid shapes to pictures of them

Framework objectives

- *Visualise common 2D shapes and 3D solids; identify shapes from pictures of them in different positions and orientations; sort, make and describe shapes, referring to their properties*
- Speak with clarity and use appropriate intonation when reading and reciting texts

Teacher notes

Preparation
Make a collection of everyday objects shaped like cubes (a dice), cuboids (a cereal box), cylinders (a straw), spheres (a ball), cones (a funnel). Photocopy PCM 37, and cut out the cards.

Getting started
Put a collection of 3D objects in middle of the table. Explain that children are going to play a game. They should use the shape word (*cube*, *cuboid*, *cylinder*, *sphere*, *cone*) to describe the shape of each object, without naming the object itself. Run through the rules of the game. Use the flashcards on PCM 37 to support children with the vocabulary if necessary.

Activity
Child A starts the game by saying: *I went shopping and bought one cube*. They place a cube-shaped object in the basket. They pass it to Child B saying: *Here is the basket with one cube in it.* Child B receives the basket and says: *Thank you for the cube. I would like to add one cone.* They add a cone-shaped object and pass the basket to Child C, saying: *I went shopping and I bought one cube and one cone.* Child C continues the game.
Children should remember what is in the basket rather than looking each time. Should a disagreement occur, items can be removed and replaced to check. If children need help remembering the shapes, they should record them by drawing them, not by writing a description.

Extra help
Practise shape names by giving each child a basket and a 'shopping list' of shapes, for example, *three cubes, two cones.* Children collect examples of the shapes and put them in the basket. A partner checks and ticks them off the list.

Further extension
Children play the game as before but they describe the properties of the shape instead, for example, *I went shopping and bought one solid shape with six square faces*.

If you have time
Make a shop in the play corner labelling all prices of objects by shape, for example, *All cubes 10p*, *All cuboids 20p*, etc.

Be aware

- Relating an everyday object to the mathematical name of the shape is difficult for some children. The broader their experiences of objects, the more likely they are to recognise shapes by their properties.
- Memorising a list of objects, then adding to it, offers repetition, and requires good listening skills. However, it's important to set the expectation.

Outcomes

- I can use the names of 3D shapes in a game.
- I can listen to others and wait for my turn.

Supporting resources

Children can check shape words with an interactive maths dictionary:
- http://www.amathsdictionaryforkids.com/

D2: naming common 3D shapes; sorting and describing 3D shapes; subtracting multiples of 10; adding and subtracting 9, 11, 19 and 21

Summary

Y2 ☆ D2.2	**The shape sorter**
	Pairs working independently
	Year 2 Challenge Textbook page 26
	Year 2 Challenge PCM 38 (optional)
	A collection of different shaped boxes

Abacus Evolve objectives

- Sort 3D shapes and describe their features: number of faces and corners
- Use the names of common 3D shapes, including: cube, cuboid, cylinder, sphere, cone
- Relate solid shapes to pictures of them
- Classify and describe common 2D and 3D shapes

Framework objectives

- *Visualise common 2D shapes and 3D solids; identify shapes from pictures of them in different positions and orientations; sort, make and describe shapes, referring to their properties*
- Present solutions to puzzles and problems in an organised way; explain decisions, methods and results in pictorial, spoken or written form, using mathematical language and number sentences

Teacher notes

Preparation
Make a collection of different boxes including several cubes, cuboids, etc.

Getting started
Show children the shape sorter on Textbook page 26. Point out the six 3D shapes along the top of the page: cube, cuboid, pyramid, cone, cylinder, sphere. *We are going to tip these six shapes into the shape sorting machine and it is going to tell us which shape is which.* Use an example of a cylinder. Take it through the first two questions of the shape sorter to show how it works. *Now you can work out which shapes should go in the empty boxes.*

Activity
Children work from Textbook page 26. They draw and name the missing shape that goes in each empty box. They discuss their choices, and agree together whether their answers make sense.

Further extension
Children can make their own collection of shapes and use PCM 38 to create their own shape sorter to sort the shapes. When children have tested out their own diagram they can give it to a partner to check whether it works.

Be aware

- To sort the shapes effectively it is important to use questions with yes / no answers. Being able to use such questions is a key skill when sorting information.

Outcomes

- I can recognise the features of some 3D shapes.
- I can use a tree diagram to solve a shape problem.

Supporting resources

Children can practise naming shapes with the Number Crew 3: Changing Faces:

- http://www.teachers.tv/video/25381

Summary

Y2 ☆ D2.3 **Packaging**

A small group working with an adult

3D packaging; large boxes; large tubes

Abacus Evolve objectives

- Sort 3D shapes and describe their features: number of faces and corners

Framework objectives

- *Visualise common 2D shapes and 3D solids; identify shapes from pictures of them in different positions and orientations; sort, make and describe shapes, referring to their properties*
- Present solutions to puzzles and problems in an organised way; explain decisions, methods and results in pictorial, spoken or written form, using mathematical language and number sentences
- Use language and gesture to support the use of models, diagrams or displays when explaining

Teacher notes

Preparation
Collect a lot of 3D shape packaging, for example, tins, cereal packets, tubes of crisps, etc.

Activity
- Look together at the packaging. Children discuss which shapes they can see and describe them.
- Ask a pair to collect together all the cubes. Encourage them to explain their reasoning, using properties of the shapes. Ask another pair to collect together all the cylinders and explain their reasoning.
- *You are going to design some packaging to send large numbers of items to the supermarket. Your package will contain only one product, for example boxes of cereal.* Each pair chooses one product. *You have an order for 20 of these products. How will you package them? What shape do you think will be the most efficient use of space?*
- Give children time to explore ideas and test them out using bigger boxes and tubes. Ask questions such as: *Do you think that a large tube is the best shape to pack in or do you think a box is best? Why?* Children record their ideas by drawing sketches.
- Children then present their findings to the group, explaining their reasoning. Encourage the group to ask questions about how efficiently each idea uses space and resources. *Which is the best shape for packing cubes? Why? Which is the best shape for packing tubes? Why?*

Extra help
Offer children one product to package. As a group they pack several into a bigger box. *What shape box is best?*

Further extension
Look at the empty spaces around the smaller products when they have been packaged. *What shapes are left empty? Why? Can you think of a more efficient use of the space?*

If you have time
Discuss the advantages and disadvantages of different shapes of packaging in a shop.

Be aware

- Packing quantities of one shape into another requires an understanding of volume and shape, focussing on relationship between faces, corners of shapes and impact they have on their 'fit' together.

Outcomes

- I can think of ways to package several 3D shapes together.

Supporting resources

Read more about using stacking in maths here:
- http://nrich.maths.org/public/viewer.php?obj_id=5602

Challenge Plan: Year 2

D2: naming common 3D shapes; sorting and describing 3D shapes; subtracting multiples of 10; adding and subtracting 9, 11, 19 and 21

Summary

Y2 ☆ D2.4 — **Egg boxes**

Individuals or pairs working independently

Year 2 Challenge PCM 39

Different-sized egg boxes

Abacus Evolve objectives

- Subtract a multiple of 10 from a 2-digit number by counting back in 10s

Framework objectives

- *Add or subtract mentally a one-digit number or a multiple of 10 to or from any two-digit number; use practical and informal written methods to add and subtract two-digit numbers*
- Solve problems involving addition, subtraction, multiplication or division in contexts of numbers, measures or pounds and pence
- Present solutions to puzzles and problems in an organised way; explain decisions, methods and results in pictorial, spoken or written form, using mathematical language and number sentences

Teacher notes

Preparation
Photocopy PCM 39, one copy per child or pair.

Getting started
Provide some real egg boxes and ask children to sort them into groups by size. *There is a new design of egg box, which holds 10 eggs. Supermarkets now only order eggs in 10s. Mr Phipps' chickens have laid 83 eggs. The supermarket wants to buy 70 eggs. How many eggs will he have left?* Remind children about counting forwards and backwards in 10s. Give children PCM 39.

Activity
Children work from PCM 39. They use the diagrams of empty egg boxes to help them think through the problem and find an answer. They then show their working on a 1–100 number line.

Extra help
Mr Phipps collects 27 eggs. The mini-market wants to buy 10 eggs. How many eggs has Mr Phipps got left?

Further extension
A dozen means 12. Eggs are often still sold in dozens. How different would the problem be if Mr Phipps only sold his eggs in dozens? (The supermarket would have to buy 60 or 72 eggs. They would not be able to buy 70.)

If you have time
How many different ways are there of putting 20 eggs in three baskets? Discuss your answer with a partner and then decide if you have found all the possible ways of organising them.

Information
It is thought that a dozen was used because there are 12 finger knuckles on one hand.

Be aware

- Children may find it difficult to subtract multiples of 10. Make sure they use the picture to reinforce the concept of grouping in 10s.

Outcomes

- I can subtract a multiple of 10 from a 2-digit number.
- I can explain my decisions to a partner.

Supporting resources

Children could watch The Number Crew practise filling boxes of 10 things:
- http://www.teachers.tv/video/25375

Summary

Y2 ☆ D2.5 — **How much change?**

A small group working with an adult

Year 2 Challenge Textbook page 27

Plastic or real money; items for the play shop; labels for pricing

Abacus Evolve objectives

- Add and subtract 9 and 11 by adding and subtracting 10
- Begin to add and subtract 19 and 21 by adding and subtracting 20
- Recognise all coins and begin to use £.p notation for money
- Solve 'real-life' problems involving money (paying an exact sum)

Framework objectives

- *Add or subtract mentally a one-digit number or a multiple of 10 to or from any two-digit number; use practical and informal written methods to add and subtract two-digit numbers*
- Solve problems involving addition, subtraction, multiplication or division in contexts of numbers, measures or pounds and pence
- Listen to a talk by an adult, remember some specific points and identify what they have learned

Teacher notes

Preparation
Set up a play shop with items priced 9p, 11p, 19p, 21p, 29p, 31p, 39p, 41p, 49p, 51p.

Activity
- Children role play buying items in the play shop, noting how much change is given each time. *Prices in the shop always end in 1p or 9p.*
- Children work from Textbook page 27. *Can you think of any quick ways of working out how much change each child should get?* Establish that it is useful to add or subtract to 10. Children work out how much change each person gets.
- *Mr McKenzie owns this shop. But he never has enough change. Why do you think that is? He comes up with a plan to sell half the items in the shop for 11p and half for 9p. Then he thinks he won't have to give so much change. Do you think that is true?* Children choose two items and work out how much they cost together. (Mr McKenzie will only have to give less change if customers buy one item that ends in 9p and one item that ends in 1p.)
- *Then Mr McKenzie decides to price everything at 10p. Will he have more change then? Why?*

Extra help
Price all items at 10p and practise giving change from 50p. Once children are familiar with this, change all prices to 9p. *Can you work out the change now?* Remind children how easy it was when everything was 10p. Suggest they imagine selling for 10p then adjust the total.

Further extension
Price four items at 19p, 29p, 39p, 49p. Ask children to work out the change from £2. *How did you use an easy calculation to work out a difficult calculation?*

If you have time
Create scenarios where people are 'short-changed'. For example, *A toy costs 29p. Tom pays 50p and gets 20p change. Is this right? Who lost out? Who gained? How can you put it right?*

Be aware

- Some children have little experience of handling money. Support them in understanding change: overpaying and compensating. Use subtractions and number lines to introduce the concept of money.

Outcomes

- I can add and subtract 9p and 11p.

Supporting resources

Children can practise counting on to 10 by watching The Number Crew buy ice creams for 9p:
- http://www.teachers.tv/video/25376

Challenge Plan: Year 2

D2: naming common 3D shapes; sorting and describing 3D shapes; subtracting multiples of 10; adding and subtracting 9, 11, 19 and 21

Summary

Y2 ☆ D2.6 — **Question swap**

Pairs working independently

Year 2 Challenge PCMs 40 and 41

Abacus Evolve objectives

- Begin to add and subtract 19 and 21 by adding and subtracting 20

Framework objectives

- *Add or subtract mentally a one-digit number or a multiple of 10 to or from any two-digit number; use practical and informal written methods to add and subtract two-digit numbers*
- Listen to others in class, ask relevant questions and follow instructions

Teacher notes

Preparation
Photocopy PCM 40, one copy per pair. Photocopy PCM 41, one copy per child.

Getting started
Look together at PCM 40. *Mrs Patil wrote some number sentences on the board. By mistake she wrote the answers on the board too!* Explain that instead of finding answers, children will be checking answers. *Then you will write your own questions and ask your partner to tell you how to work out the answers!*

Activity
Children work from PCM 40. They check the answers, giving reasons for why they are correct or not. (Two of the answers are incorrect.)
Children then work from PCM 41. Child A writes a number in the first empty box of each number sentence. Child B then solves the questions, but does not write anything down. Instead they explain to Child A how to work out the answers. Child A jots down Child B's workings and answers. Child A must not help Child B find the answers! Children then discuss what makes some number sentences harder than others. Pairs swap so that Child B sets questions. Children discuss what they have learned from each other's methods.

Extra help
Fill in the first number of each number sentence on PCM 41 yourself, choosing easier calculations.

Further extension
Give each pair some number sentences with empty boxes using $+$ or $-$ and $=$. Ask children to write any calculation they want, choosing numbers to make it very difficult or very easy for their partner.

If you have time
Ask children to make up scenarios that fit the number sentences. *What might be happening in the number story?*

Be aware

- The concepts of difficult and easy are complex as what is difficult for one child may be easy for another. It is helpful to have that conversation with children. Some children may be reluctant to take risks with more challenging questions. Encourage fun settings where the pressure of getting things right or wrong is lessened and discussion of challenging calculations can be explored.

Outcomes

- I can make up number sentences for others to solve.
- I can explain how to work out a calculation.

Challenge Plan: Year 2

E2: counting on in 2s, 5s or 10s; understanding multiplication as 'lots of'; multiplication as repeated addition; division as grouping

Summary

Y2 ☆ E2.1 — **Exploring multiples**

Pairs working independently

Year 2 Challenge Textbook page 28

Year 2 Challenge PCM 42

Coloured pencils

Abacus Evolve objectives

- Count on in 2s, 5s or 10s up to 100
- Begin to recognise odd and even numbers up to at least 100
- Know by heart the multiplication facts for 2, 5 and 10 times tables
- Begin to recognise 2-digit multiples of 2, 5 and 10

Framework objectives

- Read and write 2- and 3-digit numbers in figures and words; describe and extend number sequences and recognise odd and even numbers
- Derive and recall multiplication facts for the 2, 5 and 10 times tables and the related division facts; recognise multiples of 2, 5 and 10
- Describe patterns and relationships involving numbers or shapes, make predictions and test these with examples
- Explain their views to others in a small group; decide how to report the group's views to the class

Teacher notes

Preparation
Photocopy PCM 42, one copy per child.

Getting started
Ask children to explain what is meant by a multiple of 2. Explain to them that they are going to mark multiples of 2 and multiples of 5 onto the first part of a 1–100 square. Explain that they are going to look for patterns and use any patterns they notice to make predictions. Look at the Textbook page. Ask a child to read the first set of instructions aloud. Make sure everyone understands what they need to do.

Activity
Children work from Textbook page 28. In pairs, they count in 2s to 50, circling the numbers on the number grid on PCM 42. They describe any patterns that they notice, and use these patterns to predict a few numbers above 60 that they think will be a multiple of 2. Children then do the same for multiples of 5, drawing squares around the numbers on the number grid. They then think about which numbers appear in both sets.

Extra help
If children are struggling to notice or describe the patterns, suggest that they ask the rest of the group to describe what they have noticed. Children can then try to record a description of the patterns, and use them to predict further numbers in the count.

Further extension
Ask children to investigate multiples of other pairs of numbers, such as 2 and 4, using another copy of the PCM.

Information
The numbers that are multiples of both 2 and 5 are called *common multiples* of 2 and 5. The set of common multiples of 2 and 5 is equivalent to the set of multiples of 10. For some children, you may feel it is appropriate to introduce this new vocabulary.

Be aware

- Make sure that children understand and can use the words *multiple* and *predict*.

Outcomes

- I can count in 2s and 5s.
- I can recognise multiples of 2, 5 and 10.
- I can describe patterns and make predictions.

E2: counting on in 2s, 5s or 10s; understanding multiplication as 'lots of'; multiplication as repeated addition; division as grouping

Summary

Y2 ☆ E2.2	**Multiplication race**
	Pairs working independently
	Year 2 Challenge PCM 43
	Calculators; coloured pencils; 2p, 5p and 10p coins (optional)

Abacus Evolve objectives

- Introduce multiplication as 'lots of'
- Know by heart the multiplication facts for 2, 5 and 10 times tables
- Begin to recognise 2-digit multiples of 2, 5 and 10

Framework objectives

- Represent repeated addition and arrays as multiplication, and sharing and repeated subtraction (grouping) as division; use practical and informal written methods and related vocabulary to support multiplication and division, including calculations with remainders
- Derive and recall multiplication facts for the 2, 5 and 10 times tables and the related division facts; recognise multiples of 2, 5 and 10
- Ensure everyone contributes, allocate tasks, consider alternatives and reach agreement

Teacher notes

Preparation
Photocopy PCM 43, one or two copies per child.

Getting started
Give each pair one copy of the PCM. Put the spares in a pile in the middle of the table (children can use these if they have time to play the game a second time). Ask a child to read aloud the rules of the game. Make sure everyone understands how to play. If necessary, ask one pair to take a turn each to model how to play. Give each pair two different coloured pencils and a calculator.

Activity
Children work from PCM 43. They play the following game in pairs:
- Player A chooses a number from the grid. They say a multiplication fact from the 2, 5 or 10 times table that has their chosen number as the answer.
- Player B checks that fact on a calculator.
- If Player A is right, they colour the number on the grid.
- Player B has their turn.
- Children continue to take turns until one of them has coloured a path from one side of the grid to the other.

If children have time, they could play again, perhaps trying out a different strategy.

Extra help
If children are not sure whether to use a fact from the 2, 5 or 10 times table, encourage them to look at the units digit. *If a number is in the 2/5/10 times table, what must it end in? Is this number in the 2/5/10 times table?*
Children could use coins to support counting in 2s, 5s or 10s.

Further extension
Create a new version of the grid including multiples of 2, 3, 4, 5 and 10.

If you have time
Ask children to play the game again using division. They should say a division fact that starts with their chosen number. The answer must be a whole number. For example, for the number 14 a child could say *14 ÷ 2 = 7*. This activity would encourage children to begin to understand the inverse nature of multiplication and division.

Be aware

- Encourage children to use their knowledge of the possible units digits in multiples of 2, 5 and 10 to identify appropriate multiplication tables.

Outcomes

- I can recognise multiples of 2, 5 and 10.
- I can give a multiplication fact with an answer that is in the 2, 5 or 10 times table.

Challenge Plan: Year 2

E2: counting on in 2s, 5s or 10s; understanding multiplication as 'lots of'; multiplication as repeated addition; division as grouping

Summary

Y2 ☆ E2.3 — **Known multiplication facts**

Individuals or pairs working independently

Year 2 Challenge Textbook page 29

Abacus Evolve objectives

- **Y3** Know by heart the multiplication facts for the 2 times table
- **Y3** Recognise multiples of 10, 100 and 50
- **Y3** Use known facts to multiply a multiple of 10 by a 1-digit number

Framework objectives

- **Y3** Derive and recall multiplication facts for the 2, 3, 4, 5, 6 and 10 times tables and the corresponding division facts; recognise multiples of 2, 5 or 10 up to 1000
- **Y3** Use practical and informal written methods to support multiplication and division of 2-digit numbers (e.g. 13×3, $30 \div 4$); round remainders up or down, depending on the context
- **Y3** Identify patterns and relationships involving numbers or shapes, and use these to solve problems

Teacher notes

Getting started
Explain to children that they are going to count in steps of £2 and then £20. Practise this briefly together for the first few numbers in each count. Ask children to compare the count so far for £2 steps and £20 steps and discuss what they notice. Explain that they are going to use this link to answer multiplication facts for the 20 times-table.

Activity
Children work from Textbook page 29. They write a sequence counting up in £2 steps from £2 to £20. They then write a sequence counting up in £20 steps from £20 to £200. Children complete linked pairs of multiplication facts, from the 2 and 20 times-tables. They describe what they notice. They write some other linked pairs of facts from the 2 and 20 times-tables, then go on to write some linked pairs of facts from other times-tables.

Extra help
If children struggle to complete 20 times-tables facts, encourage them to count along the row of £20s on the Textbook page. Ask questions such as: *What is 9 × 2? What is 9 × 20? Look at the two answers. What is the same? What is different?*

Further extension
Children can be given multiplication facts involving multiples of 10 such as 8×50 or 4×30 and asked what times-table facts they know that could help them answer these. Initially, encourage children to record the known fact that they use as well as the answer to the original question.

Be aware

- Help children to understand the link between, for example, 6 and 60: 6 is six units; 60 is six tens. 60 is therefore 10 times as large as 6.

Outcomes

- I can use the 2 times-table to answer questions about the 20 times-table.

Supporting resources

- Some children may benefit from using money. Pieces of scrap paper could be used to represent £20 notes.

Challenge Plan: Year 2

E2: counting on in 2s, 5s or 10s; understanding multiplication as 'lots of'; multiplication as repeated addition; division as grouping

Summary

Y2 ☆ E2.4 **Multiplication monsters**

A small group working with an adult

Year 2 Challenge PCMs 44 and 45

Matchsticks or straws cut into pieces; scissors; individual whiteboards and pens

Abacus Evolve objectives

- Introduce multiplication as 'lots of'
- Introduce multiplication as repeated addition or as describing an array
- Record multiplication facts using × and = in number sentences

Framework objectives

- Represent repeated addition and arrays as multiplication, and sharing and repeated subtraction (grouping) as division; use practical and informal written methods and related vocabulary to support multiplication and division, including calculations with remainders
- *Use the symbols +, −, ×, ÷ and = to record and interpret number sentences involving all four operations; calculate the value of an unknown in a number sentence (e.g. 30 − □ = 24, □ ÷ 2 = 6)*
- Present solutions to puzzles and problems in an organised way; explain decisions, methods and results in pictorial, spoken or written form, using mathematical language and number sentences

Teacher notes

Preparation
Photocopy PCMs 44 and 45, one copy of each per pair.
Each pair will need about 20 'monster legs' (matchsticks or short pieces of drinking straw).

Activity
- Give each pair a set of 12 square monster cards from PCM 44. *Square monsters each have four legs.* Give each pair about 20 matchsticks or pieces of straw. *These are the monsters' legs.*
- *How many square monsters altogether have 12 legs?* Encourage pairs to lay 'legs' on top of cards until they have completed three monsters, giving a total of 12 legs.
- Repeat for 20 legs. Ask pairs to write a multiplication sentence to show this (5 × 4 = 20 or 4 × 5 = 20), and show their working.
- Give each pair a set of 12 triangle monster cards from PCM 45. *Triangle monsters each have three legs.*
- *How many triangle monsters altogether have nine legs?* When pairs have worked it out, ask them to jot down a multiplication sentence that could represent this situation and show their working.
- Repeat for 15 legs.
- *A group of monsters altogether have 17 legs: some are triangle monsters and some are square. How many of each must there be?* Once pairs have worked this out, ask them to record their answer in their own way.
- Give them a different number of legs to investigate, for example, 11 or 19.
- Towards the end of the session, bring the group back together. Ask children to compare methods and discuss different strategies for solving the problems.

Extra help
If children cannot find a set giving the exact number of legs required, suggest they start by finding a solution that is quite close. For example, when trying to find 17 legs they might find that two triangle monsters and three square monsters have a total of 18 legs. *Does this group have too many or too few legs? How many fewer/more legs are needed? What could you change to make this happen?* Help children to see that swapping one sort of monster for the other will add/subtract a leg each time.

Information
It is possible to create a set of monsters for each number of legs greater than 6. For some numbers there will be more than one possible solution.

Be aware

- Encourage children to use 3 and 4 times-table facts to work efficiently without counting individual legs.

Outcomes

- I can work out problems that involve multiplication.
- I can record my results in my own way.

Challenge Plan: Year 2

E2: counting on in 2s, 5s or 10s; understanding multiplication as 'lots of'; multiplication as repeated addition; division as grouping

Summary

Y2 ☆ E2.5	**Plates of fruit**
	Individuals or pairs working independently
	Year 2 Challenge Textbook page 30
	Coins (optional)

Abacus Evolve objectives

- Introduce multiplication as 'lots of'
- Introduce multiplication as repeated addition or as describing an array
- Record multiplication facts using × and = in number sentences

Framework objectives

- Represent repeated addition and arrays as multiplication, and sharing and repeated subtraction (grouping) as division; use practical and informal written methods and related vocabulary to support multiplication and division, including calculations with remainders
- *Use the symbols +, −, ×, ÷ and = to record and interpret number sentences involving all four operations; calculate the value of an unknown in a number sentence (e.g. 30 − □ = 24, □ ÷ 2 = 6)*
- Identify and record the information or calculation needed to solve a puzzle or problem; carry out the steps or calculations and check the solution in the context of the problem

Teacher notes

Getting started
Look at the Textbook page. *You are going to work out the price for different plates of fruit.* Look at the first example together. *What would you work out first?* Take feedback. Agree that it will be sensible to work out how much one type of fruit would cost first. Ask children what calculation they would do to find the cost of the grapes on the plate. Establish that the calculation is 4 × 2p because there are four grapes each costing 2p. Ask children to record this calculation and the answer. *What do you need to do next?* Establish that they need to work out the cost of the two cherries, then find the total for the grapes and the cherries together. Explain that children should record each calculation and any other jottings they need to do to find the answer.

Activity
Children work from Textbook page 30. Children read about a snack shop where you pay for each item of fruit you put on your plate. They are shown the prices for the three types of fruit. They are shown pictures of four plates of fruit, and they must work out the total cost of each plate. Since the prices of the individual pieces of fruit are 2p, 5p and 10p, children will need to use 2, 5 and 10 times-table facts. Each plate contains at least two types of fruit, so finding the total cost of each plate involves several steps. Children should record their working.

Extra help
If children struggle to work out the totals, encourage them to use coins to match the cost of the fruit on each plate. These children would also benefit from discussing methods and recording with a partner.

If you have time
Children could set up a shop and role play buying several items at once.

Information
It is important that children begin to understand how multiplication sentences can replace those involving repeated addition as this leads to more efficient recording.

Be aware

- Some children may use repeated addition rather than multiplication, for example, recording the cost of four grapes as *2p + 2p + 2p + 2p*. If so, encourage them to vocalise the scenario as '... lots of ...p' and ask them how to record this using multiplication.

Outcomes

- I can solve problems involving money.
- I can record the steps to solve a problem using number sentences.

Challenge Plan: Year 2

E2: counting on in 2s, 5s or 10s; understanding multiplication as 'lots of'; multiplication as repeated addition; division as grouping

Summary

Y2 ☆ E2.6 **Remainder game**

A small group working with an adult

Year 2 Challenge PCM 46

Thin card; linking cubes; individual whiteboards and pens

Abacus Evolve objectives

- Begin to understand division as grouping
- Understand that division sometimes leaves a remainder
- Introduce the ÷ sign

Framework objectives

- Represent repeated addition and arrays as multiplication, and sharing and repeated subtraction (grouping) as division; use practical and informal written methods and related vocabulary to support multiplication and division, including calculations with remainders
- *Use the symbols +, −, ×, ÷ and = to record and interpret number sentences involving all four operations; calculate the value of an unknown in a number sentence (e.g. 30 − □ = 24, □ ÷ 2 = 6)*
- Listen to others in class, ask relevant questions and follow instructions

Teacher notes

Preparation
Copy PCM 46 onto thin card. Cut out the number cards.

Activity
- Place a collection of cubes on the table. Divide the number cards into two sets: 1-digit numbers and 2-digit numbers. Place both sets face down on the table. Spread them out, but make sure you keep the two sets separate.
- Ask a child to pick a card from each set, for example, 21 and 4. Ask them to write a division sentence with the larger number first, for example, *21 ÷ 4. How could you use grouping to answer this question?* Encourage them to take 21 cubes and organise them into groups or towers of four. *How many groups of four have you made? How many cubes are left over?* Ask the child to record this, for example, *21 ÷ 4 = 5 r 1*.
- *In this game, you win any remainders. If you wrote a division with a remainder of 1, you would win one cube. The person with the most cubes at the end of the game wins.*
- Give children a chance to have a go at picking one card from each set and recording the division sentence.
- Look at the division sentences together. *Whose answer has the largest remainder? Did any have no remainder? Can you predict whether a division will or won't have a remainder? How?*
- Play the game as a group, with children taking turns to pick cards and work out the division.

Extra help
Some children find it hard to interpret a division sentence such as 21 ÷ 4 as 'How many 4s make 21?' To help these children, write the question *How many …s make …?* onto a whiteboard and use this to prompt them.

Further extension
Include other number cards such as 6 or 7 as divisors.

If you have time
Play the game slightly differently by placing cards onto the table face up so children can choose their cards. This becomes more strategic as children will begin to predict which calculations give larger remainders. Ask questions such as: *Why did you choose that number? If you choose to divide a number by 2, what would be the biggest possible remainder you could get?*

Be aware

- Children can become confused between division by sharing and division by grouping. Avoid using the word 'share' during this session.

Outcomes

- I can work out division calculations by grouping.
- I can find remainders when dividing.

Summary

Y2 ☆ A3.1	**HTU game**
	A small group working with an adult
	Year 2 Challenge PCM 47
	Digit cards 0–9; bags; A4 paper

Abacus Evolve objectives

- Begin to partition 3-digit numbers into H, T and U
- Begin to read and write numbers up to 1000 in figures

Framework objectives

- *Count up to 100 objects by grouping them and counting in 10s, 5s or 2s; explain what each digit in a 2-digit number represents, including numbers where 0 is a place holder; partition 2-digit numbers in different ways, including into multiples of 10 and 1*
- Read and write 2- and 3-digit numbers in figures and words; describe and extend number sequences and recognise odd and even numbers
- Adopt appropriate roles in small or large groups and consider alternative courses of action

Teacher notes

Preparation

Photocopy PCM 47, one copy per pair.

Activity

- Give each pair a copy of PCM 47 and a set of digit cards 0–9 in a bag. *We are going to play a game, using digit cards to make 3-digit numbers. We will be trying to make the highest and lowest possible numbers.*
- Model one round of the game, asking one child to be your opponent:
  - *The winner will be the person who makes the higher number.*
  - Take a digit card at random from the bag. *I have to put this card on my grid. I need to decide whether to put it in the hundreds, tens or units column. Where do you think I should put it?* If it is a high number, explain that it is best to put it in the hundreds column. If it is a low number, explain that it might be best to put it in the units column.
  - Now it is the other player's turn. Encourage them to verbalise their thinking, and encourage the rest of the group to help them to make a good decision.
  - Take turns until you have each made a 3-digit number. *Whose number is higher?* Write the winning number where everyone can see it.
- Ask children to play against each other in pairs. In the first round, they aim to make the highest number; in the second round they aim to make the lowest number. They continue to alternate like this. After each round, they write the winning number on a piece of paper.
- When you say *Stop*, pairs order their winning numbers from lowest to highest, and show them to the group.
- *Which pair found the highest number? Which pair found the lowest number?*
- Ask pairs to answer the two questions on the PCM.

Extra help

Support decisions about where to place each digit by asking questions such as: *Which digits are left? Are there more higher or lower digits left? Do you think you are more likely to get a higher or lower digit next time?*

Further extension

Extend the game to 4-digit numbers. Children place a thousands digit card to the left of the hundreds digit.

Be aware

- The rule about not moving a card once it is placed is significant. It will help to prevent arguments as children may try to justify why they should be allowed to rearrange their digits.

Outcomes

- I can partition numbers into hundreds, tens and units.

Challenge Plan: Year 2

A3: partitioning 3-digit numbers into H, T, U; rounding to the nearest 10; adding by bridging a multiple of 10; finding the difference by counting on

Summary

Y2 ☆ A3.2	**Number chains**
	Pairs working independently
	Year 2 Challenge PCM 48
	Bags; raffle tickets 0–1000; 0–1000 number line (optional)

Abacus Evolve objectives

- **Y3** Read and write numbers up to 1000 in figures and words
- **Y3** Order numbers up to at least 1000
- **Y3** Partition 3-digit numbers into H, T and U
- **Y3** Know what each digit in a 3-digit number represents, including 0 as a place holder

Framework objectives

- **Y3** Read, write and order whole numbers to at least 1000 and position them on a number line; count on from and back to zero in single-digit steps or multiples of 10
- **Y3** *Partition 3-digit numbers into multiples of 100, 10 and 1 in different ways*
- **Y3** Use talk to organise roles and actions

Teacher notes

Preparation
Photocopy PCM 48, one copy per child. Make two extra copies for demonstration.
Provide a bag or envelope per pair, large enough for a child to put their hand in easily without seeing the contents. Prepare a set of raffle tickets from 0 to 1000 and put a handful of them into each bag or envelope.

Getting started
Give each child a copy of the PCM. Give each pair a bag containing 32 raffle tickets (chosen at random).
You are going to play a game in which you take numbers from your bag, and try to write them in order. But you won't see all the numbers before trying to order them! You are going to play two versions of the game – a shorter version and a longer version.
Model playing the shorter version, asking one child to be your opponent:

- Take a raffle ticket at random from the bag. *I have to decide which of the six boxes I should write this number in. My aim is to write all my six numbers in a chain, in order from smallest to largest. So if it is a low number, I might want to write it in the first box. But if I write it in the first box, and then choose a smaller number later, I won't be able to write that number in my chain.* Demonstrate making a sensible choice based on your chosen number.
- Now it is the other player's turn. Encourage them to verbalise their thinking, and encourage the rest of the group to help them to make a good decision.
- Continue to take turns, adding numbers to the chain when you can, and discarding numbers if you are unable to place them in order. On each turn, justify your decision and accept advice from the rest of the group.
- Stop when you have taken six numbers each. *Who has more numbers in their chain?*

Activity
Children work from PCM 48. They play the game in pairs. They start by playing the shorter game (six numbers), and then play the longer game (10 numbers). At the end of both games, pairs write all of their 32 numbers in order, and answer the questions on the PCM.

Extra help
Children may find a 0–1000 number line useful.
For a simpler game, children can play with just the numbers 0–100.

Be aware

- For the game to play out well, it may be necessary to make sure there are several numbers with the same hundreds digit in each bag.

Outcomes

- I can write numbers up to 1000.
- I can write 3-digit numbers in order.

Summary

Y2 ☆ A3.3 **5 up, 50 up**

A small group working with an adult

Year 2 Challenge PCM 49

Large 0–100 number line; number cards 0–100; bag; tack; 0–1000 number line (optional)

Abacus Evolve objectives

- **Y3** Round numbers less than 100 to the nearest 10
- **Y3** Begin to round 3-digit numbers to the nearest 100 and 10

Framework objectives

- **Y3** Round 2- or 3-digit numbers to the nearest 10 or 100 and give estimates for their sums and differences
- **Y3** Actively include and respond to all members of the group

Teacher notes

Preparation

Photocopy PCM 49, one copy per pair. Make a large 0–100 number line, with divisions for each integer, and the multiples of 10 labelled. Put number cards 0–100 in a bag.

Activity

- Show children the 0–100 number line.
- Ask each child to take a number card at random from the bag. Ask them to find its place on the number line, and stick the card above the correct place using tack. Ask them to draw a line to join the card to its exact place on the line.
- When all the children have placed a number on the line, go through each number in turn and ask children to round it to the nearest 10. They should discuss and agree as a group before giving an answer.
- *When rounding to the nearest 10, we have to look at the units digit. Any number with a 5, 6, 7, 8 or 9 at the end should be rounded up. An easy way to remember this is '5 up'.*
- Ask children to round a couple of numbers to the nearest 100, for example 180 and 330.
- *When rounding to the nearest 100, we have to look at the tens digit. Any number from 50 upwards should be rounded up. An easy way to remember this is '50 up'.* Draw a horizontal arrow above the number line, pointing right from 50 to 100. Draw a second horizontal arrow above the number line, pointing left from 49 to 0. *All the numbers from 50 to 99 round up to 100. All numbers from 1 to 49 round down to 0.*
- Pairs work from PCM 49. They complete the four wheels, rounding 3-digit numbers to the nearest 10 and 100.

Extra help

Give children a 0–1000 number line to help them with rounding the 3-digit numbers.

Further extension

What could the reminder be for rounding to the nearest 1000? Or 10 000? Or 100 000? Or 1 000 000?

If you have time

Children can design a poster reminding them to round '5 up' or '50 up'.

Be aware

- Children are often confused by numbers with 0 units if rounding to the nearest 10, or 0 tens and units if rounding to the nearest 100. In effect, they are already at the nearest 10 or 100 so the number need not change.

Outcomes

- I can round 2- and 3-digit numbers to the nearest 10 and 100.

Summary

Y2 ☆ A3.4 — **Frog additions**

Individuals or pairs working independently

Year 2 Challenge Textbook page 31

0–100 number lines; laminated 0–100 number line (optional); whiteboard pens (optional)

Abacus Evolve objectives

- Add a 1-digit number to a 2-digit number, crossing a multiple of 10 (rehearse)
- Begin to add by bridging a multiple of 10 (36 + 8 = 36 + 4 + 4)

Framework objectives

- *Add or subtract mentally a single-digit number or a multiple of 10 to or from any 2-digit number; use practical and informal written methods to add and subtract 2-digit numbers*

Teacher notes

Getting started
Ask a few quick questions to revise number bonds to 10, such as: *What goes with 7 to make 10? Give me two numbers that add to make 10. Can you think of two more? What about another two?*
Look at the Textbook page. Together work through Freddy's method of adding 36 + 8. Point to 36 on the number line. *How many more to get to 40? How many did Freddy need to add in the first place? So how many more must he add?*
Give each child or pair a 0–100 number line.

Activity
Children work from Textbook page 31. They solve the number sentences, using the two-jump method. They use their number line to help them work out the two jumps.

Extra help
A laminated 0–100 number line is a useful support as it can be drawn on with a whiteboard pen and wiped clean if necessary.

If you have time
Discuss how you might extend this method to add larger numbers on the number line, for example, 36 + 19.

Information
It is not necessary for the numbers to be positioned exactly on the number line, as long as they are labelled correctly to help children keep track of their progress.

Be aware

- Children often know the number bonds to 10 extremely well, but find it hard to use them in calculations such as these. A set of cards with the number bonds on may be useful at first.

Outcomes

- I can add a 1-digit number to a 2-digit number, using two jumps.

Summary

Y2 ☆ A3.5	**Kangaroo additions**
	Individuals or pairs working independently
	Year 2 Challenge Textbook page 32
	0–100 number lines; cards showing number bonds to 10 (optional)

Abacus Evolve objectives

- Add two 2-digit numbers using an appropriate strategy
- Begin to add by bridging a multiple of 10 (36 + 8 = 36 + 4 + 4)

Framework objectives

- *Add or subtract mentally a single-digit number or a multiple of 10 to or from any 2-digit number; use practical and informal written methods to add and subtract 2-digit numbers*

Teacher notes

Preparation
Provide one 0–100 number line per child.

Getting started
Ask a few quick questions to revise number bonds to 10.
Look at the Textbook page. Together work through Kim's method of adding 57 + 17. Point to 57 on the number line. *How many more to get to 60?* (3) *How many to get to another multiple of 10?* (10) *How much did Kim need to add in the first place?* (17) *So how many more must she add?* (4)
Give each child or pair a 0–100 number line.

Activity
Children work from Textbook page 32. They solve the number sentences, using the three-jump method. They use their number line to help them work out the three jumps. For some of the additions, they will need to jump more than one multiple of 10 in the middle step.

Extra help
Provide cards showing the number bonds to 10.

Further extension
Ask children to write additions that add a 2-digit number to a 3-digit number. They swap additions with a partner and try to solve each others, recording all the steps. If children get stuck ask: *What is different about these number sentences compared to the previous ones? What could you do to account for that?*

Be aware

- Some children may need support with the middle jump, especially in additions such as 43 + 29 (in which the middle jump should be 20 rather than 10).

Outcomes

- I can add two 2-digit numbers.

A3: partitioning 3-digit numbers into H, T, U; rounding to the nearest 10; adding by bridging a multiple of 10; finding the difference by counting on

Summary

Y2 ☆ A3.6	**Difference**
	Individuals, pairs or groups working independently
	Year 2 Challenge PCM 50
	Digit cards 3–9; 0–100 number line or 1–100 square (optional)

Abacus Evolve objectives

- Extend understanding of relationship of subtraction to difference
- Find the difference between two numbers by counting on
- Use the +, − and = signs to record addition and subtraction sentences

Framework objectives

- Understand that subtraction is the inverse of addition and vice versa and use this to derive and record related addition and subtraction number sentences
- *Use the symbols +, −, ×, ÷ and = to record and interpret number sentences involving all four operations; calculate the value of an unknown in a number sentence (e.g. 30 − □ = 24, □ ÷ 2 = 6)*
- Present solutions to puzzles and problems in an organised way; explain decisions, methods and results in pictorial, spoken or written form, using mathematical language and number sentences

Teacher notes

Preparation
Photocopy PCM 50, one copy per child, pair or group.

Getting started
Give each child, pair or group the PCM and a set of digit cards 3–9. Ask a child to read aloud the instructions on the PCM. Make sure that everyone understands what to do.

Activity
Children work from PCM 50. They shuffle digit cards 3–9 and place them in a pile face down. They turn over the top card, for example, 4. This is their target difference. They then turn over the rest of the digit cards, and look for four cards to make a pair of 2-digit numbers with the given difference, for example, 73 and 69. They try to find all the pairs of numbers with that difference. They then shuffle the cards, choose a new difference, and find all the pairs of numbers with the new difference.

Extra help
Children could use a 0–100 number line or a 1–100 square to help with checking the calculations.

Information
The activity cannot be extended to finding two 3-digit numbers with a specific number since there is only one of each digit. The hundreds digits could not be the same so there are only a few numbers which would work. To extend to 3-digit numbers, differences would have to be high 2-digit numbers.

Be aware

- Each of the two 2-digit numbers must have different tens digits, since there is only one of each digit. This forces the calculation to bridge a multiple of 10. Check that children are comfortable working with calculations bridging a multiple of 10.

Outcomes

- I can find two 2-digit numbers with a given difference.

Summary

Y2 ☆ B3.1	**Carpet tiles**
	Pairs working independently
	Year 2 Challenge PCMs 51 and 52

Abacus Evolve objectives

- Use the names of common 2D shapes, including: pentagon, hexagon, octagon
- Classify and describe common 2D and 3D shapes
- Make models, shapes and patterns and describe their features

Framework objectives

- *Visualise common 2D shapes and 3D solids; identify shapes from pictures of them in different positions and orientations; sort, make and describe shapes, referring to their properties*
- Identify and record the information or calculation needed to solve a puzzle or problem; carry out the steps or calculations and check the solution in the context of the problem

Teacher notes

Preparation
Photocopy PCM 51, two copies per child. Photocopy PCM 52, one copy per pair. Cut out the shapes.

Getting started
Look at PCM 51. Ask children to name the five shapes. *You are going to design a carpet tile pattern using these shapes. There must be a shape in each square. You can only use each shape once in each row and each column.*

Activity
Children work from PCM 51. They design a pattern using five 2D shapes, making sure that each shape only appears once in each row and each column. They practise with the cut-out shapes from PCM 52 to find a correct pattern, which they then draw on. They then describe their pattern to a partner, using the shape names. Their partner tries to copy the design onto a second copy of PCM 51. Children then colour their design, using different colours, and describe their colour pattern to their partner. Children look for similarities and differences between the shape pattern and the colour pattern.

Extra help
Provide a 4 × 4 grid for children to make a design using just four shapes.

Further extension
Children can try to design a 6 × 6 tile pattern using the same rule. *What new shape will you use?*

Be aware

- In order to follow the rule that each shape can only appear once in each row and each column, children will need to be systematic and keep checking and thinking more than one step ahead.

Outcomes

- I can name some 2D shapes.
- I can describe shape patterns using words.

Supporting resources

Children can classify shapes here:

- http://www.primaryresources.co.uk/online/powerpoint/2Dshapes.swf/

Challenge Plan: Year 2

B3: 2D and 3D shapes; halves and quarters of shapes and numbers; pairs of multiples of 10 that total 100; making the next multiple of 10

Summary

Y2 ☆ B3.2 — **Halving shapes**

A small group working with an adult

Different coloured A4 paper; scissors

Abacus Evolve objectives

- Begin to recognise halves and quarters of shapes
- Begin to recognise that two halves or four quarters make one whole

Framework objectives

- Find one half, one quarter and three quarters of shapes and sets of objects
- Describe patterns and relationships involving numbers or shapes, make predictions and test these with examples
- Listen to others in class, ask relevant questions and follow instructions

Teacher notes

Activity

- Organise children into pairs. Give each child a coloured sheet of A4 paper and a pair of scissors.
- Show children a piece of A4 paper. Explain that for this activity they are going to need squares, not rectangles. *How can we make a square from this rectangle?* Give children time to talk together about this and then ask them to share their ideas as a group. Show them how to fold along the diagonal so that they use the edge as a way of 'measuring' the same length along the long side.

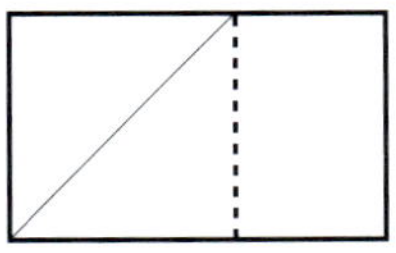

- Ask children to turn their A4 paper into a square.
- *We are going to investigate what different shapes we can make from the square if we cut it exactly in half.* In pairs children experiment with their squares to see what shapes they can make when they cut it in half. Ask children to record what they are doing so that they can explain what they have done to the rest of the class.
- *Have you managed to make some different shapes? Have you noticed any patterns?* Children share ideas with the group and identify any general statements. For example: *You can cut a square into two right-angled triangles. You can cut a square into two rectangles.*

Extra help

Give children a ready-made square. Ask them to describe the properties of the square before they start.

Further extension

Ask children to think about a quarter of each shape. Children predict what shapes they could make if they cut their half-shapes in half. Children test their ideas and record the outcomes using diagrams. *What has happened to the lengths of the sides now you have cut the shapes in half twice? What about the angles?*

Be aware

- This activity focuses on halving the shape. Children will need to cut the shape symmetrically each time to make sure they are cutting it exactly in half. Ensure children understand the significance of this.

Outcomes

- I can turn a rectangle into a square.
- I can cut shapes exactly in half.
- I can describe patterns when halving shapes.

Supporting resources

Children can practise working with fractions with this 'Fun Fractions' activity:

- http://www.primaryresources.co.uk/maths/pdfs/funfractions.pdf

Summary

Y2 ☆ B3.3 **Queuing at the supermarket**

Pairs working independently

Year 2 Challenge Textbook page 33

Abacus Evolve objectives

- Begin to recognise halves and quarters of small numbers of objects
- Recognise that two quarters and one half are equivalent
- Recognise halving as the inverse of doubling
- Know by heart doubles for numbers up to at least 15 and the corresponding halves

Framework objectives

- Find one half, one quarter and three quarters of shapes and sets of objects
- Understand that halving is the inverse of doubling and derive and recall doubles of all numbers to 20, and the corresponding halves
- Present solutions to puzzles and problems in an organised way; explain decisions, methods and results in pictorial, spoken or written form, using mathematical language and number sentences
- Use language and gesture to support the use of models, diagrams or displays when explaining

Teacher notes

Getting started
Look at the Textbook page. Run through the scenario of the supermarket queue. Make sure children understand that increasing the number of tills will reduce the size of the queues.

Activity
Children work from Textbook page 33. They work out how many people are in the supermarket queues each time the manager opens a new till. They represent this by drawing diagrams and explain what is happening.

Extra help
Draw a diagram of a supermarket with two tills, only one of which is open. Draw four people queuing for the till. Then illustrate opening the second till, and dividing the people between the two tills. Discuss halving the number of people in the queue if you double the number of tills.

Further extension
Change the number of people in the queue to 48. *What happens to the number of people at each till now?*
Ask children to devise their own *What if...* questions to go with this supermarket scenario.

If you have time
Create a play shop for children to role-play supermarket queues and see what happens when the number of tills increases.

Be aware

- Some children will be able to use fraction notation but, if they do, check that they can give you a sentence in words that explains the context of their fraction statement. For example, *$\frac{1}{4}$ of 24 means there are 24 people in the supermarket and four tills are open. So a quarter of the people are at each till.*

Outcomes

- I can find halves and quarters of the number of people in a queue.

Supporting resources

You can access several activities about fractions here:
- http://www.ncetm.org.uk/resources/8856

Summary

Y2 ☆ B3.4 — **Clothes problems**

A small group working with an adult

Abacus Evolve objectives

- Understand that subtraction is the inverse of addition, using missing number sentences
- State the subtraction corresponding to a given addition, and vice versa

Framework objectives

- Understand that subtraction is the inverse of addition and vice versa and use this to derive and record related addition and subtraction number sentences
- Solve problems involving addition, subtraction, multiplication or division in contexts of numbers, measures or pounds and pence
- Listen to a talk by an adult, remember some specific points and identify what they have learned

Teacher notes

Activity

Mum is sorting out her wardrobe. She has a box for the unwanted clothes. There are already five items in the box.

- Organise children into pairs. *I'm going to tell you what else she put in the box. Listen carefully and write down any useful calculations as we go along.*
  - *Mum puts 10 T-shirts in the box.* (5 + 10)
  - *Then she takes three out.* (−3)
  - *She puts four jumpers in.* (+4)
  - *Then she takes one of them out.* (−1)
  - *She puts two pairs of trousers in.* (+2)
  - *Then she takes five T-shirts out.* (−5)
  - *How many items are in the box now?* (12)
- Children investigate the problem, looking at the operations and the chain of numbers that they generate. Ask each child to use what they have found to set their own clothes problem like this and try it on the group.

Extra help

Start by only using numbers up to 5.

Further extension

Challenge children to create a problem like this using addition, subtraction, doubling and halving.

Be aware

- It is important for children to notice that every operation performed can be 'undone'. You may like to introduce the term *inverse operation* if you feel it is appropriate.

Outcomes

- I can solve problems by performing operations and then 'undoing' them.

Supporting resources

Children can try some maths 'magic tricks' here:

- http://nrich.maths.org/public/viewer.php?obj_id=2289

Challenge Plan: Year 2

B3: 2D and 3D shapes; halves and quarters of shapes and numbers; pairs of multiples of 10 that total 100; making the next multiple of 10

Summary

Y2 ☆ B3.5 — **Matching outfits**

Individuals, pairs or groups working independently

Year 2 Challenge Textbook page 34

Till receipts (optional); items for the play shop (optional); labels for pricing (optional); plastic or real money (optional)

Abacus Evolve objectives

- **Y3** Rehearse pairs of multiples of 10 that total 100
- **Y3** Know by heart pairs of multiples of 100 that total 1000
- **Y3** Use pairs that total 100 to make the next multiple of 100

Framework objectives

- **Y3** *Derive and recall all addition and subtraction facts for each number to 20, sums and differences of multiples of 10 and number pairs that total 100*
- **Y3** Represent the information in a puzzle or problem using numbers, images or diagrams; use these to find a solution and present it in context, where appropriate using £.p notation or units of measure

Teacher notes

Getting started
Look at the Textbook page. *You are going to solve some shopping problems.* Ask a child to read aloud the instructions. Make sure everyone understands what they need to do.
It may be helpful to show children some till receipts so that they can understand the conventions of billing by totalling for each item and then finding the final total of all items.

Activity
Children work from Textbook page 34. They match socks to make pairs that total 100 and gloves to make pairs that total 1000. They then explore which items could have been bought for £100. They record the different combinations in the form of a bill to show that they have found all the options.

Extra help
Give children time at the beginning of the activity to practise pairs of numbers that total 10, 100 and 1000.

Further extension
I have three pairs of trousers and four jumpers. If I wear one pair of trousers and one jumper each time, how many different outfits can I make?
I have been shopping and I have bought one more pair of trousers. How many different outfits can I make now?

If you have time
Make a play shop and label the items with prices up to £1. Give each child a budget, and ask them to choose which items they want to buy. *Make sure you have enough money! How much change will you get?*

Be aware

- When children are working out the possible shopping bills they will need to use a variety of methods to calculate the totals. Support children in finding 'easy' options such as adding pairs that make a multiple of 10 or doubling numbers.

Outcomes

- I can use pairs of numbers to solve shopping problems.

Challenge Plan: Year 2

B3: 2D and 3D shapes; halves and quarters of shapes and numbers; pairs of multiples of 10 that total 100; making the next multiple of 10

Summary

Y2 ☆ B3.6 — **Spokes and wheels**

Pairs working independently

Year 2 Challenge PCMs 53 and 54

Abacus Evolve objectives

- Know by heart addition and subtraction facts for pairs of numbers that total 20
- Rehearse addition and subtraction facts for pairs of numbers that total 10
- Use pairs that total 10 to make the next multiple of 10

Framework objectives

- *Derive and recall all addition and subtraction facts for each number to at least 10, all pairs with totals to 20 and all pairs of multiples of 10 with totals up to 100*
- Identify and record the information or calculation needed to solve a puzzle or problem; carry out the steps or calculations and check the solution in the context of the problem
- Ensure everyone contributes, allocate tasks, consider alternatives and reach agreement

Teacher notes

Preparation
Photocopy PCMs 53 and 54, one copy of each per pair.

Getting started
Look at PCM 53. Explain how the wheel works: *A spoke runs from one side of the wheel to the other, going straight through the middle. In these wheels, each spoke has a number at either end. The pair of numbers on each spoke add up to the same total. In this case, the total is 20. The total of each spoke is shown in the middle of the wheel.*

Activity
Children work from PCMs 53 and 54. They start by filling in the missing numbers on the wheel on PCM 53. They add up all the outside numbers, then try to find a quick way to find this total. (Each spoke has a total of 20 and there are four spokes, so the total of all the numbers is $20 \times 4 = 80$.)
Children then move on to PCM 54. They fill in the missing numbers on the first wheel, finding the middle number as they go, and then find the total of all the outside numbers. The second wheel is blank, but children know that the total of all the outside numbers is 40. They use this information to work out the middle number, and then find spoke numbers that work. Pairs should compare their completed wheel with other pairs.

Further extension
Children could investigate how many different ways there are of making a wheel with an outside total of 100 if they can only use each number once.

If you have time
Ask children to devise their own wheels with missing numbers for a partner to fill in. *How much information do you need to give to your partner so that they can complete the wheel?*

Be aware

- It is important for children to understand the context of this activity and relate it to addition and subtraction sentences. Addition and subtraction sentences can be recorded if that helps children to make the connection.

Outcomes

- I can use pairs of numbers to solve problems.

Supporting resources

Children can try another number problem here:
- http://nrich.maths.org/public/viewer.php?obj_id=2782

Challenge Plan: Year 2

C3: estimating and measuring capacity; capacities in litres and millilitres; adding/subtracting a 1-digit number to/from a multiple of 100; tables

Summary

Y2 ☆ C3.1	**Litre line**
	Pairs working independently
	Year 2 Challenge PCM 55
	Products measured in millilitres and litres, up to 2 litres; 0–1000 number line (optional)

Abacus Evolve objectives

- **Y3** Measure and compare capacities using standard units: litres, millilitres
- **Y3** Know the relationship between litres and millilitres
- **Y3** Read a capacity scale to the nearest labelled and unlabelled division

Framework objectives

- **Y3** Know the relationships between kilometres and metres, metres and centimetres, kilograms and grams, litres and millilitres; choose and use appropriate units to estimate, measure and record measurements
- **Y3** *Read, to the nearest division and half-division, scales that are numbered or partially numbered; use the information to measure and draw to a suitable degree of accuracy*
- **Y3** Develop and use specific vocabulary in different contexts

Teacher notes

Preparation
Photocopy PCM 55, one copy per pair.

Getting started
Provide a selection of products which have the capacity given in millilitres and/or litres. Be careful not to use any toxic products that children might be able to open.
Hold up one of the products. *Can anyone find out what the capacity of this product is?* Pass the product around to allow all children to identify the measurement written on the label. Remind them that *ml* stands for millilitre and *l* stands for litre. *How many millilitres are in a litre? How many millilitres in half a litre?*
Give each pair PCM 55. Ask a child to read aloud the instructions. Make sure everyone knows what to do.

Activity
Children work from PCM 55. In pairs, they find the capacity of each product and discuss where the product should go on the litre line. They mark and label each product in the appropriate place on the line. When they have done this, they work out the total capacity of all the products labelled on their line.

Extra help
Children may find a 0–1000 number line useful. You could write *ml* after *1000*, and *1 litre* below *1000 ml.*

Further extension
Ask children to write some number sentences about the capacities of the products using greater than (>) and less than (<).

Be aware

- You may need to check the product labels before the activity to make sure all items are labelled in millilitres or litres, rather than grams for example.
- Children may assume that the greatest capacity on the number line is the total capacity, rather than adding all the capacities together. If necessary encourage them to make a list of all the capacities on another piece of paper and add them using a method of their choice.

Outcomes

- I can position items on a number line by their capacity.

C3: estimating and measuring capacity; capacities in litres and millilitres; adding/subtracting a 1-digit number to/from a multiple of 100; tables

Summary

Y2 ☆ C3.2 **Fruit cocktail**

Pairs working independently

Year 2 Challenge PCMs 56 and 57

Thin card; bags; rulers; crayons; 0–1000 number line (optional); 1 l measuring jug (optional); water (optional); paper cups (optional)

Abacus Evolve objectives

- Estimate, measure and compare capacities using standard units: litres, millilitres
- Read a simple capacity scale to the nearest labelled and unlabelled division

Framework objectives

- Estimate, compare and measure lengths, weights and capacities, choosing and using standard units (m, cm, kg, litre) and suitable measuring instruments
- Read the numbered divisions on a scale, and interpret the divisions between them, e.g. on a scale from 0 to 25 with intervals of 1 shown but only the divisions 0, 5, 10, 15 and 20 numbered; use a ruler to draw and measure lines to the nearest centimetre
- Ensure everyone contributes, allocate tasks, consider alternatives and reach agreement

Teacher notes

Preparation
Photocopy PCM 56 onto thin card, one copy per pair. Cut out the cards. Place each set of cards in a bag.
Photocopy PCM 57, one copy per child.

Getting started
Show children the capacity cards from PCM 56. Talk about the amounts shown. Choose four cards at random, and ask children to put them in order from the smallest to the largest capacity. They must work as a group, agreeing the order together.
Give each child PCM 57. *You are going to play a game in pairs in which you will take turns to pick a capacity card and colour in the matching quantity on the measuring jug. The first person to reach 1 litre is the winner.* If nobody reaches exactly 1 litre, then the person closest to 1 litre is the winner. If necessary, remind children that there are 1000 ml in 1 l.
Give each child a ruler and a pencil. Have a selection of coloured crayons available.

Activity
Children work from PCM 57. They play the game in pairs: they take turns to take a capacity card at random from the bag. They add the matching amount to their measuring jug by drawing a straight line across the correct line using a crayon, and colouring the section below the line to represent liquid. The winner is the first child to reach 1 litre or get closest to it.

Extra help
Children may find a 0–1000 number line useful. You could write *ml* after *1000*, and *1 litre* below *1000 ml.*

Further extension
Show children a litre of water in a measuring jug. *How much juice do you think you would need to make a fruit cocktail for six children?* Encourage answers around 250 ml (approximately half a pint) per child, or 1500 ml in total. Allow children to pour the water into cups to help inform their decision. *What juices could go in it? How much of each juice do we need?*

Be aware

- Children often do not realise that the surface of a liquid is flat and therefore may not draw a straight line. Encourage children to use a ruler when adding juice to their jug.

Outcomes

- I can add different amounts of millilitres to make 1 litre.
- I know there are 1000 ml in a litre.

Supporting resources

- A set of 1 litre containers of different shapes will show children that 1 litre of water can look very different. Try putting food colouring in the water so it is easier to see.

Summary

Y2 ☆ C3.3 **Water lines**

A small group working with an adult

A bucket of water; 20 ml pipettes; metre sticks, a trundle wheel or a measuring tape

Abacus Evolve objectives

- Estimate, measure and compare capacities using standard units: litres, millilitres
- Estimate, measure and compare lengths using standard units: centimetres
- Estimate, measure and compare lengths using standard units: metres
- Use a ruler to draw and measure lines to the nearest centimetre

Framework objectives

- Estimate, compare and measure lengths, weights and capacities, choosing and using standard units (m, cm, kg, litre) and suitable measuring instruments
- Read the numbered divisions on a scale, and interpret the divisions between them, e.g. on a scale from 0 to 25 with intervals of 1 shown but only the divisions 0, 5, 10, 15 and 20 numbered; use a ruler to draw and measure lines to the nearest centimetre
- Adopt appropriate roles in small or large groups and consider alternative courses of action

Teacher notes

Preparation
Make sure the playground is available for this activity and that the ground is dry. Fill a bucket with water and take it outside.

Activity
- Take children outside. Give each child a 20 ml pipette. Explain that each of them will draw a long, continuous line using water from their pipettes. *Everyone has exactly the same amount of water, so the challenge is to make your line as long as possible!*
- Demonstrate filling a pipette with exactly 20 ml of water from the bucket. Squirt the water onto the ground to show how small a puddle 20 ml makes.
- Each child fills their pipette and practises squirting the water onto the ground to make a line. They will need to coordinate their movements to squirt continuously and move the pipette at the same time.
- Ask children to refill their pipettes. Find a convenient starting point. Children try to make the longest water line they can. They can try one after another or all at the same time.
- Support children in measuring their lines in metres and centimetres. Record the length of each child's line for the group to see.
- Repeat several times and compare results to see which child has drawn the longest line.

Extra help
Lay out a measuring tape or metre sticks for children to draw next to, to keep their lines straight.

If you have time
Challenge children to write their full name with 20 ml of water.

Be aware

- If it is sunny, the water may evaporate so the lines will need to be measured quickly.

Outcomes

- I can draw and measure a line of water.

Supporting resources

- Provide various containers for pouring and comparing.

Summary

Y2 ☆ C3.4 **Subtraction towers**

A small group working with an adult

Year 2 Challenge Textbook page 35

Squared paper; 0–1000 number line (optional)

Abacus Evolve objectives

- Add and begin to subtract a 1-digit number to and from multiples of 10 and 100
- Begin to partition 3-digit numbers into H, T and U
- Use patterns of similar calculations

Framework objectives

- *Add or subtract mentally a single-digit number or a multiple of 10 to or from any 2-digit number; use practical and informal written methods to add and subtract 2-digit numbers*
- *Count up to 100 objects by grouping them and counting in 10s, 5s or 2s; explain what each digit in a 2-digit number represents, including numbers where 0 is a place holder; partition 2-digit numbers in different ways, including into multiples of 10 and 1*
- Describe patterns and relationships involving numbers or shapes, make predictions and test these with examples
- Listen to others in class, ask relevant questions and follow instructions

Teacher notes

Preparation
Provide two or three sheets of squared paper for each child.

Activity
- Look together at the first subtraction tower on the Textbook page. Focus on the highlighted calculation on the ground floor.
- *What has changed in the calculation on the next floor?* Make sure children see that since the number that 7 is being subtracted from is 10 less, the answer is also 10 less.
- Look at the rest of the 'floors' together. Encourage children to discuss the pattern.
- Look at the first calculation in the second tower. *What has changed in the calculation on the next floor?* (Since the number that 4 is being subtracted from is 10 more, the answer is also 10 more.)
- *You are going to draw your own subtraction towers on squared paper. Be careful – if you make a mistake, the rest of the tower will be incorrect as you will be following a different pattern.*
- Children work from Textbook page 35. They use the start calculations on the bricks to draw subtraction towers like the examples.
- As children draw each tower, ask them to check that a mistake has not been made by looking at the number patterns.

Extra help
Children may find a 0–1000 number line useful.

If you have time
Children can swap their work with a partner who checks the number patterns, and corrects any mistakes.

Be aware

- Children may well make a mistake without noticing. For that reason it is important to make sure each tower is checked before children move on to the next.

Outcomes

- I can subtract a 1-digit number from a multiple of 10 up to 1000.
- I can find number patterns and continue them.

Summary

Y2 ☆ C3.5 **Digit tree**

Pairs working independently

Year 2 Challenge PCM 58

0–1000 number line (optional)

Abacus Evolve objectives

- Add and begin to subtract a 1-digit number to and from multiples of 10 and 100
- Begin to partition 3-digit numbers into H, T and U
- Use patterns of similar calculations

Framework objectives

- Add or subtract mentally a 1-digit number or a multiple of 10 to or from any 2-digit number; use practical and informal written methods to add and subtract 2-digit numbers
- *Count up to 100 objects by grouping them and counting in 10s, 5s or 2s; explain what each digit in a 2-digit number represents, including numbers where 0 is a place holder; partition 2-digit numbers in different ways, including into multiples of 10 and 1*
- Describe patterns and relationships involving numbers or shapes, make predictions and test these with examples
- Ensure everyone contributes, allocate tasks, consider alternatives and reach agreement

Teacher notes

Preparation
Photocopy PCM 58, one copy per child.

Getting started
Look at the PCM. *What do you notice about the calculations?* Focus on the fact that they all involve multiples of 10. *Which number bond to 10 has a 3 in it*? (3 + 7 = 10) Ask some questions to check that children recognise the pattern of the calculations: *What is 10 − 3? What is 20 − 3? 30 − 3? 100 − 3? 200 − 3? 220 − 3?* Explain that children will complete the digit tree individually then swap with a partner to check each other's answers.

Activity
Children work from PCM 58. They complete the four branches of calculations in the digit tree. They then swap their tree with a partner and check each other's answers, making any corrections where necessary.

Extra help
Children may find a 0–1000 number line useful.
Support children by asking questions such as: *Which digit must always be in the units space? How many tens are in the question? How many tens will be in the answer? How many hundreds?*

Be aware

- Children may find subtracting a 1-digit number from a 3-digit multiple of 10 difficult. Encourage them to think carefully about the digits, one at a time. Make sure they understand that, in these subtractions, more than one digit will change.

Outcomes

- I can subtract a 1-digit number from a multiple of 10 up to 1000.

C3: estimating and measuring capacity; capacities in litres and millilitres; adding/subtracting a 1-digit number to/from a multiple of 100; tables

Summary

Y2 ☆ C3.6 **Raffle ticket table**

Individuals or pairs working independently

Year 2 Challenge Textbook page 36

Year 2 Challenge PCM 59

Abacus Evolve objectives

- Organise information in a table
- Interpret information from a table
- Begin to recognise odd and even numbers up to at least 100
- Compare two or more 2-digit numbers; introduce the greater than (>), less than (<) signs

Framework objectives

- Answer a question by collecting and recording data in lists and tables; represent the data as block graphs or pictograms to show results; use ICT to organise and present data
- *Use lists, tables and diagrams to sort objects; explain choices using appropriate language, including 'not'*
- Read and write 2- and 3-digit numbers in figures and words; describe and extend number sequences and recognise odd and even numbers
- Order 2-digit numbers and position them on a number line; use the greater than (>), less than (<) signs
- Follow a line of enquiry; answer questions by choosing and using suitable equipment and selecting, organising and presenting information in lists, tables and simple diagrams

Teacher notes

Preparation
Photocopy PCM 59, one copy per child or pair.

Getting started
Look at the Textbook page. Briefly discuss the features of the numbers on the raffle tickets. *I would like you to keep a record of what you know about the numbers on these tickets.* Show the PCM. *We can make a note of our number facts in this table.* Show that the ticks for ticket 264 have already been filled in. *Now you can fill in the rest of the table for the other raffle tickets.*

Activity
Children work from Textbook page 36. They complete the table on PCM 59 by writing the numbers in the left-hand column, and putting ticks in the relevant boxes. After completing the table, they look at the number of ticks each number has been given and say which ticket has the lowest number of ticks and which has the highest number of ticks, and why.

Extra help
Encourage children to start by sorting the numbers into numerical order, then enter them in the table in that order. This will make it easier to identify which columns to tick.

Be aware

- If children are unsure of what some of the headings mean, they may find it difficult to complete the table. If necessary run through the terms before children start the activity.

Outcomes

- I can organise information in a table.
- I can spot number patterns using my table.

Summary

Y2 ☆ D3.1 — **The cruise 1**

A small group working with an adult

Year 2 Challenge Textbook page 37

Year 2 Challenge PCM 60

Dice; cubes or model people

Abacus Evolve objectives

- Add a 1-digit number to a 2-digit number, bridging a multiple of 10 without crossing 100
- Add two 2-digit numbers using an appropriate strategy
- Partition additions into T and U, then recombine

Framework objectives

- *Add or subtract mentally a one-digit number or a multiple of 10 to or from any two-digit number; use practical and informal written methods to add and subtract two-digit numbers*
- Present solutions to puzzles and problems in an organised way; explain decisions, methods and results in pictorial, spoken or written form, using mathematical language and number sentences

Teacher notes

Preparation
Photocopy PCM 60, one copy per pair. Provide one dice per pair.

Activity
- Check if children are familiar with the concept of a cruise and explain if necessary.
- Arrange children into pairs. Each child draws a small picture of a ship and cuts it out. One child in each pair colours their ship blue, and the other red. Pairs turn to Textbook page 37. Place cubes or model people on the islands ready to be 'picked' up as passengers. The number of passengers on each island is given on PCM 60. Explain the rules of the game.
- Pairs use the game board on Textbook page 37. They place their ships at the port. The blue and red ships move in different directions, indicated by the arrows. Children take turns to roll a dice and move their ship. They visit the islands, and pick up the correct amount of passengers using the information on PCM 60. Passengers can only be picked up once, so if the blue ship picks up the passengers at Splash Island, the red ship will have no passengers to pick up from that island. Both ships must visit all islands. Passengers do not leave the ship. When each ship reaches an island, children fill in their passenger log on PCM 60 to show how many passengers they have.
- When all children have finished playing, ask the group to discuss their logs, talking about which methods of recording worked well.

Extra help
Make a new list of passenger bookings, with 12 passengers at the port, and single-digit numbers of passengers at each island. Remove the competitive element of the game by allowing both children to pick up the same number of passengers from all four islands.

Further extension
Use numbers beyond 100. *What is the best way to record the total number of passengers at each island?*

If you have time
Children can draw their own game board and devise a new game to play with a partner.

Be aware

- Each child takes responsibility for generating their own calculations and explaining how they kept a log of the passenger numbers. Children should be encouraged to discuss this without getting too absorbed in the competitive element of the game.

Outcomes

- I can add two numbers together to keep account of the passenger numbers.
- I can discuss my methods with a partner.

Challenge Plan: Year 2

D3: adding 1- and 2-digit numbers; subtracting 2-digit numbers; using units of time; reading the time to the quarter hour

Summary

Y2 ☆ D3.2	**The cruise 2**
	Pairs or groups working independently
	Year 2 Challenge Textbook page 37
	Year 2 Challenge PCM 61
	Dice; cubes or model people

Abacus Evolve objectives

- Add two 2-digit numbers using an appropriate strategy
- Subtract one 2-digit number from another using an appropriate strategy
- Understand that subtraction is the inverse of addition, using missing number sentences

Framework objectives

- *Add or subtract mentally a one-digit number or a multiple of 10 to or from any two-digit number; use practical and informal written methods to add and subtract two-digit numbers*
- Present solutions to puzzles and problems in an organised way; explain decisions, methods and results in pictorial, spoken or written form, using mathematical language and number sentences

Teacher notes

Preparation
Photocopy PCM 61, one copy per pair. Provide one dice per pair.

Getting started
Check if children are familiar with the concept of a cruise and explain if necessary. Arrange children into pairs. Each child draws a small picture of a ship and cuts it out. One child in each pair colours their ship blue, and the other red. Pairs turn to Textbook page 37. Place cubes or model people on the islands ready to be 'picked' up as passengers. PCM 61 shows the passenger bookings at each island. In this game passengers may get on or off at each island. Explain the rules of the game.

Activity
Pairs use the game board on Textbook page 37. They place their ships at the port. The blue and red ships move in different directions, indicated by the arrows. Children take turns to roll a dice and move their ship. They visit the islands, and pick up and drop off the correct amount of passengers using the information on PCM 61. Passengers can only be picked up/dropped off once, so if the blue ship picks up the passengers at Splash Island, the red ship will have no passengers to pick up at that island. Both ships must visit all islands. When each ship reaches an island, children fill in their passenger log on PCM 61 to show how many passengers they have picked up, how many they have dropped off and how many they have in total. When both ships are back at the port children discuss the logs, talking about which methods of recording worked well.

Extra help
If necessary adjust the number of passengers to meet the ability level of children.

Further extension
Use numbers beyond 100. *What is the best way to record the total number of passengers at each island?*

If you have time
Children can use a map to look up names of real islands, then find out about them and write a cruise brochure.

Be aware

- Calculations can be simplified by taking account of the difference between the number of passengers getting on and off before adding this to the total. It is important that children arrive at this 'short-cut' by themselves as this supports understanding of the impact of applying inverse operations to numbers.

Outcomes

- I can decide which calculations are needed to solve a problem.
- I can use addition and subtraction to find the total number of passengers.

Supporting resources

Children can watch The Number Crew use a range of number operations in Landing on the Island:
- http://www.teachers.tv/video/25380

D3: adding 1- and 2-digit numbers; subtracting 2-digit numbers; using units of time; reading the time to the quarter hour

Summary

Y2 ☆ D3.3 — **Misprints**

Individuals or pairs working independently

Year 2 Challenge PCM 62

Abacus Evolve objectives

- Add two 2-digit numbers using an appropriate strategy
- Subtract one 2-digit number from another using an appropriate strategy
- Understand that subtraction is the inverse of addition, using missing number sentences

Framework objectives

- *Add or subtract mentally a one-digit number or a multiple of 10 to or from any two-digit number; use practical and informal written methods to add and subtract two-digit numbers*
- Solve problems involving addition, subtraction, multiplication or division in contexts of numbers, measures or pounds and pence

Teacher notes

Preparation
Photocopy PCM 62, one copy per child.

Getting started
Arrange children into pairs. *I've made some worksheets, but I'm very disappointed because the printer has broken and some of the numbers are missing! Read through the number sentences and try to fill in the missing numbers.* Show children PCM 62 and explain what to do in each section. You may need to check that children understand what a digit is.

Activity
Children work from PCM 62. They correct the misprints. Children then make a similar page for a partner. Children swap sheets and solve each other's missing-number sentences.

Extra help
Complete all but one of the missing digits in the second section of PCM 62 before photocopying.

Further extension
Children can make up a scenario for each number sentence. *What might it mean? What would make a good story to explain the number sentence?*

If you have time
Children can try to make up some impossible missing number sentences, for example, 12 − □ = 2□. Ask them to explain why they are impossible.

Be aware

- Some children may be unclear about the differences between numbers and digits and may need some clarification of the link between the two.
- It is important for children to know that sometimes there is more than one right answer.

Outcomes

- I can work out missing numbers in number sentences.
- I can decide which calculation is needed.

Supporting resources

Children can play 'Secret Number' in pairs, using additions and subtractions as clues:

- http://nrich.maths.org/public/viewer.php?obj_id=5651

D3: adding 1- and 2-digit numbers; subtracting 2-digit numbers; using units of time; reading the time to the quarter hour

Summary

Y2 ☆ D3.4 — **It's ready!**

Pairs or groups working independently

Year 2 Challenge PCM 63

Food packaging with microwave cooking instructions (optional)

Abacus Evolve objectives

- Use units of time and know the relationship between them: hours, minutes, seconds
- Recognise addition as counting on
- Extend understanding of subtraction as taking away

Framework objectives

- *Use units of time (seconds, minutes, hours, days) and know the relationships between them; read the time to the quarter hour; identify time intervals, including those that cross the hour*
- *Add or subtract mentally a one-digit number or a multiple of 10 to or from any 2-digit number; use practical and informal written methods to add and subtract 2-digit numbers*
- Understand that subtraction is the inverse of addition and vice versa and use this to derive and record related addition and subtraction number sentences

Teacher notes

Preparation
Photocopy PCM 63, one copy per pair.

Getting started
Explain that children are going to work in pairs to begin with, then share their ideas as a group.
Give children PCM 63. Explain that the timer on the microwave oven only has + and − buttons, and if you press these buttons it adds or subtracts 1 second. Remind children that there are 60 seconds in a minute.

Activity
Children work from PCM 63. In pairs they solve the microwave time problems. Children then discuss the questions and answers as a group, and compare methods.

Extra help
Use 1-digit numbers to calculate. For example, 10 seconds take away 3 seconds.

Further extension
The meal that I am cooking takes 1 minute to cook. I set the timer on the microwave to 1 minute. However, the instructions say that it needs stirring half-way through cooking. What will the timer say when I need to stir it? Ask children to make up word problems like this for other children to solve. The problems should include amounts of time in minutes and seconds.

If you have time
Provide some food packages that provide microwave cooking instructions. Children can make up some subtraction calculations using the information on the packets.

Be aware

- Some children may not be familiar with microwave ovens so the example may need some explanation. However, the maths is the same for any timing device so children could be encouraged to make up their own contexts and timings instead.

Outcomes

- I can use units of time to think about cooking.

Challenge Plan: Year 2

D3: adding 1- and 2-digit numbers; subtracting 2-digit numbers; using units of time; reading the time to the quarter hour

Summary

Y2 ☆ D3.5 — **Waiting for hours**

A small group working with an adult

Year 2 Challenge PCM 64

Watches; clocks; stopwatches; sand timers

Abacus Evolve objectives

- Use units of time and know the relationship between them: hours, minutes, seconds
- Read the time to the quarter hour on analogue and 12-hour digital clocks

Framework objectives

- *Use units of time (seconds, minutes, hours, days) and know the relationships between them; read the time to the quarter hour; identify time intervals, including those that cross the hour*

Teacher notes

Preparation

Photocopy PCM 64, one per child. Collect together watches, clocks, stopwatches and sand timers.

Activity

- *Can you remember feeling so excited that you couldn't wait for something to happen, like a birthday or a holiday? Does time seem to pass slowly or quickly when you are waiting for something?*
- Display the range of timing devices you have collected and discuss how they work and similarities and differences between them.
- Show a stopwatch and tell children you will use it to time 1 minute. Ask children to sit in silence with their eyes closed. Tell them you will start timing 1 minute and you want them to put their hand up when they think a minute has passed. Watch as children raise their hands to see who has estimated it well and who has misjudged it.
- *Did time pass slowly? Why do you think that was?* Ask children to discuss the idea of time passing quickly and slowly. *What does it mean? Is there such a thing as time going slowly?*
- Tell children a story about you waiting for a bus on a cold, wet Monday morning. Tell them it felt like you were waiting for hours and hours at the bus stop. Hand out PCM 64 and ask children to find out exactly how long you waited. *Was it really hours? How could you find out?*

Extra help

Use times that relate to a complete hour or minute.

Further extension

Ask children to consider the school timetable. *How long are the lessons? How long is assembly? How long is the school day? Which parts of the day pass quickly for you? Which pass more slowly?*

If you have time

Ask children to make their own sand timer (see instructions at the bottom of PCM 64).

Ask children to time each other doing a range of activities that last a minute. For example, how many times can children jump up and down in one minute? Or throw and catch a ball?

Be aware

- Many children find it hard to understand that there are 60 minutes in an hour and 60 seconds in a minute and children may find the concept of time passing difficult to estimate. Developing an awareness of time passing is an important skill and may help children to become more efficient in their work with time.

Outcomes

- I can use units of time.
- I understand the relationship between seconds and minutes.

Challenge Plan: Year 2

D3: adding 1- and 2-digit numbers; subtracting 2-digit numbers; using units of time; reading the time to the quarter hour

Summary

Y2 ☆ D3.6 — **The clock shop**

Individuals or pairs working independently

Year 2 Challenge Textbook page 38

Year 2 Challenge PCM 65 (optional)

Assorted clocks and watches; clock with moveable hands

Abacus Evolve objectives

- Read the time to the quarter hour on analogue and 12-hour digital clocks

Framework objectives

- *Use units of time (seconds, minutes, hours, days) and know the relationships between them; read the time to the quarter hour; identify time intervals, including those that cross the hour*

Teacher notes

Preparation
Display a collection of clocks and watches. Photocopy PCM 65, one copy per child who is likely to reach the Further extension.

Getting started
Show children some clock faces. If possible, give them a clock with moveable hands so they can practise turning the hands to different times. *Imagine you are trying to teach a young child to read the time. How would you teach them? What could you show them to help them to understand a clock?*
Explain about the speaking clock. Set a range of times on the clocks and watches and select children to be the 'speaking clock'. Others 'ring in' to find out the time.
Show children Textbook page 38, and explain what to do.

Activity
Children work from Textbook page 38. They read about Mr Wheeler's clock shop. Children confirm that all the clocks say the same time (09:15). They then consider what each of the clocks would look like if they were one hour slow. They draw this time on an analogue clock and a digital clock. Children can work on the Textbook page individually, and then discuss their thoughts in pairs.

Extra help
Use the blank clock faces on PCM 65 to set the clocks in Mr Wheeler's shop at a time that is appropriate for children, for example, 09:00 rather than 09:15.

Further extension
Use PCM 65 to set times for your partner to read that are at 10 past the hour. What time will it be in half an hour?

If you have time
Children can find out about British Summer Time. *When does it change? Why?*

Be aware

- Children can be confused by the different ways of displaying and telling the time. It may help to consider together how clocks can look different and what information they are giving.
- Using real clocks helps children to understand that time is constantly moving. It is important for children to notice that the hour hand and the minute hand are both moving all the time but at different rates.

Outcomes

- I can read times such as quarter past nine.

Supporting resources

Find out more about The BT Speaking Clock here:
- http://www.telephonesuk.co.uk/speaking_clock.htm

E3: multiplication as repeated addition; 2, 5 and 10 times tables; doubling and halving multiples of 5 and 10; halves and quarters

Summary

Y2 ☆ E3.1	**Multiplying then dividing**
	Individuals or pairs working independently
	Year 2 Challenge Textbook page 39
	Year 2 Challenge PCM 66
	Linking cubes; squared paper (optional)

Abacus Evolve objectives

- Begin to understand multiplication as repeated addition or as describing an array
- Begin to understand division as the inverse of multiplication
- Use patterns of similar calculations

Framework objectives

- Represent repeated addition and arrays as multiplication, and sharing and repeated subtraction (grouping) as division; use practical and informal written methods and related vocabulary to support multiplication and division, including calculations with remainders
- Describe patterns and relationships involving numbers or shapes, make predictions and test these with examples

Teacher notes

Preparation
Photocopy PCM 66, one copy per child or pair.

Getting started
Put some linking cubes out on the table. Children may wish to use these to help them to work out the multiplication and division facts. Look at the Textbook page. *You are going to investigate multiplying and dividing using function machines.* Look together at the two function machines. Track the numbers through the machines, making sure children understand how they work. *What methods did you use to work out each step?*
Now you are going to put some numbers through different function machines to see what happens when you multiply then divide by the same number.

Activity
Children work from Textbook page 39. They use what they have learned about function machines to take a number from 6 to 9 through the function machines on PCM 66. These machines all multiply and divide by the same number. Children describe what happens to the numbers, and try to explain why this happens.

Extra help
Encourage children to use the cubes to help them. They may also find squared paper useful, for drawing arrays.

If you have time
What do you think would happen if the function machines were the other way round, and you divided then multiplied by the same number? Children can consider this, using examples where the answer to the division will be a whole number.

Information
Multiplication and division are inverse operations so when you multiply and then divide by the same number (or vice versa) the two operations cancel each other out and you get back to your start number.

Be aware

- If children spot the pattern early, make sure that they still perform the multiplication and division calculations to check that their predictions are correct.

Outcomes

- I can multiply a 1-digit number by 2, 3, 4 and 5.
- I can divide a 2-digit number by 2, 3, 4 and 5.
- I can explain what happens when I multiply then divide by the same number.

Challenge Plan: Year 2

E3: multiplication as repeated addition; 2, 5 and 10 times tables; doubling and halving multiples of 5 and 10; halves and quarters

Summary

Y2 ☆ E3.2 **Multiplication and division arrays**

A small group working with an adult

Year 2 Challenge PCM 67

Linking cubes; squared paper; coloured pencils

Abacus Evolve objectives

- Introduce multiplication as 'lots of'
- Begin to understand multiplication as repeated addition or as describing an array
- Begin to understand division as the inverse of multiplication

Framework objectives

- Represent repeated addition and arrays as multiplication, and sharing and repeated subtraction (grouping) as division; use practical and informal written methods and related vocabulary to support multiplication and division, including calculations with remainders
- Present solutions to puzzles and problems in an organised way; explain decisions, methods and results in pictorial, spoken or written form, using mathematical language and number sentences
- Listen to talk by an adult, remember some specific points and identify what they have learned

Teacher notes

Preparation
Photocopy PCM 67, one copy per pair.

Activity
- Look together at the arrays on the PCM. Discuss how they are similar and how they are different.
- Look at the different number sentences used to describe each addition. *What is happening in each number sentence?* Focus on ideas relating to repeated addition, multiplication and division.
- *Which number sentence tells us that the 12 squares are grouped into 3s?* (3 + 3 + 3 + 3 = 12) *Which number sentence tells us there are 3 lots of 4?* (3 × 4 = 12)
- As children are talking, record any key vocabulary for the group to see.
- Children work from PCM 67. They draw arrays of squares to match the numbers shown, and write number sentences to describe them. Children can use cubes to find each array before they draw it. Encourage children to describe their array as they are drawing it, before they write the number sentences.
- As children are working, ask questions such as: *How many squares are there in each row/column? How many rows/columns are there? How many sets has the array been divided into?*

Extra help
If children are unsure of how to find or describe their arrays, or what number sentences to write, refer them to the key vocabulary that you wrote up. This might include terms such as: *added; times; lots of; divided into groups of; shared equally into*.

If you have time
Children can make a poster of an array with all the ways of describing it they can think of, including descriptions in words as well as number sentences.

Be aware

- Some children may get mixed up with where to place each number in a number sentence. Encourage them to describe the array in words then translate this into a number sentence.

Outcomes

- I can draw arrays to show multiplications and divisions.
- I can describe an array in different ways using number sentences.

Supporting resources

- Provide practical equipment for creating arrays such as peg boards or square tiles.

Summary

Y2 ☆ E3.3 **Totals with 2p and 5p coins**

Groups working independently

Large sheets of paper; 2p and 5p coins; tack

Abacus Evolve objectives

- Know by heart the multiplication facts for 2, 5 and 10 times tables
- Use the + and = signs to record addition sentences
- Record multiplication facts using × and = in number sentences
- Find totals of sets of coins: relate to adding three or more numbers

Framework objectives

- Derive and recall multiplication facts for the 2, 5 and 10 times tables and the related division facts; recognise multiples of 2, 5 and 10
- *Use the symbols +, −, ×, ÷ and = to record and interpret number sentences involving all four operations; calculate the value of an unknown in a number sentence (e.g. 30 − □ = 24, □ ÷ 2 = 6)*
- Present solutions to puzzles and problems in an organised way; explain decisions, methods and results in pictorial, spoken or written form, using mathematical language and number sentences
- Adopt appropriate roles in small or large groups and consider alternative courses of action

Teacher notes

Preparation
Make a recording sheet on a large sheet of paper. Write the heading: *Which totals can be made with 2p and 5p coins?* Draw a large table with two columns and 10 rows, about 8 cm high. Write the totals *1p*, *2p*, *3p*, ... *10p* in order down the left-hand column.

Getting started
Put the recording sheet on the table, along with 2p and 5p coins and tack.
You are going to investigate which totals can be made using 2p and 5p coins. Is it possible to make 1p using 2p and 5p coins? Establish that it isn't, so the box by the 1p total stays empty.
Give a child one 5p coin and two 2p coins. Ask children to work out the total. (9p) Stick the coins on the recording sheet in the box next to the 9p total. *How many 5p coins are there?* Write *1 × 5p* next to the set of coins. *How many 2p coins are there?* Write *2 × 2p* next to the first calculation. *How do we find the total?* Write an addition symbol between the two calculations so that the number sentence reads *1 × 5p + 2 × 2p.*
Explain to children that they will complete the table like this. Remind them that there may be more than one way to make some amounts (for example 10p) and they should aim to find all the possible ways of making each total. Encourage children to look for and use patterns in the table to help find answers.

Activity
Children work together to complete the table. They find all the possible ways of making totals from 1p to 10p (or more) using 2p and 5p coins, and investigate which totals can be made and which cannot. Where totals can be made in more than one way, they aim to find all the possible solutions. They record their results on the recording sheet using coins and number sentences.

Further extension
Make another recording sheet for children to continue the investigation with totals up to 20p.

Information
It is possible to make every total of 4p or above. As children add solutions to the table, patterns will emerge. For example, any set of coins should appear again two rows below with another 2p added.

Be aware

- Children may find it difficult to approach this in an organised way as a group. Encourage teamwork to find solutions and, if necessary, allocate a task to each child. For example, child A sticks the coins on, child B writes the number sentences, child C does the calculations to check the total.

Outcomes

- I can use 2 and 5 times table facts to make totals.
- I can solve a problem in an organised way.

Summary

Y2 ☆ E3.4 **Near doubles**

Individuals or pairs working independently

Year 2 Challenge Textbook page 40

Abacus Evolve objectives

- Add by identifying near doubles for multiples of 5
- Add two 2-digit numbers using an appropriate strategy

Framework objectives

- Understand that halving is the inverse of doubling and derive and recall doubles of all numbers to 20, and the corresponding halves
- *Add or subtract mentally a single-digit number or a multiple of 10 to or from any 2-digit number; use practical and informal written methods to add and subtract 2-digit numbers*

Teacher notes

Getting started
Look at the Textbook page. *You are going to test two methods of adding near doubles.* Together, read Carlo's and Anna's methods. Discuss which of them is right, and how both methods can be used to find an answer.

Activity
Children work from Textbook page 40. They compare Carlo's method for adding near doubles (*double the smaller number then add 1)* and Anna's method for adding near doubles (*double the larger number then take away 1).* Children try out each method by answering two near doubles calculations using both methods.
Children decide which method they would choose to answer the near double 45 + 46 and explain why.

Extra help
If children struggle to apply the two rules, ask questions such as: *What does the rule say to do first? Which is the smaller/larger number? How can you double this number? What do you need to do now?*

If you have time
Make a display showing children's different methods for answering near double questions. Children can then use this to support them in choosing methods in the future.

Information
Both methods for adding two consecutive numbers are correct. Children's choice of method will depend on the numbers involved, for example: 35 + 36 might be efficiently answered by using the known double of 35 then adding 1; 40 + 39 might be efficiently answered by doubling 40 and subtracting 1.
Children may need to use partitioning to work out the doubles.

Be aware

- Some children may be able to explain why both methods are correct, but it is not necessary that they are able to produce an explanation. The important thing is that they notice that both methods are good strategies for adding near doubles.

Outcomes

- I can add near doubles using different methods.
- I can choose a sensible method to answer a calculation.

Summary

Y2 ☆ E3.5 **Shape fractions**

Groups working independently

Year 2 Challenge PCMs 68 and 69

Large sheets of paper; tack; square or triangle dot paper (optional)

Abacus Evolve objectives

- Begin to recognise halves and quarters of shapes
- Begin to recognise that two halves or four quarters make one whole
- Recognise that two quarters and one half are equivalent
- Begin to recognise line symmetry
- Make symmetrical patterns by folding and cutting

Framework objectives

- Find one half, one quarter and three quarters of shapes and sets of objects
- Identify reflective symmetry in patterns and 2D shapes and draw lines of symmetry in shapes
- Use lists, tables and diagrams to sort objects; explain choices using appropriate language including 'not'
- Follow a line of enquiry; answer questions by choosing and using suitable equipment and selecting, organising and presenting information in lists, tables and simple diagrams
- Ensure everyone contributes, allocate tasks, consider alternatives and reach agreement

Teacher notes

Preparation
Photocopy PCMs 68 and 69, one copy of each per group. Cut out the shapes.
Draw a Venn diagram for each group on a large sheet of paper, with two rings headed *Shapes that can be folded in half* and *Shapes that can be folded into quarters*.

Getting started
Give each group a set of shapes cut out from PCMs 68 and 69. Explain to children that they are going to see whether each shape can be folded into halves and whether it can be folded into quarters. Show children the Venn diagram and explain that they will put each shape under the correct heading. *First you will predict where each shape belongs just by looking at it*. If there are any disagreements, children should explain their reasoning until they can agree. Once predictions have been made for all the shapes, children fold them to test their predictions, then stick the shapes onto the diagram.

Activity
Children work together to organise the shapes in the Venn diagram according to whether they can be folded into halves or halves and quarters. Children first predict where each shape should be placed, then test their predictions by folding the shapes.

Further extension
Children could use square or triangle dot paper to draw their own shapes to place in the table.

Information
This activity consolidates ideas about the symmetry of shapes. All shapes that can be folded into quarters can also be folded into halves. This means that one area of the Venn diagram will remain empty.

Be aware

- Ensure that children appreciate that for a shape to be folded into halves or quarters, the edges of the shape must match up exactly so that each piece is exactly the same size.

Outcomes

- I can recognise halves and quarters of shapes.
- I can predict and test whether a shape can be folded into halves or quarters.

E3: multiplication as repeated addition; 2, 5 and 10 times tables; doubling and halving multiples of 5 and 10; halves and quarters

Summary

Y2 ☆ E3.6 **Chomp the chocolate**

A small group working with an adult

Year 2 Challenge PCMs 70 and 71

A sharp pencil; thin card; coloured pencils or crayons

Abacus Evolve objectives

- **Y3** Begin to recognise simple equivalent fractions
- **Y3** Compare familiar fractions
- **Y3** Find unit fractions of numbers

Framework objectives

- **Y3** Read and write proper fractions (e.g. $\frac{3}{7}$, $\frac{9}{10}$), interpreting the denominator as the parts of a whole and the numerator as the number of parts; identify and estimate fractions of shapes; use diagrams to compare fractions and establish equivalents
- **Y3** Find unit fractions of numbers and quantities, e.g. $\frac{1}{2}$, $\frac{1}{3}$, $\frac{1}{4}$ and $\frac{1}{6}$ of 12 litres
- **Y3** Actively include and respond to all members of the group

Teacher notes

Preparation

Photocopy PCM 70 onto thin card. Cut out the octagon and push a pencil through the middle to make a spinner. Photocopy PCM 71, one copy per child.
Draw a simple chocolate bar, 4 squares by 2 squares, and display it for children to look at.

Activity

- Show children the drawing of a chocolate bar. *Imagine colouring one half of the chocolate bar. Show me with your fingers how many of the squares to colour.*
- Ask a child to colour half of the chocolate bar. Write $\frac{1}{2}$ on the coloured section. *How many halves make the whole chocolate bar?* Remind children that when the whole is divided into two equal pieces, each piece is called *one half*, which is written $\frac{1}{2}$.
- Repeat for $\frac{1}{4}$, using a different colour. Remind children that when the whole is divided into four equal pieces, each piece is called *one quarter*, which is written $\frac{1}{4}$.
- *What fraction of the chocolate bar is coloured altogether?* Establish that the half and the quarter together make $\frac{3}{4}$ of the shape. Ask a child to write the fraction $\frac{3}{4}$.
- *How many equal squares is the bar of chocolate divided into?* Explain that when a whole is divided into eight equal pieces, each piece is called *one eighth*, which is written $\frac{1}{8}$. Ask a child to colour in $\frac{1}{8}$ of the bar of chocolate and write the fraction. Together, count up in eighths, pointing to each eighth of the chocolate bar as you do so: $\frac{1}{8}, \frac{2}{8}, \frac{3}{8} \ldots \frac{8}{8}$.
- Show children the spinner and ask them to read out the fractions they recognise. Explain how to read any unfamiliar fractions.
- Play the 'Chomp the chocolate' game as a group. Give each child a copy of PCM 71. They take turns to spin the spinner. They say the fraction and 'chomp' that fraction of their first bar of chocolate on the PCM by colouring the appropriate number of squares. Encourage all children to think about how many squares need to be coloured each time so that they can help anyone who colours in the wrong number of squares.
- As children play, ask questions such as: *Can you explain why s/he coloured that number of squares? What is the biggest/smallest fraction on the spinner? Would you rather spin $\frac{1}{4}$ or $\frac{1}{8}$? Why? Would you rather spin $\frac{1}{2}$ or $\frac{2}{4}$? How many eighths make up $\frac{1}{2}$? What fraction of that chocolate bar is coloured altogether?*
- The first child to 'chomp up' all three chocolate bars on their game board wins.

Extra help

If children struggle to identify how many squares to colour, encourage them to refer back to the chocolate bar that the group coloured at the start of the activity.

Be aware

- Children sometimes assume that $\frac{1}{8}$ must be bigger than $\frac{1}{4}$ because 8 is bigger than 4. Use the chocolate bar images to explain why this is not true.

Outcomes

- I can find $\frac{1}{2}$, $\frac{1}{4}$ and $\frac{3}{4}$ of a shape.
- I am starting to compare fractions.

PCM Contents

Number strips

6									
8									
2									
3									
9									
1									
7									
4									
5									

How many caterpillars?

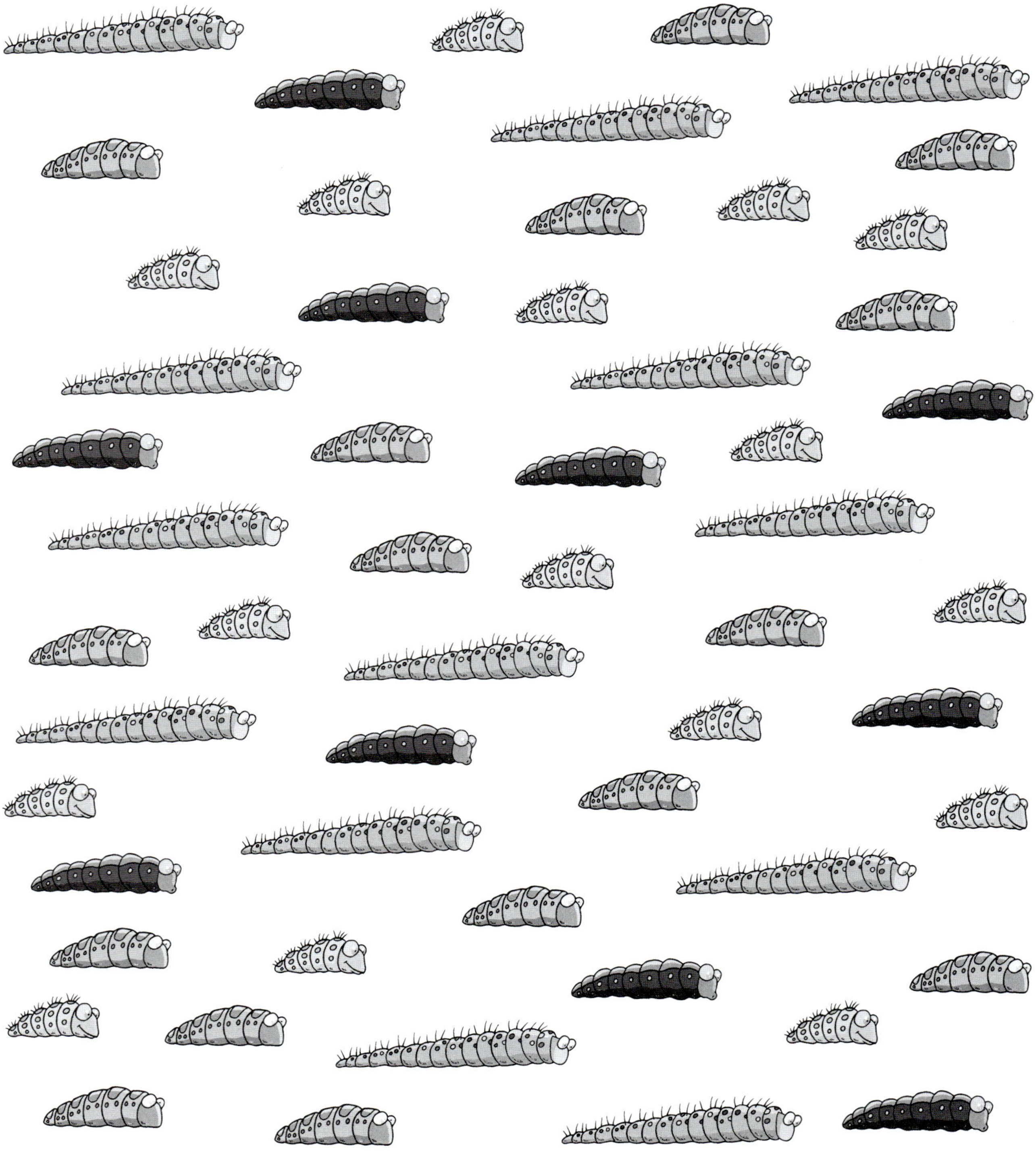

Estimate ☐ Count ☐

I counted in ____________________

How many cats?

Estimate ☐ Count ☐

I counted in ____________________

How many hands?

Estimate ☐ Count ☐

I counted in ______________________

How many ______________________?

Estimate [ ] Count [ ]

I counted in ______________________________

Moving the zero

9	9	9	9	0
8	8	8	8	0
7	7	7	7	0
6	6	6	6	0
5	5	5	5	0
4	4	4	4	0
3	3	3	3	0
2	2	2	2	0
1	1	1	1	0

Fame and fortune

Mr Moneybags

	Start amount	Extra money	Count on the 10s	Count on the 1s
Monday	£550	£0		
Tuesday	£550	£19	£560	£569
Wednesday	£569	£25		
Thursday		£9		
Friday		£12		

Miss Bigbank

	Start amount	Extra money	Count on the 10s	Count on the 1s
Monday	£500	£0		
Tuesday	£500	£27	£520	£527
Wednesday	£527	£0		
Thursday		£44		
Friday		£47		

Fill out Miss Bigbank's cheque in words and numbers.

Date______________

Pay Big Heart Charity
(Amount in words)______________

______________ £

Doughnuts 1

Here are some squares with a hole in the middle.
They look like doughnuts!
What do you notice about the rows and columns?

7	8	5
9		2
4	3	13

8	9	3
11		0
1	2	17

In these doughnuts each row and each column adds up to 20.

1 Complete these '20' doughnuts.

5		8
12		3

5	4	
		6
	8	

2 Make some different '20' doughnuts on PCM 9.
No number can be used more than once in any doughnut.

3 Make a '21' doughnut.

4 Now make a '19' doughnut.

5 What do you notice?

Doughnuts 2

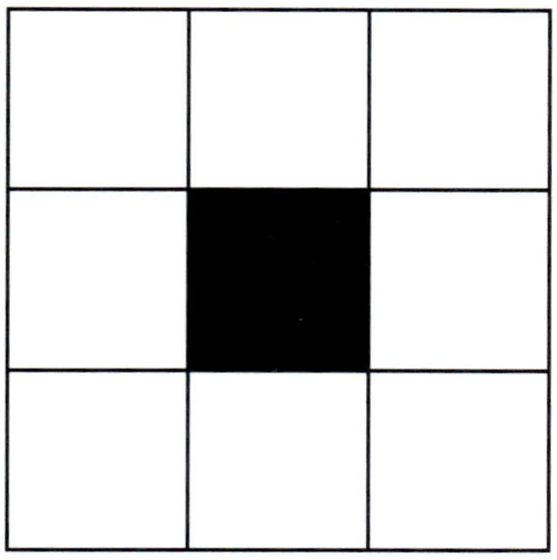

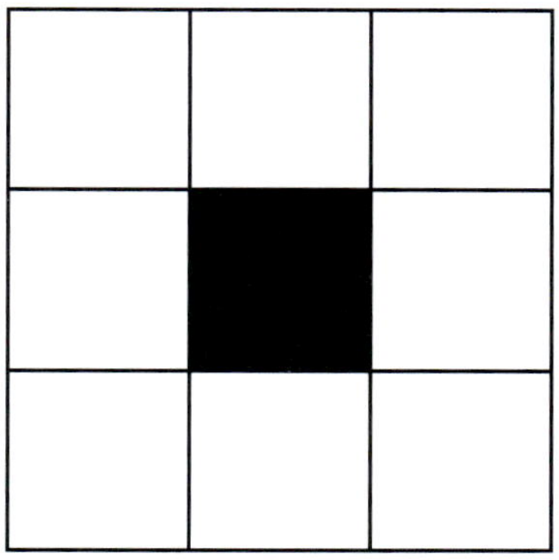

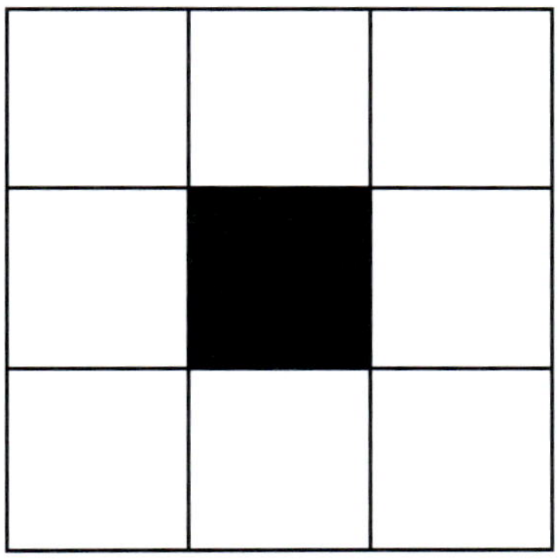

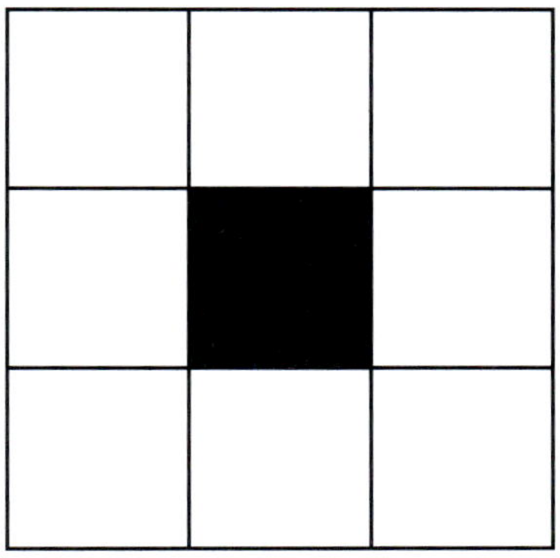

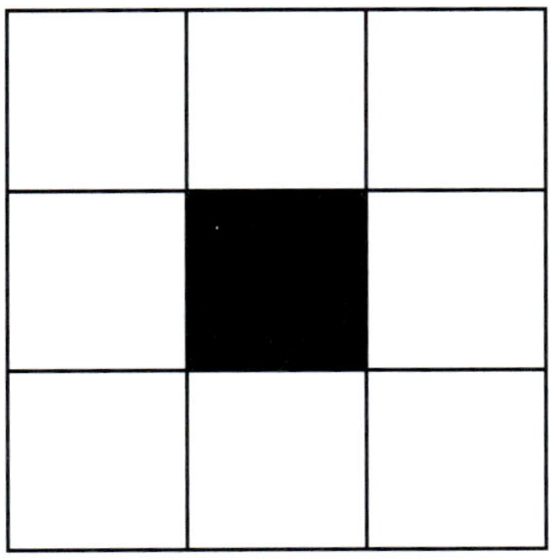

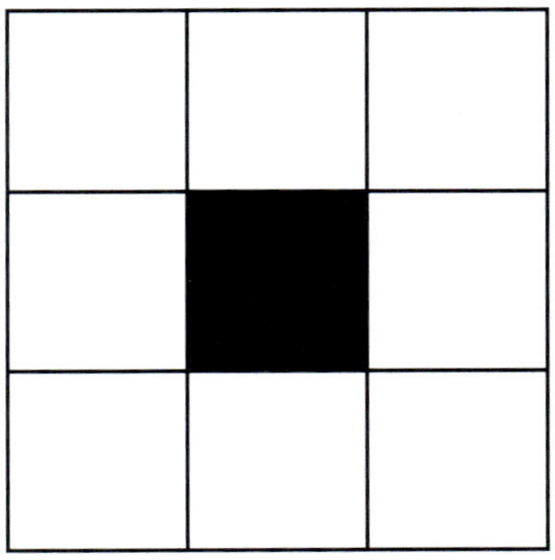

Chasing 21

- Throw the three dice.

- Find the total. Is it close to 21?

Total
11

- If you are happy with your throw, record how far it is from 21.

10 from 21

If you are not happy with your throw, you can throw one, two or all three dice again.

- Find the total. Record how far it is from 21.

Total
22

1 from 21

Take turns, writing your scores in the table.

The winner is the player whose score is closest to 0 at the end.

	Player A		Player B	
Turn	Total	How far from 21?	Total	How far from 21?
1	22	1 from 21		
2				
3				
4				
5				
	Score:		Score:	

To and fro

- Throw a dice to find a start number.
- Pair 1: add 2, then subtract 1.
  $5 + 2 = 7$ $7 - 1 = 6$
- Pair 2: add 2, then subtract 1.
  $6 + 2 = 8$ $8 - 1 = 7$
- Continue until each pair has had a go.

For example: 5

Start number: 5
Answer: 6

Start number: 6
Answer: 7

1 Play the game. Write the start numbers and answers here.

	Pair 1	Pair 2	Pair 3	Pair 4
Start number				
Answer				

2 What do you notice? Why does that happen?

3 Play again, using the rule add 3, subtract 2.
Write the start numbers and answers here.

	Pair 1	Pair 2	Pair 3	Pair 4
Start number				
Answer				

4 What do you notice? Why does that happen?

5 In pairs, think of another way to add and subtract that will give the same answers. Write your rule here.

Our rule is: ______________________________

Punctuation maths

Mrs Barton's fingers have slipped on the keyboard!

She types 3# + 4 = 40 and #3 − 60 = 3

1 Instead of # which number did she mean to type?

____

Then she types 4! + 8 = !3 and 43 − 8 = 3!

2 Instead of ! which number did she mean to type?

____

Now you know what # and ! are, work out these answers.

3 3# − ! =

4 #2 + ! =

5 Make up some more punctuation maths sentences for your partner to solve. How much information does your partner need to solve the problem?

My punctuation maths sentences:

Duck dinner time

Your pet duck eats a metre of worms a day.
Search the garden to find them!
Each time you land on a worm, collect a 10 cm worm from the worm bank.
The winner is the first to collect 1 m of worms.

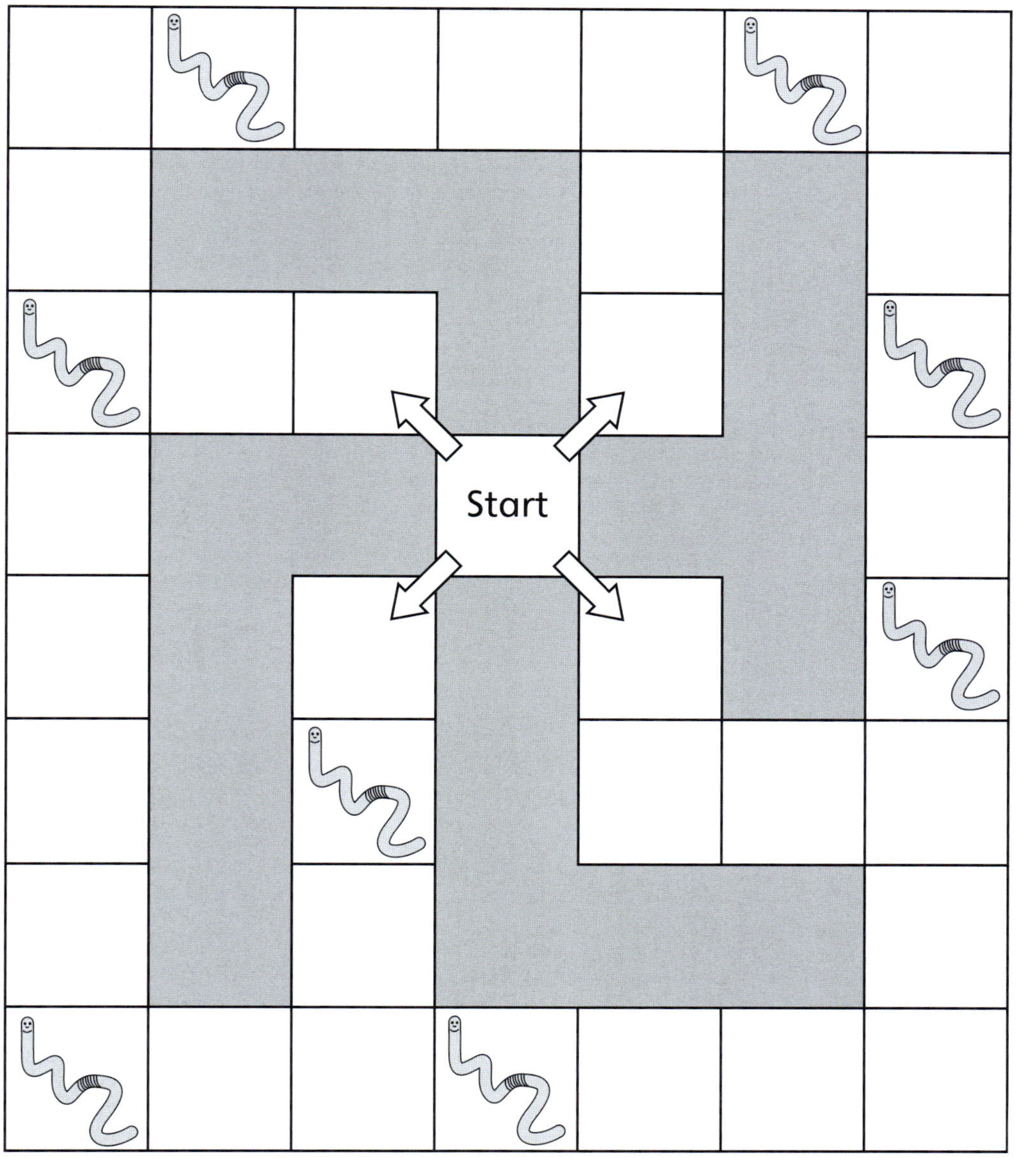

WORM BANK

My day

Pick a day. ______________________

Complete the key.

Fill in the blanks with two things you do.

Pick a colour for each activity.

Start at midnight and colour in each segment of the clock faces to show what you usually do at that time.

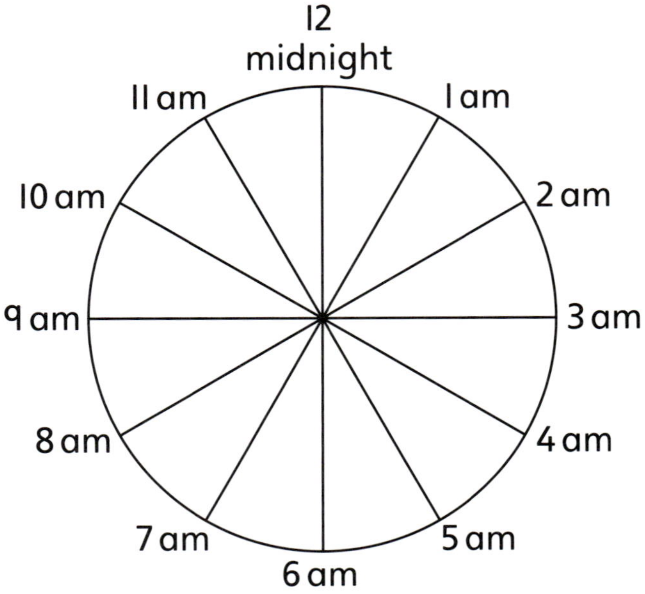

Key

asleep ☐

at school ☐

eating ☐

playing ☐

______________________ ☐

______________________ ☐

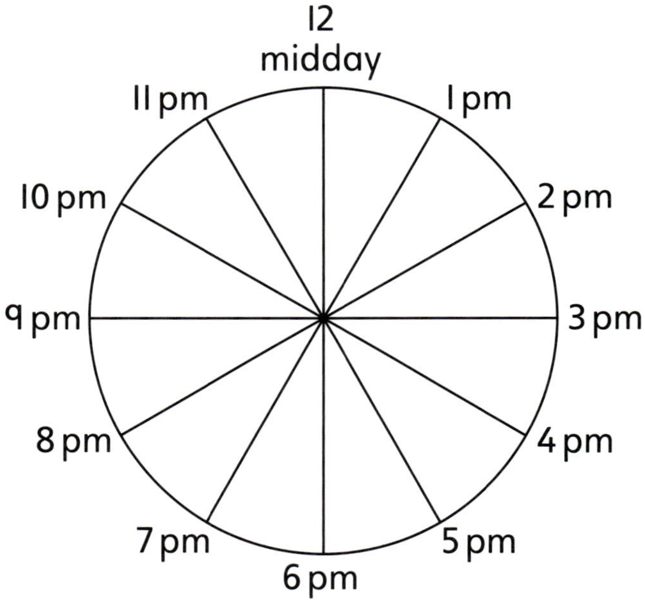

Units of time game 1

minutes	days
hours	seconds
months	weeks

Units of time game 2

January	February	April
June	August	September
November	December	Sunday
Monday	Wednesday	Friday
Saturday	school holidays	sleep
watch a DVD	lunch time	walk to school
assembly	have a shower	sing a song
make toast	yawn	brush your teeth
sneeze	clap	blink

Pass it on! 1

Pass it on! 2

Word problems 1

1 Grandma is planting bulbs ready for spring. She has a sack of 50 daffodil bulbs. She plants 3 bulbs in a pot by the front door, 6 in her window box, and 4 under the tree.

How many bulbs are left in the sack? ________________

Number sentence: ______________________________

2 After two weeks Grandma decides to plant some more bulbs. When she opens the sack, 1 bulb has been eaten by slugs and 2 have gone mouldy, so she throws these away.

How many bulbs are left in the sack? ________________

Number sentence: ______________________________

3 Freda and James arrive to visit Grandma. They offer to help with the planting. They plant 10 bulbs each.

How many bulbs are left in the sack? ________________

Number sentence: ______________________________

4 Grandma is so pleased with Freda and James that she says: "Thank you for helping me. Please take 6 bulbs each to plant in your garden."

How many bulbs are left in the sack? ________________

Number sentence: ______________________________

Word problems 2

Make up a story to explain what these number sentences might mean.

$45 - 7 = 38$

$38 - 14 = 24$

$24 - 17 = 7$

Last can!

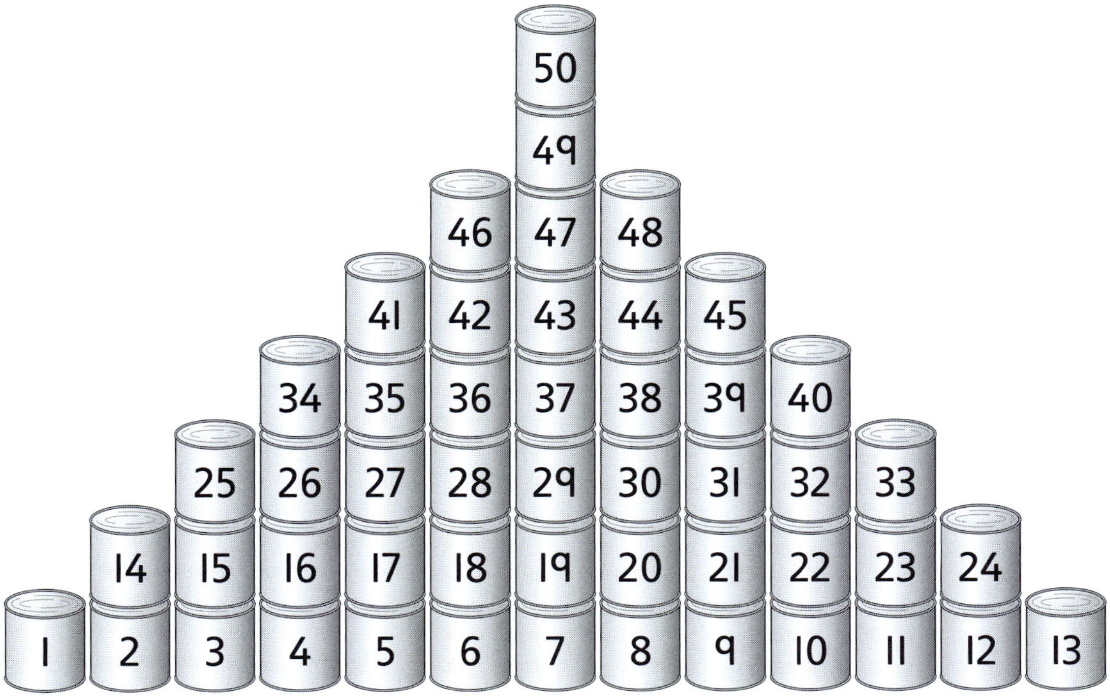

There are 50 cans in the stack.

Choose a number between 1 and 5. 3

'Knock down' this number of cans.
(Cross them out.)

Write a number sentence to match. 50 − 3 = 47

Take turns until there are no cans left.

The winner is the player who knocks down the last can!

How can you make it more likely that you will win?

Crocodile teeth

Function machines

Make up your own function machines.
Put a number from 0 to 9 through each machine.
Try predicting the end numbers before you work them out.

start end

start end

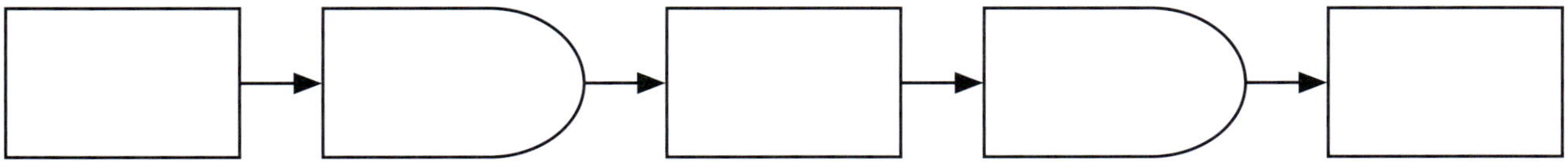

start end

start end

start end

Three in a row

Number cascades

Complete the number cascades.

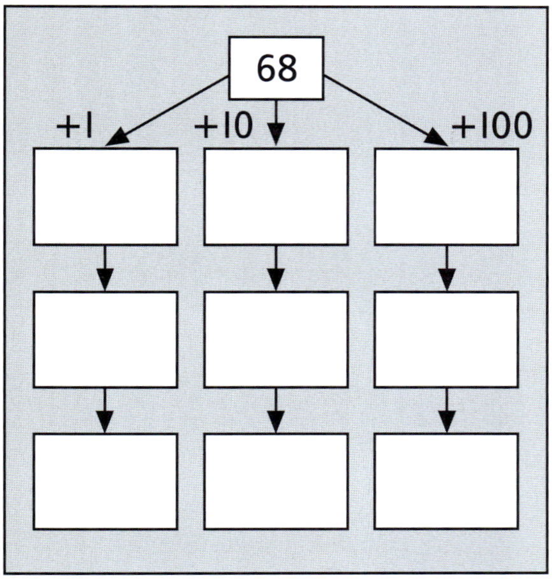

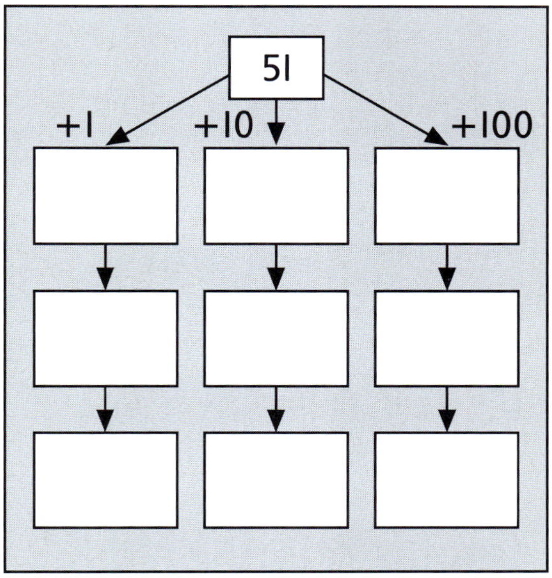

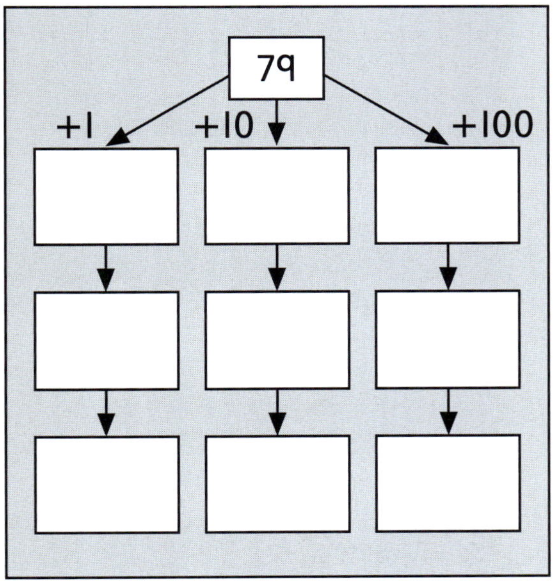

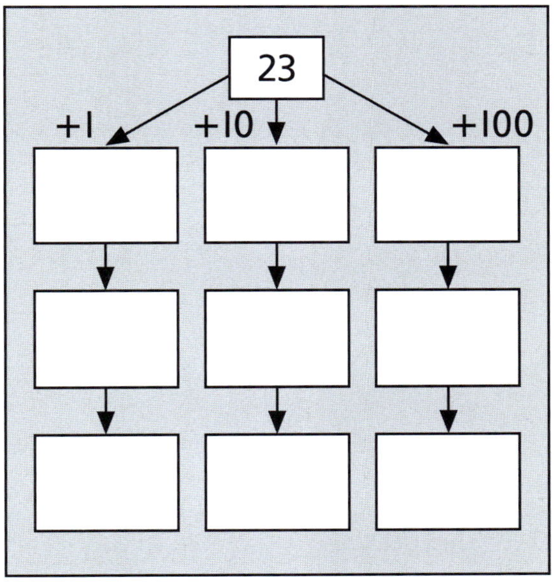

Draw your own number cascades, counting **back** in 1s, 10s and 100s. What numbers could you start from?

Walk the plank!

- Place both counters on Start.
- Take a domino from the bag.
- Add the two numbers.
- If the total is even, move one place up.
- If the total is odd, move one place down.
- Take turns to play.
- If you fall off the end of the plank, you are out!

Play again.

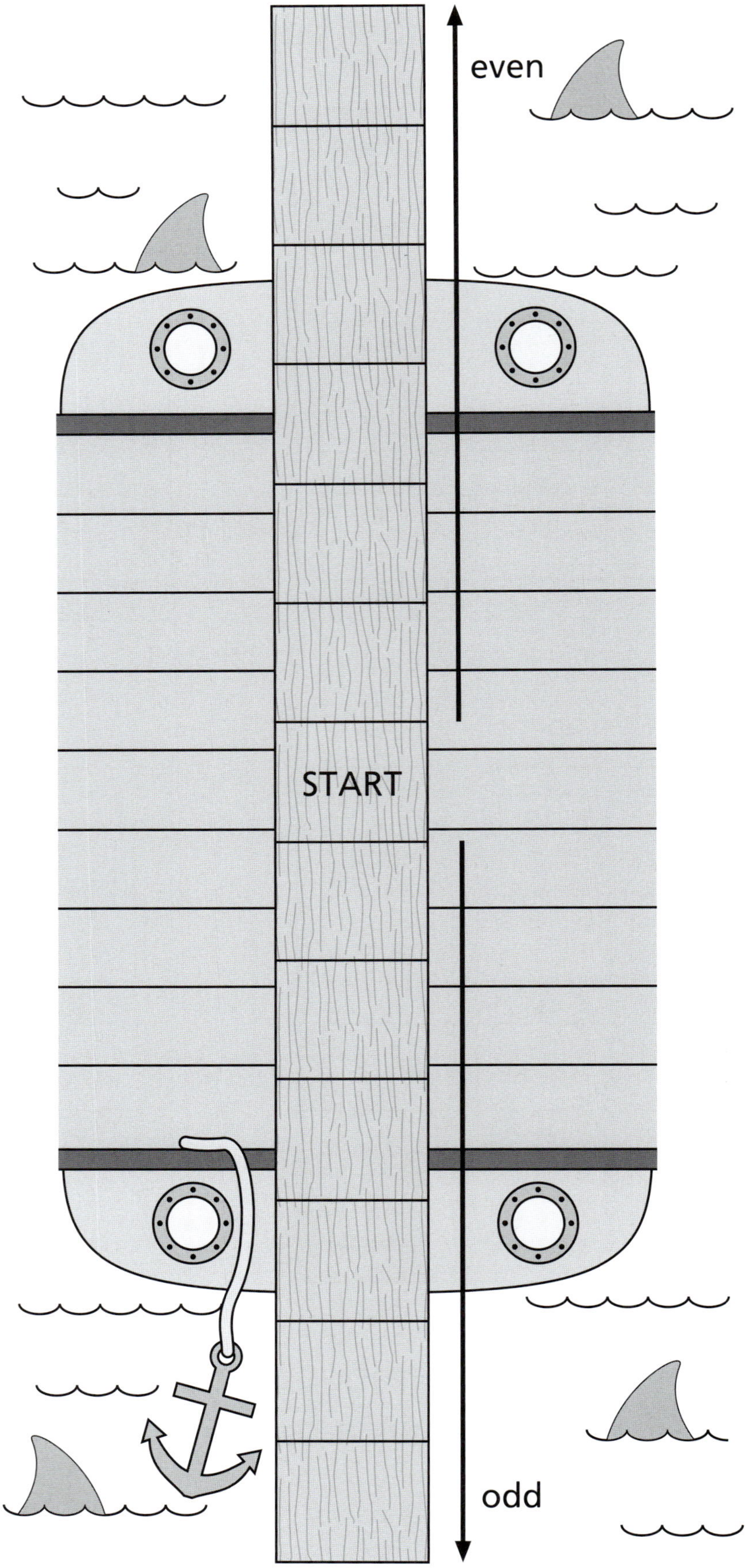

Do you usually walk off the same end of the plank? Which one? Is this what you would expect?

Number puzzles 1

Solve these number puzzles.

1	2	3	4	5	6	7	8	9	10
11	12	13	14	15	16	17	18	19	20
21	22	23	24	25	26	27	28	29	30
31	32	33	34	35	36	37	38	39	40
41	42	43	44	45	46	47	48	49	50
51	52	53	54	55	56	57	58	59	60
61	62	63	64	65	66	67	68	69	70
71	72	73	74	75	76	77	78	79	80
81	82	83	84	85	86	87	88	89	90
91	92	93	94	95	96	97	98	99	100

Which number am I?

I am less than 80.

I am more than 40.

I am not even.

My units digit is 5.

My digits add up to 12.

Which number am I?

I am > 10.

I am < 50.

I am not odd.

Neither of my digits is a 4.

My digits add up to 7.

1	2	3	4	5	6	7	8	9	10
11	12	13	14	15	16	17	18	19	20
21	22	23	24	25	26	27	28	29	30
31	32	33	34	35	36	37	38	39	40
41	42	43	44	45	46	47	48	49	50
51	52	53	54	55	56	57	58	59	60
61	62	63	64	65	66	67	68	69	70
71	72	73	74	75	76	77	78	79	80
81	82	83	84	85	86	87	88	89	90
91	92	93	94	95	96	97	98	99	100

Number puzzles 2

Write your own number puzzles.

1	2	3	4	5	6	7	8	9	10
11	12	13	14	15	16	17	18	19	20
21	22	23	24	25	26	27	28	29	30
31	32	33	34	35	36	37	38	39	40
41	42	43	44	45	46	47	48	49	50
51	52	53	54	55	56	57	58	59	60
61	62	63	64	65	66	67	68	69	70
71	72	73	74	75	76	77	78	79	80
81	82	83	84	85	86	87	88	89	90
91	92	93	94	95	96	97	98	99	100

1	2	3	4	5	6	7	8	9	10
11	12	13	14	15	16	17	18	19	20
21	22	23	24	25	26	27	28	29	30
31	32	33	34	35	36	37	38	39	40
41	42	43	44	45	46	47	48	49	50
51	52	53	54	55	56	57	58	59	60
61	62	63	64	65	66	67	68	69	70
71	72	73	74	75	76	77	78	79	80
81	82	83	84	85	86	87	88	89	90
91	92	93	94	95	96	97	98	99	100

Building monsters

Work with a partner.

Take turns to throw two dice and find the total.

You can 'buy' body parts for your monster using your total.

1 finger = **2**	1 head = **10**
1 body = **7**	1 arm = **5**
1 toe = **1**	1 hand = **4**
1 leg = **6**	1 foot = **3**

My Monster

Draw each body part as you buy it.
Write your score and what you bought in the table.

	My score	What I bought
1		
2		
3		
4		
5		

Making squares

Choose three numbers in a line from the grid. Find their total.

Ask your partner to check your answer.

If your partner agrees you are correct, you can colour those three squares.

Now it is your partner's turn.

2	6	4	4	4	2	0	1	2
9	3	3	3	7	9	9	9	3
4	7	4	1	8	0	8	2	4
8	1	5	5	5	1	7	8	5
2	1	5	7	6	9	6	4	6
1	2	1	8	4	7	5	6	7
4	6	4	6	6	3	8	2	8
6	4	6	7	3	7	3	9	9
4	6	4	3	7	3	4	2	10

Keep taking turns.

Your aim is to create a square with three numbers on each side, like this.

3	3	7
4	1	8
5	5	5

So on your next turn, you may want to colour in another side of the square.

Watch out – your partner may try to stop you!

Darts

Your aim is to end up with a score as close as possible to 23.

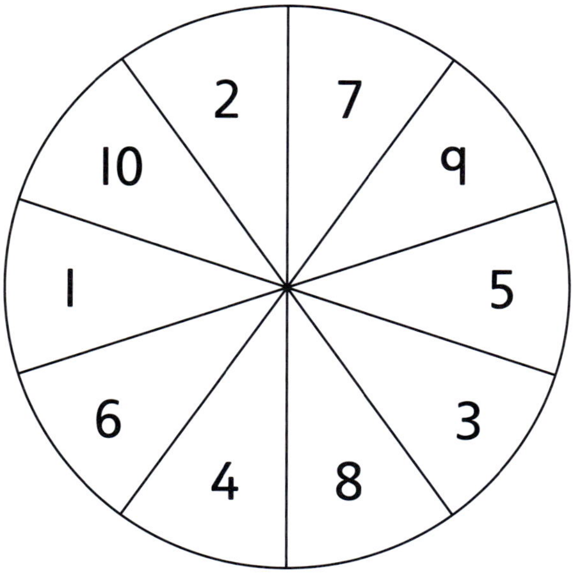

Player 1	Player 2
0	0

- You have three darts (counters).
- On each turn, choose three numbers to throw your darts at (put your counters on the numbers).
- Choose whether to add or subtract each number from your total.
- You both start with a total of 0.
- Have four turns each.
- At the end of each turn, record your new total in the table.
- Who is closest to 23 at the end?

Choose a different target number and play again.

Ice-skating

clockwise	clockwise	clockwise
anticlockwise	anticlockwise	anticlockwise
whole turn	whole turn	whole turn
half turn	half turn	half turn
quarter turn	quarter turn	quarter turn
right angle	right angle	right angle

How heavy?

Colour the best estimate for the weight of each item.

40 kg | 40 g | 400 g

250 kg | 250 g | 25 g

300 g | 30 g | 3 kg

20 kg | 200 g | 200 kg

5 g | 500 g | 5 kg

25 g | 250 g | 25 kg

More or less?

Draw three products. For each product write its labelled weight and its actual weight. Find the differences.

	Labelled weight	Difference
	Actual weight	More or less?
	Labelled weight	Difference
	Actual weight	More or less?
	Labelled weight	Difference
	Actual weight	More or less?

Which product has the biggest weight difference?

Why do you think that might be?

Changing times

Work out the new times and show them on both clocks.

Two hours later than seven o'clock

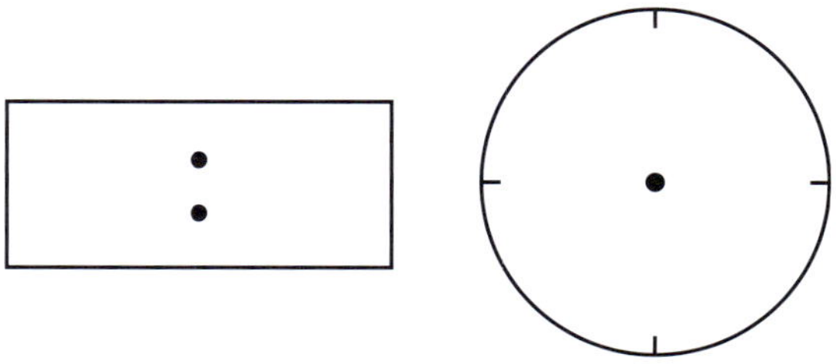

Three hours earlier than half past eight

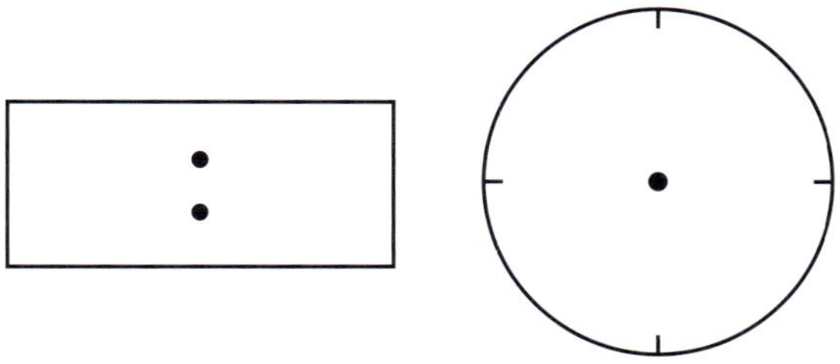

Four and a half hours later than two o'clock

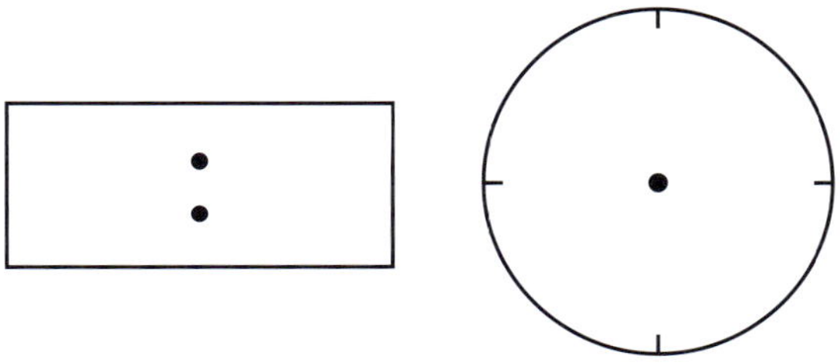

Two and a half hours later than five o'clock

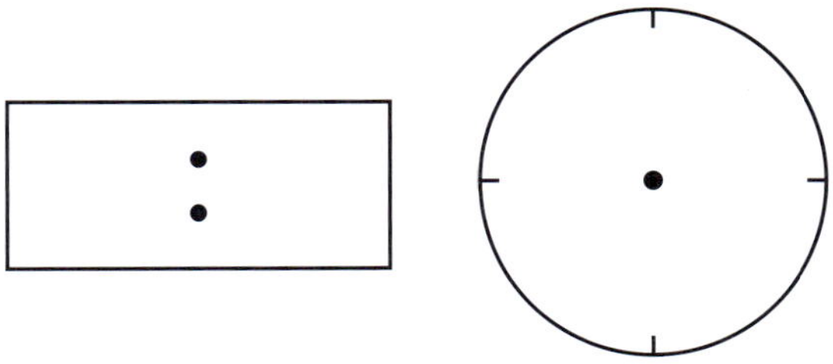

One and a half hours earlier than half past nine

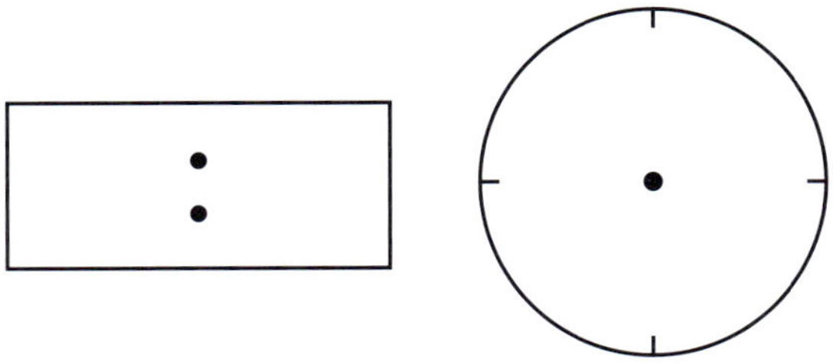

Six and a half hours later than half past three

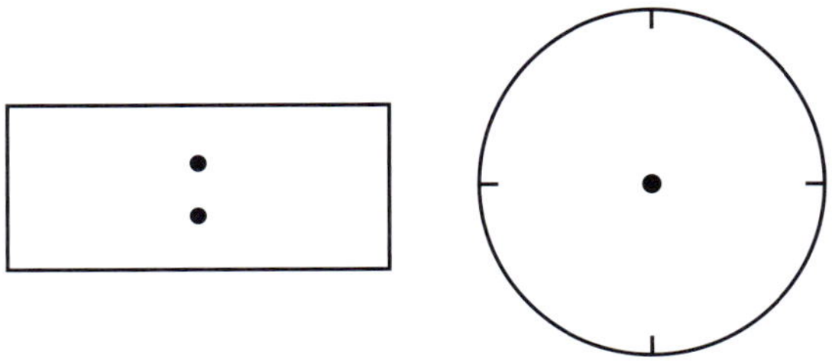

Names in our class

Number of letters in Class ______ first names

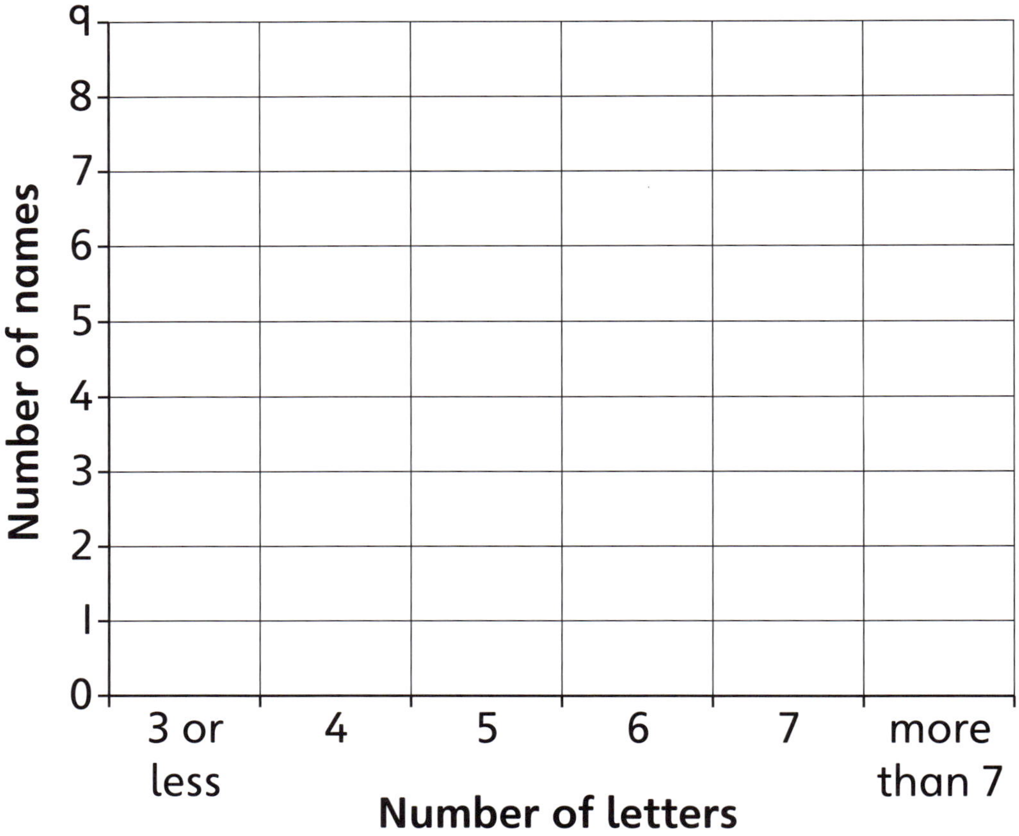

1 How many names have 7 letters? ____________

2 What number of letters is most common? ____________

3 How many children in the class altogether? ____________

4 What is the total number of letters in each column?

5 What is the total number of letters in everyone's names? ____________

In my basket

I went shopping and bought one

________ .

Here is the basket with one ________ in it.

Thank you for the ________ .

I would like to add one ________ .

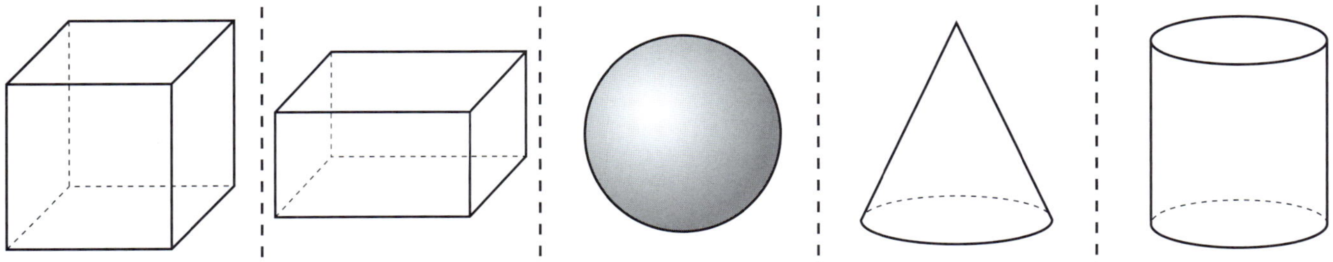

cube	cuboid	sphere	cone	cylinder

The shape sorter

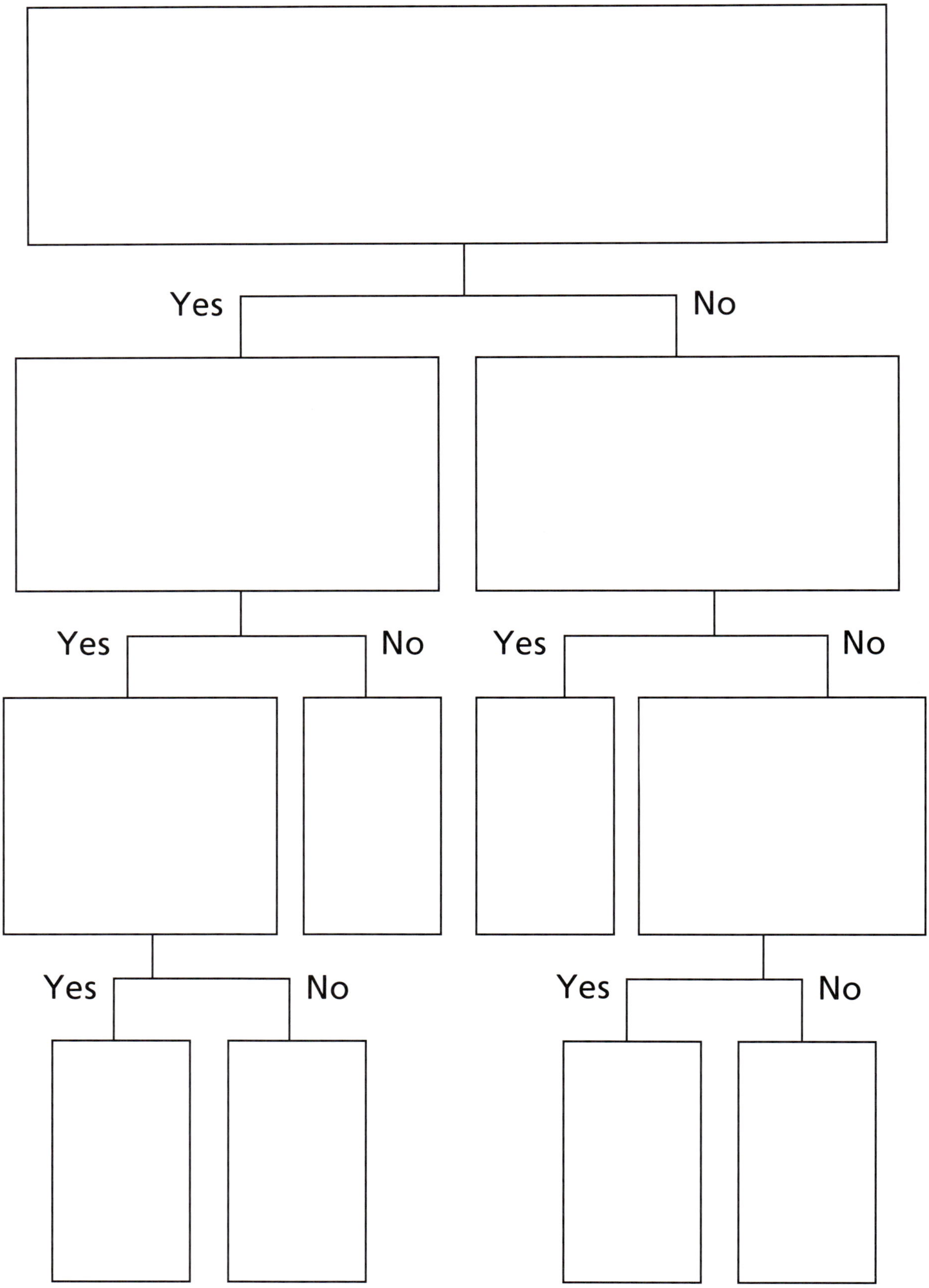

Egg boxes

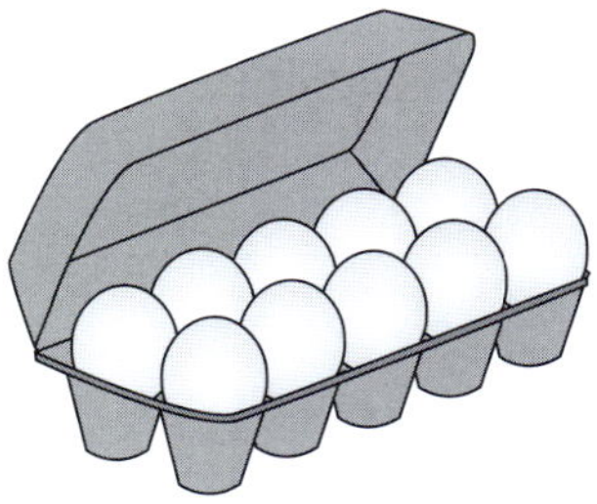

Mr Phipps collects 83 eggs from his chickens on Monday.
The supermarket wants to buy 70 eggs.
Mr Phipps only sells boxes of 10 eggs.

1 How many boxes will the supermarket need? ___________

2 How many eggs will Mr Phipps have left? ___________
Use these egg boxes to help you answer the questions.

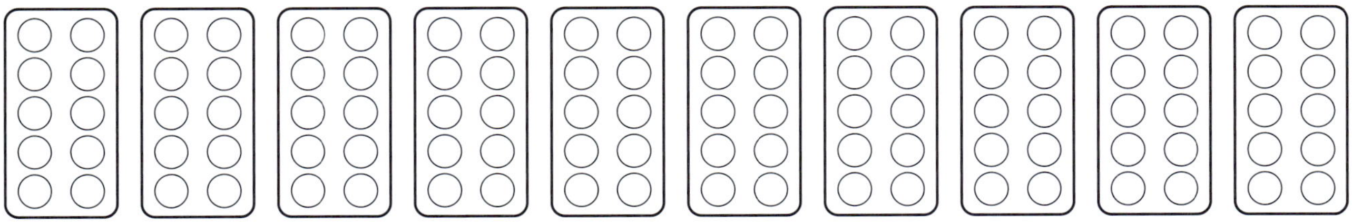

3 Show how you worked it out on the number line.

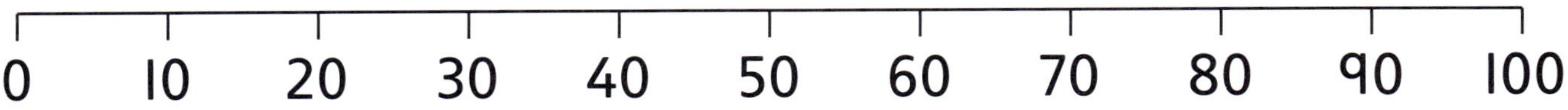

These are the numbers of eggs Mr Phipps collects one week:

Monday	Tuesday	Wednesday	Thursday	Friday
87 eggs	63 eggs	52 eggs	35 eggs	91 eggs

The supermarket has ordered another 250 eggs to be delivered on Friday afternoon.

4 Has Mr Phipps got enough eggs to complete that order? How do you know? Discuss your answer with a partner.

Question swap 1

Mrs Patil is a teacher.
She wrote some number sentences on the board.
By mistake she wrote the answers on the board too!

Check to see if the answers are right. Explain how you know.

		✓ or ✗	How do you know?
1	43 + 19 = 62		
2	65 − 21 = 47		
3	88 − 19 = 69		
4	94 + 21 = 113		

Question swap 2

1 Write a number in the first box of each number sentence.

Workings

☐ + 21 = ☐

☐ − 21 = ☐

Make this number sentence the easiest you can think of.

☐ + 19 = ☐

Make this number sentence the hardest you can think of.

☐ − 19 = ☐

2 Give your sheet to a partner. They must find the answers to your number sentences without writing anything down! You must do their writing for them.

3 What makes some number sentences harder than others?

___

Exploring multiples

1	2	3	4	5	6	7	8	9	10
11	12	13	14	15	16	17	18	19	20
21	22	23	24	25	26	27	28	29	30
31	32	33	34	35	36	37	38	39	40
41	42	43	44	45	46	47	48	49	50

Multiplication race

- Take turns to choose a number on the grid.
- Say a multiplication fact in the 2, 5 or 10 times table which has your number as the answer.
- Your partner checks the fact on a calculator.
- If you are correct, colour in the number.
- The winner is the first person to make a path in their colour from one side of the grid to the other.

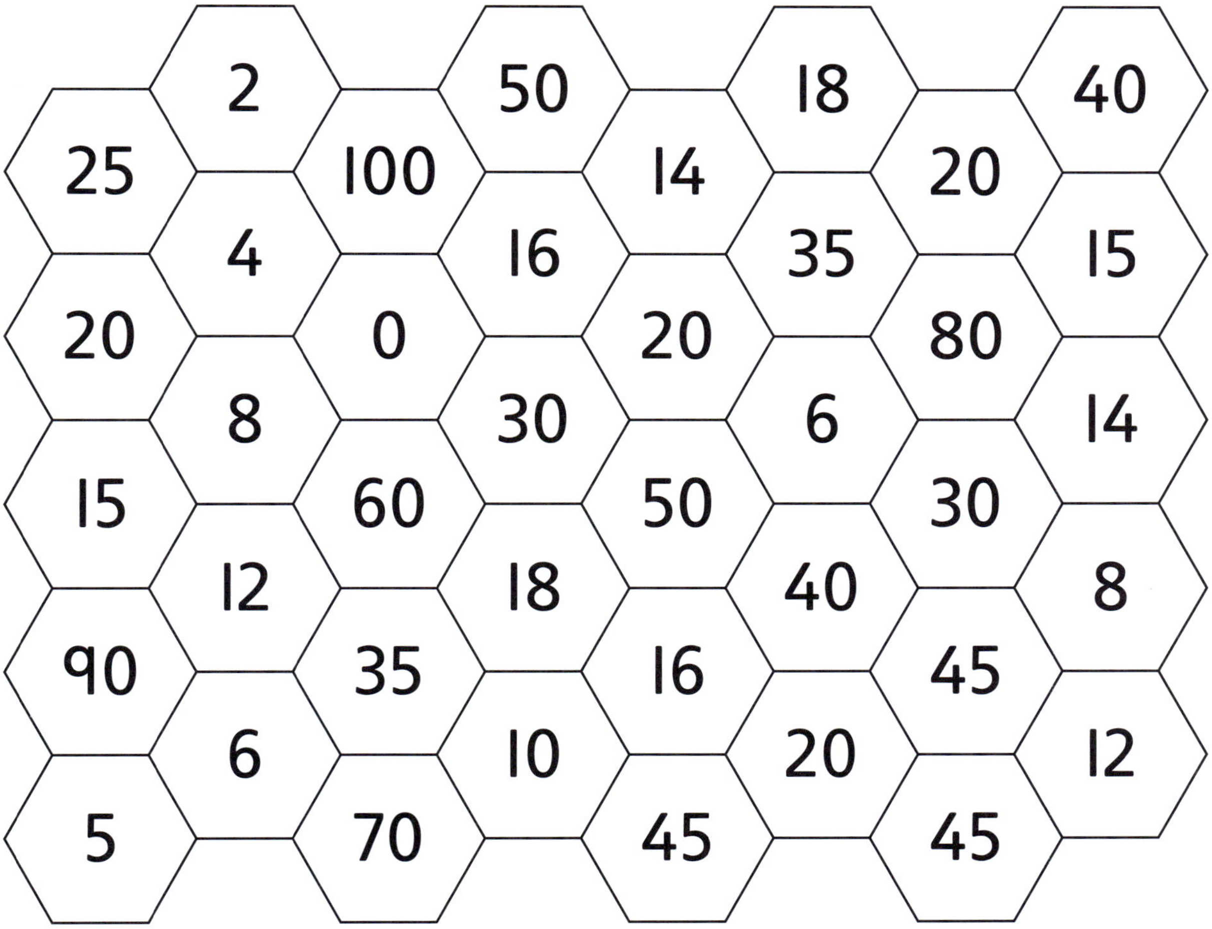

Multiplication monsters I

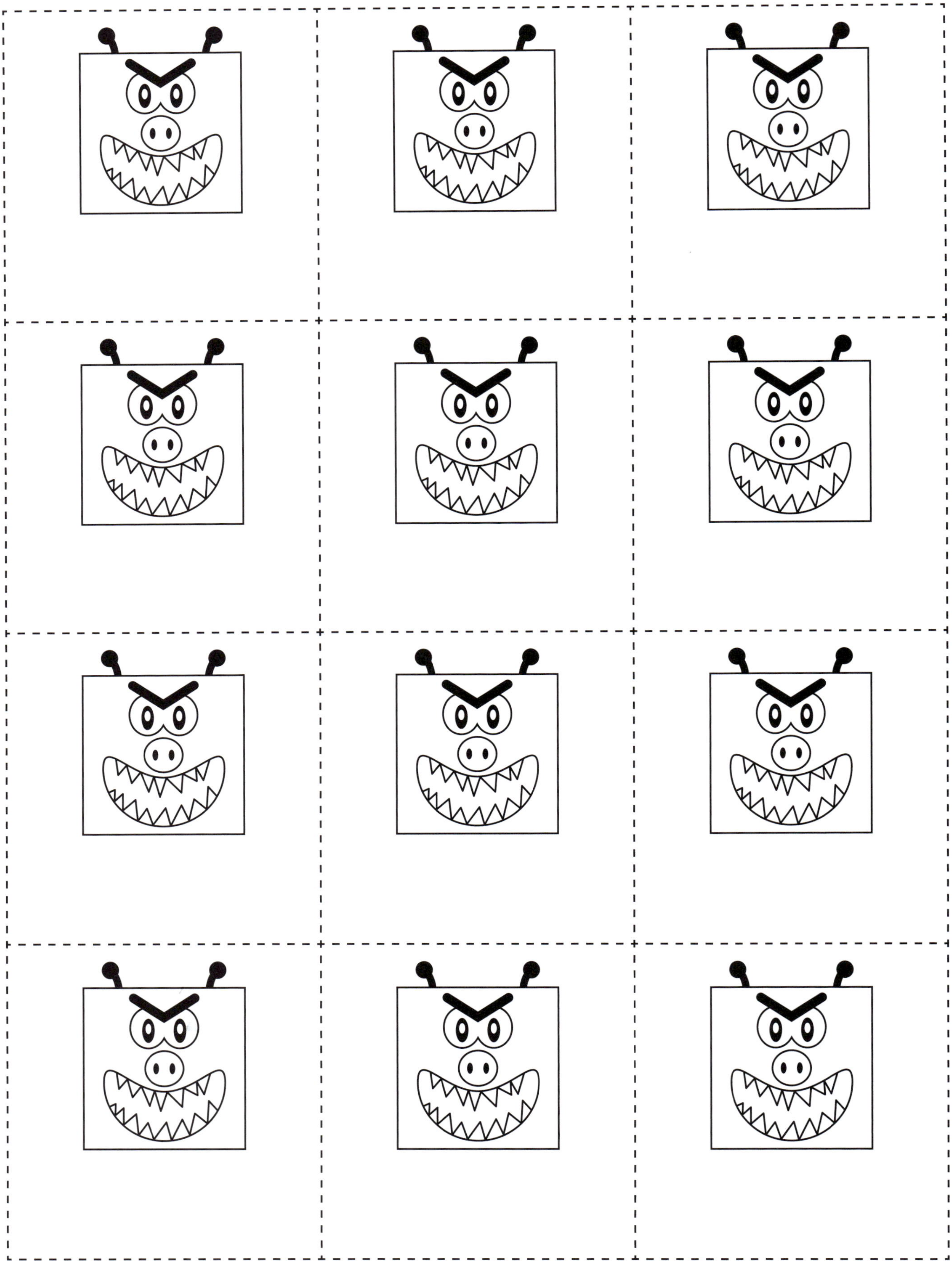

Multiplication monsters 2

Remainder game

2	3	4	5
2	3	4	5
2	3	4	5
13	14	15	16
17	18	19	20
21	22	23	24

HTU game

Player 1

hundreds	tens	units

Player 2

hundreds	tens	units

What is the smallest number you could make?

____

What is the highest number you could make?

____

Number chains

Write all 32 numbers in order, to make one long chain.

What is the largest number in your chain?

What is the smallest?

5 up, 50 up

Write each number to the nearest 10 or the nearest 100.

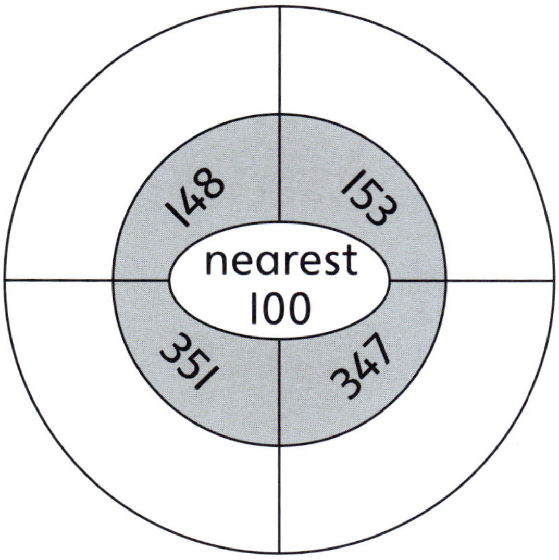

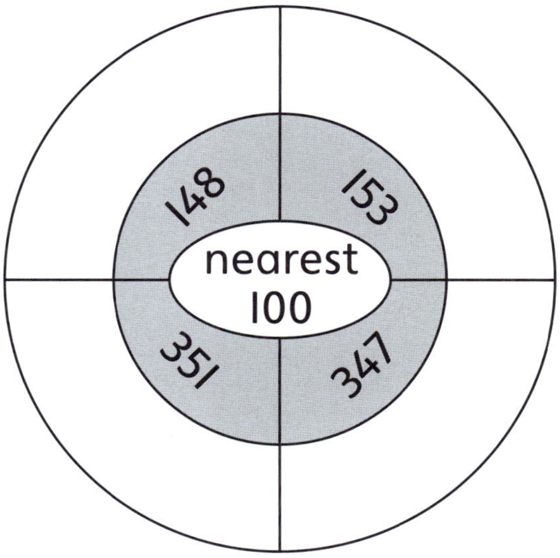

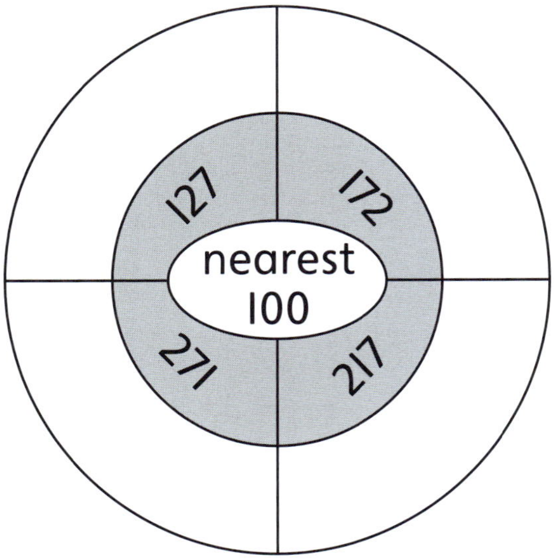

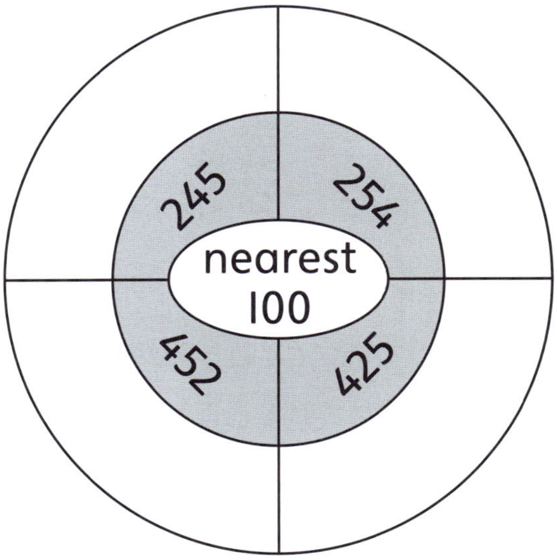

Difference

- Shuffle digit cards 3–9. Place them face down.
- Turn over the top card. This is your difference card.
- Turn over the other seven cards. Choose four cards to make two 2-digit numbers with the given difference.

For example:

7	3	–	6	9	=	4

How many correct number sentences can you make with your chosen difference? Record your working here.

Shuffle the cards and pick a new difference card.
Find as many correct number sentences as you can.

Carpet tiles 1

On each square carpet tile there is one of these shapes.

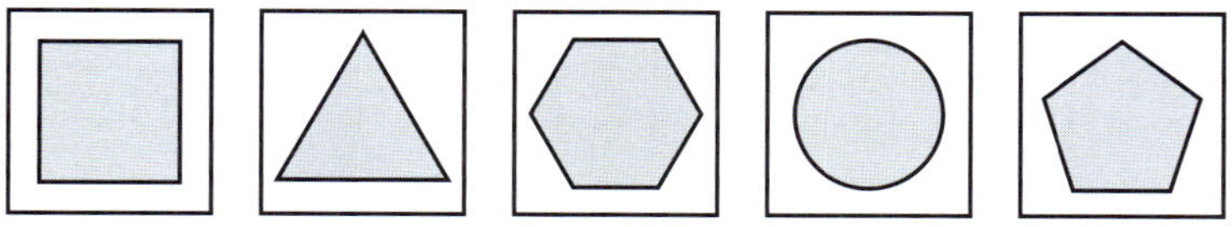

There are five different carpet tiles and five of each tile.

They need to fit into this square space and each shape can only appear once in each row and each column.

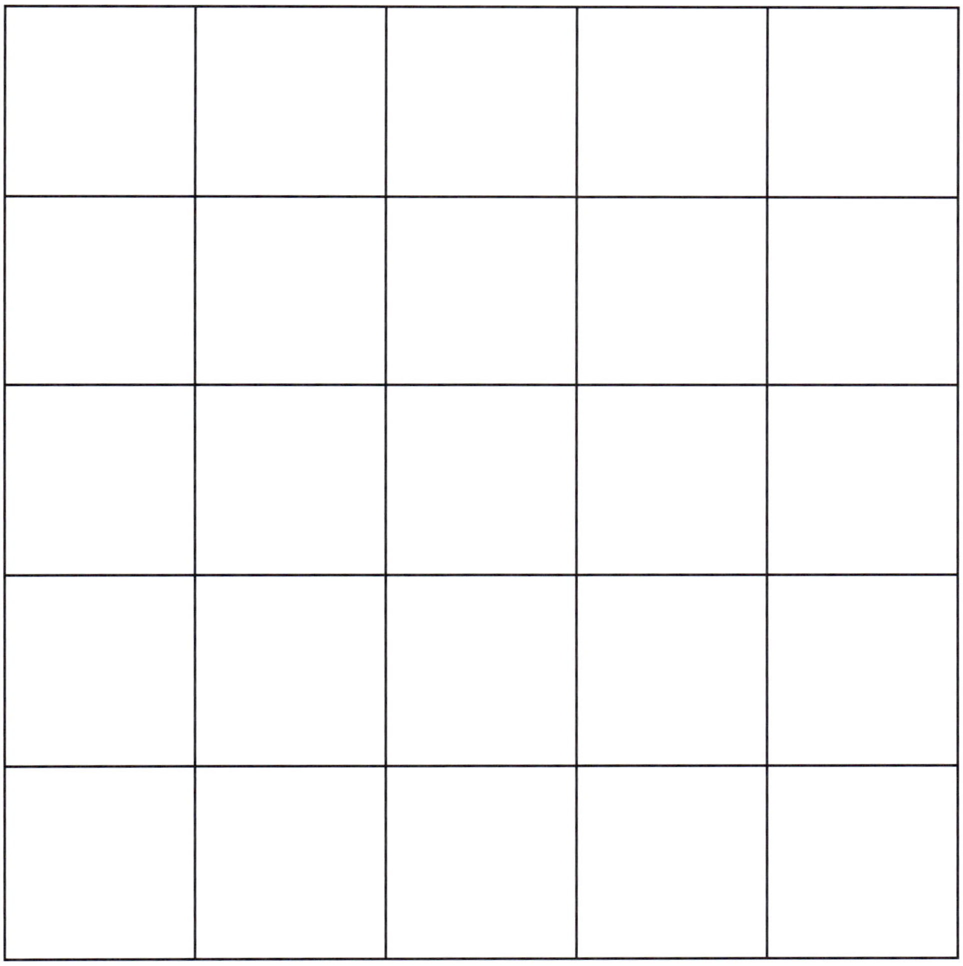

Describe your pattern to your partner, using the names of the shapes. Can they copy it from your description?

Colour your design. Describe the colour pattern to your partner. Is it the same as the shape pattern?

Carpet tiles 2

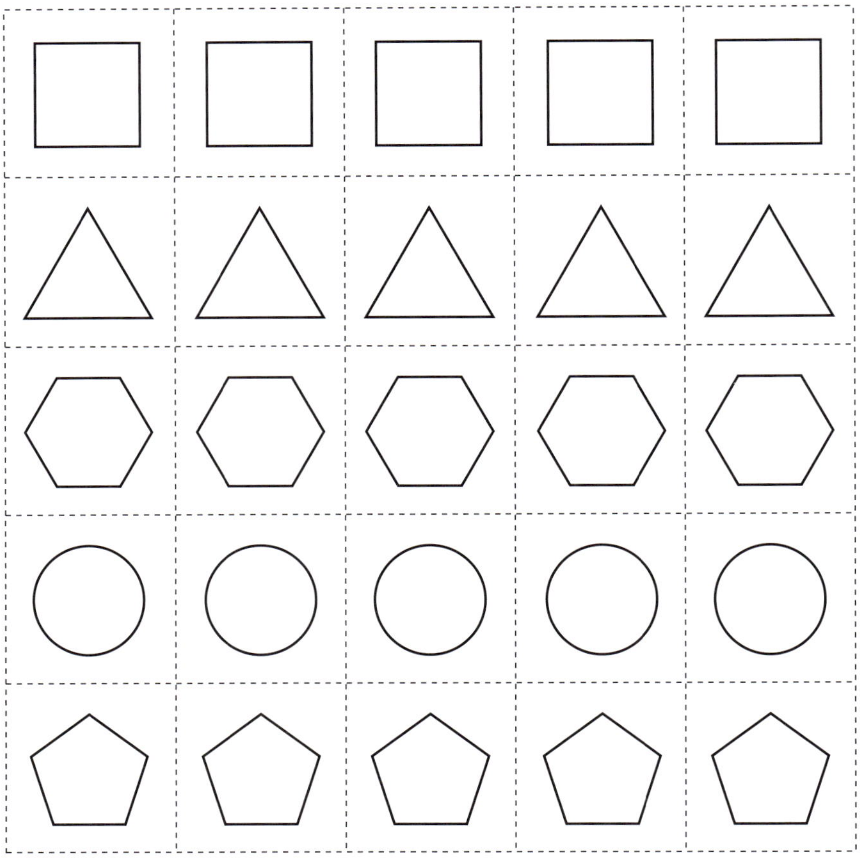

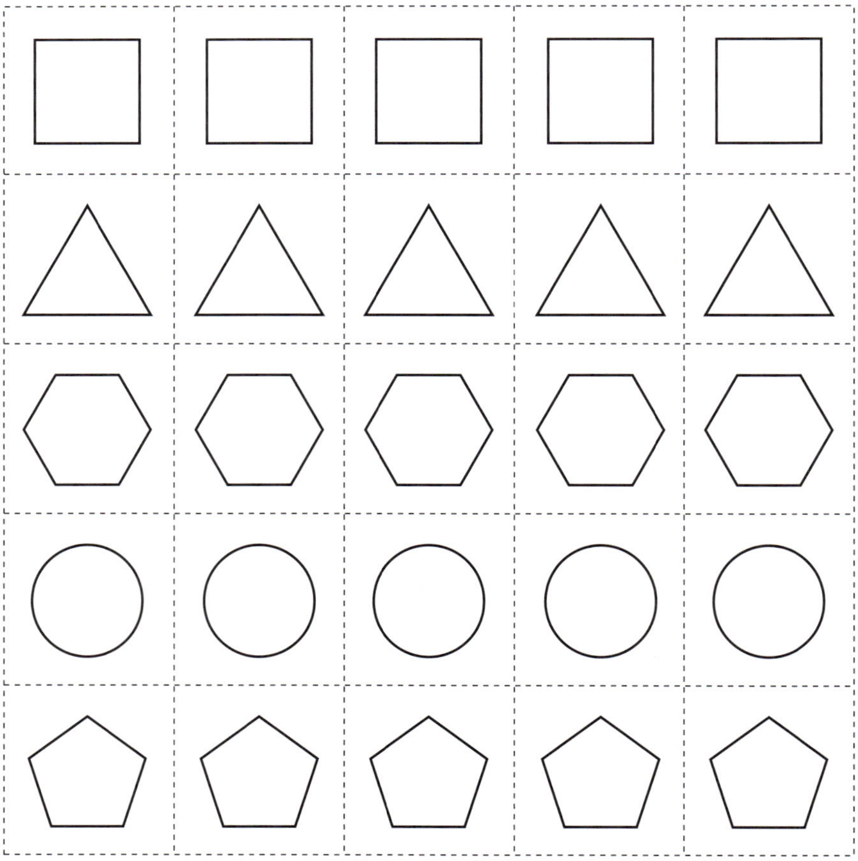

Spokes and wheels 1

Each spoke on this wheel has a total of 20.

Fill in the missing numbers.

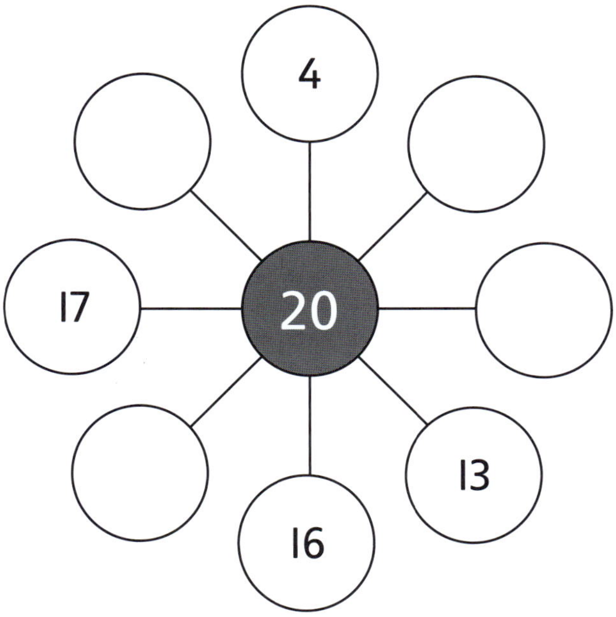

Add up the outside numbers.

What is the total for this wheel?

Is there a quick way to work it out? What is it?

Spokes and wheels 2

Fill in the missing numbers on this wheel.

You cannot use a number more than once.

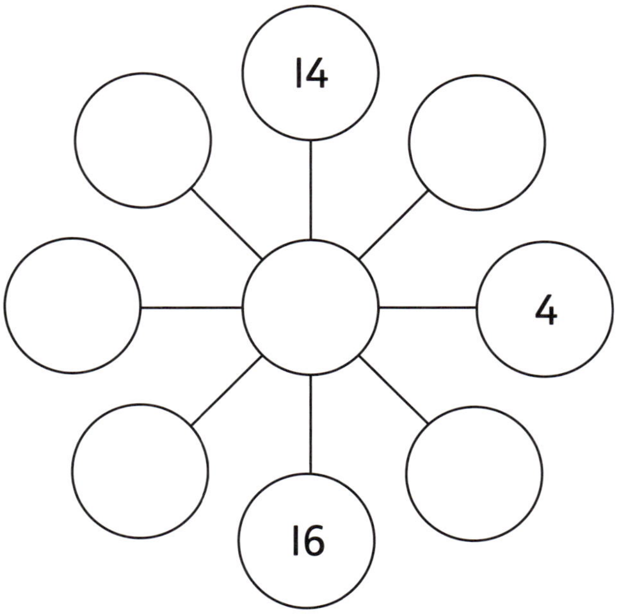

What is the middle number?

____

What is the total of all the outside numbers

____

For this wheel, the total of all the outside numbers is 40.

What is the middle number?

____

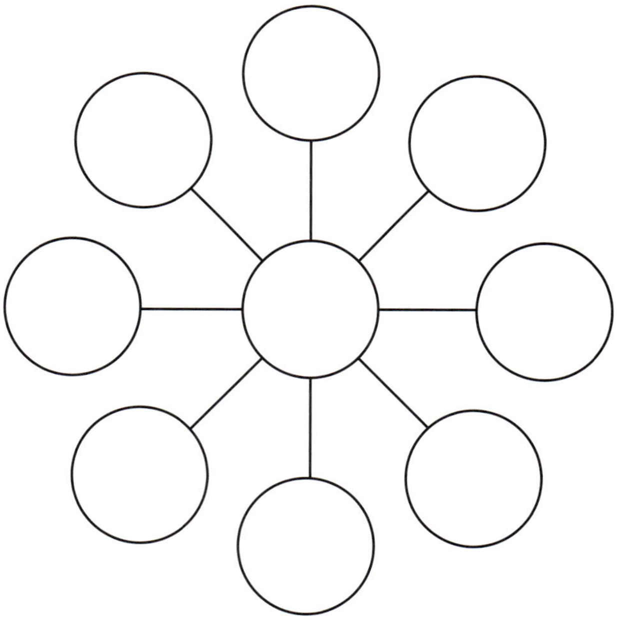

Litre line

Look at a range of products.

How much does each product contain?

Mark and label each product in the correct place on the litre line.

How many litres have you marked on the line altogether?

____

Fruit cocktail cards

50 ml of orange juice	50 ml of cranberry juice
50 ml of pineapple juice	50 ml of apple juice
50 ml of peach juice	100 ml of grape juice
100 ml of mango juice	100 ml of cherry juice
100 ml of lemon juice	100 ml of grapefruit juice
100 ml grapefruit juice	100 ml lemon juice
100 ml cherry juice	200 ml of mango juice
200 ml of grape juice	250 ml of peach juice
250 ml of apple juice	250 ml pineapple juice
250 ml of cranberry juice	250 ml of orange juice

Fruit cocktail jug

Take turns to pick a fruit juice card.

Add the correct amount of juice to your jug.

The first person to have exactly 1 litre of juice in their jug is the winner.

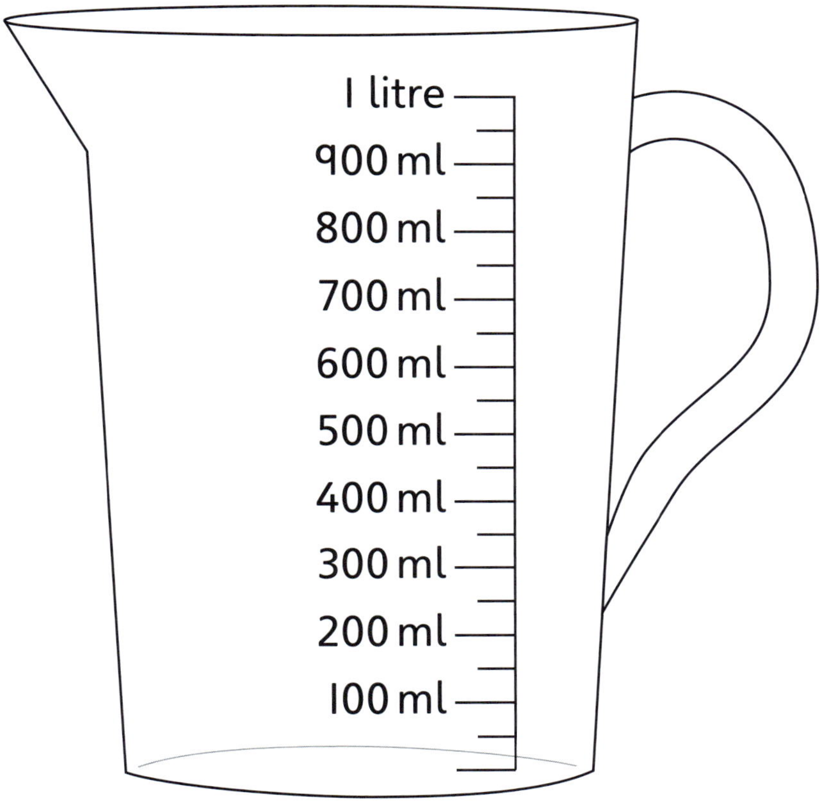

Write your own recipe for a litre of fruit cocktail.

Use at least three different fruit juices.

Digit tree

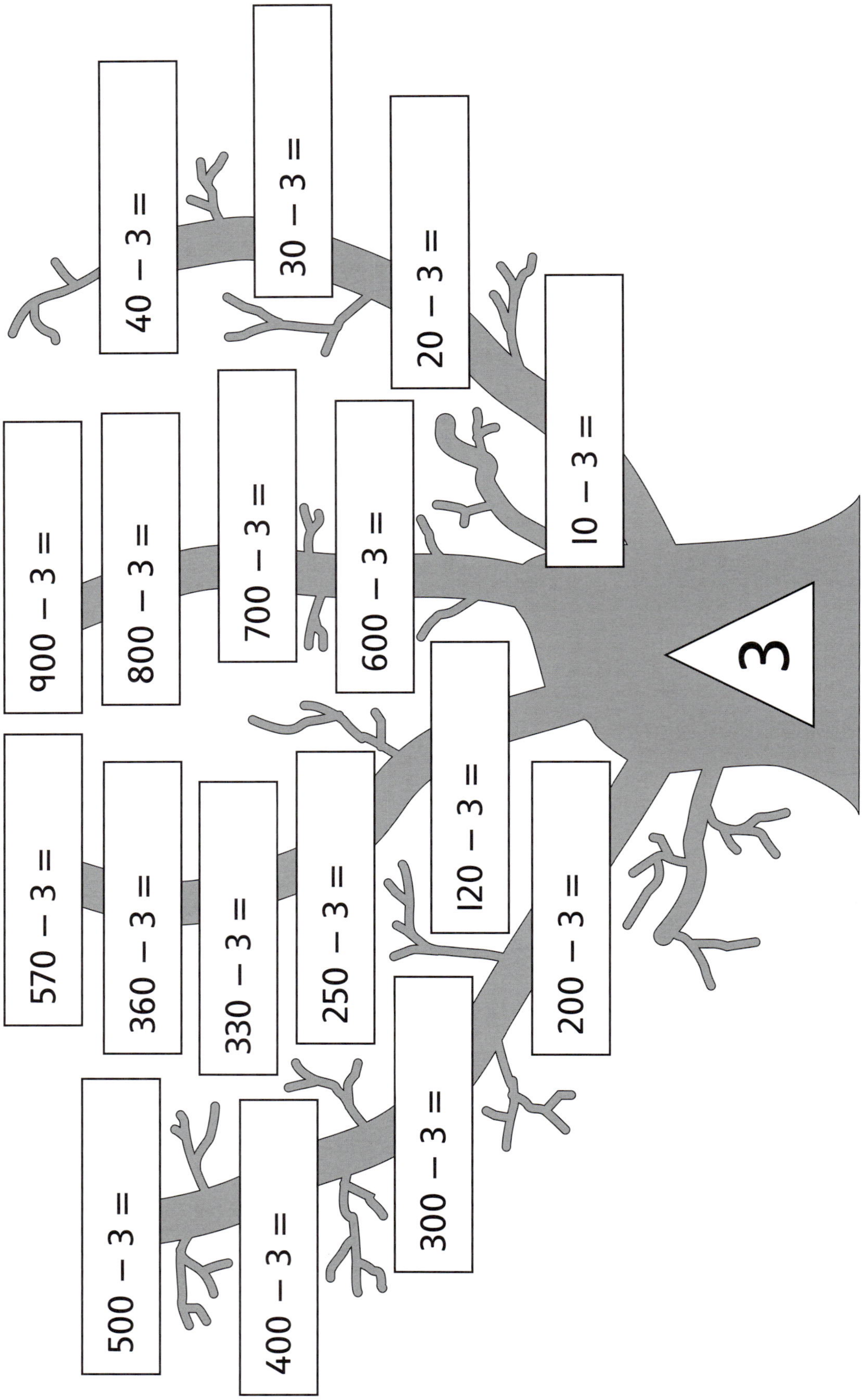
3
10 – 3 =
20 – 3 =
30 – 3 =
40 – 3 =
600 – 3 =
700 – 3 =
800 – 3 =
900 – 3 =
120 – 3 =
250 – 3 =
330 – 3 =
360 – 3 =
570 – 3 =
200 – 3 =
300 – 3 =
400 – 3 =
500 – 3 =

Raffle ticket table

Complete the table for the tickets on Textbook page 36.

	Odd	Even	Multiple of 10	> 99	All even digits	Two digits	Three digits
264		✓		✓	✓		✓

The cruise I

Passenger bookings

Pick-up point	Number of passengers
Port	56
Splash Island	10
Palm Island	12
Flower Island	8
Parrot Island	6

Passenger logs

How many passengers did you have at each point?

	Blue ship
Port	56
Splash Island	
Palm Island	
Flower Island	
Parrot Island	
Port	

	Red ship
Port	56
Parrot Island	
Flower Island	
Palm Island	
Splash Island	
Port	

The cruise 2

Passenger bookings

Pick-up point	Number of passengers boarding	Number of passengers getting off
Port	87	0
Splash Island	2	13
Palm Island	10	22
Flower Island	3	14
Parrot Island	9	28

Passenger logs

How many passengers did you have at each point?

	Blue ship
Port	87
Splash Island	
Palm Island	
Flower Island	
Parrot Island	
Port	

	Red ship
Port	87
Parrot Island	
Flower Island	
Palm Island	
Splash Island	
Port	

Misprints

The printer has broken and some of the numbers are missing! Fill in the missing numbers.

1 95 − ___ = 25

2 ___ + 13 = 72

3 85 − ___ = 26

4 54 + 37 = ___

Working

Some of these digits are hidden by ink splodges. Each splodge is hiding one digit. Write in the missing digits.

5 1___ + 9 = ___3

6 2___ − ___ = 14

7 Is there more than one way to complete these number sentences?

____

____

8 On another sheet of paper, make up your own missing-digit number sentences and give them to your partner. Can they work them out?

It's ready!

I want to cook popcorn. The packet says to cook the popcorn for 32 seconds.

My microwave is set to 39 seconds.

The timer has a + button and a – button to add or subtract 1 second.

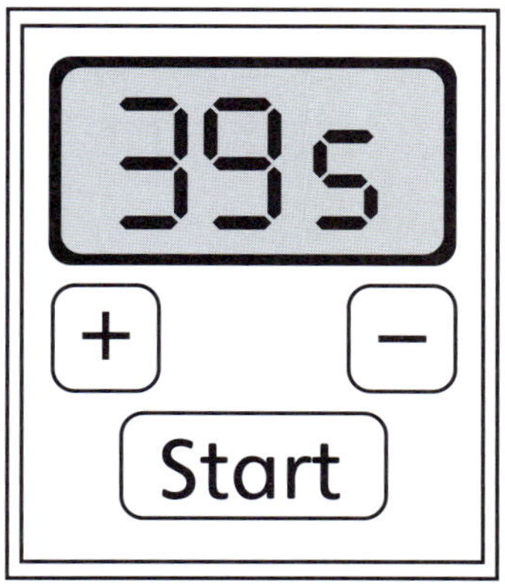

1 How do I change the time to cook my popcorn for 32 seconds?

____

2 Write down what you did as a number sentence.

☐ – ☐ = ☐

The popcorn is not ready so I put it in for 1 more minute.

3 How many seconds has the popcorn cooked for?

____

These are instructions for cooking carrots in a microwave:

- Cook for 1 minute.
- Leave to stand for 90 seconds.
- Cook for $1\frac{1}{2}$ minutes. Serve.

4 How long are the vegetables cooked for?

____

5 On another sheet of paper, make up some cooking instructions for 22 + 5 + 3 = 30.

Waiting for hours

1 I arrive at the bus stop in time to catch the 7 o'clock bus to school.

Leaving	Arriving
07:00	07:30

But the bus is late.

When it arrives I look at my watch.

2 What time will I get to school?

____

3 How long did I wait for the bus?

____

4 Show the sequence of events on this timeline.

Make your own sand timer. Choose a plastic bottle and fill it with dry sand. Turn it upside down and count how long it takes for all the sand to come out. Test different plastic bottles and see how long they take to empty. Which one takes the longest time? The shortest time?

The clock shop

Multiplying then dividing

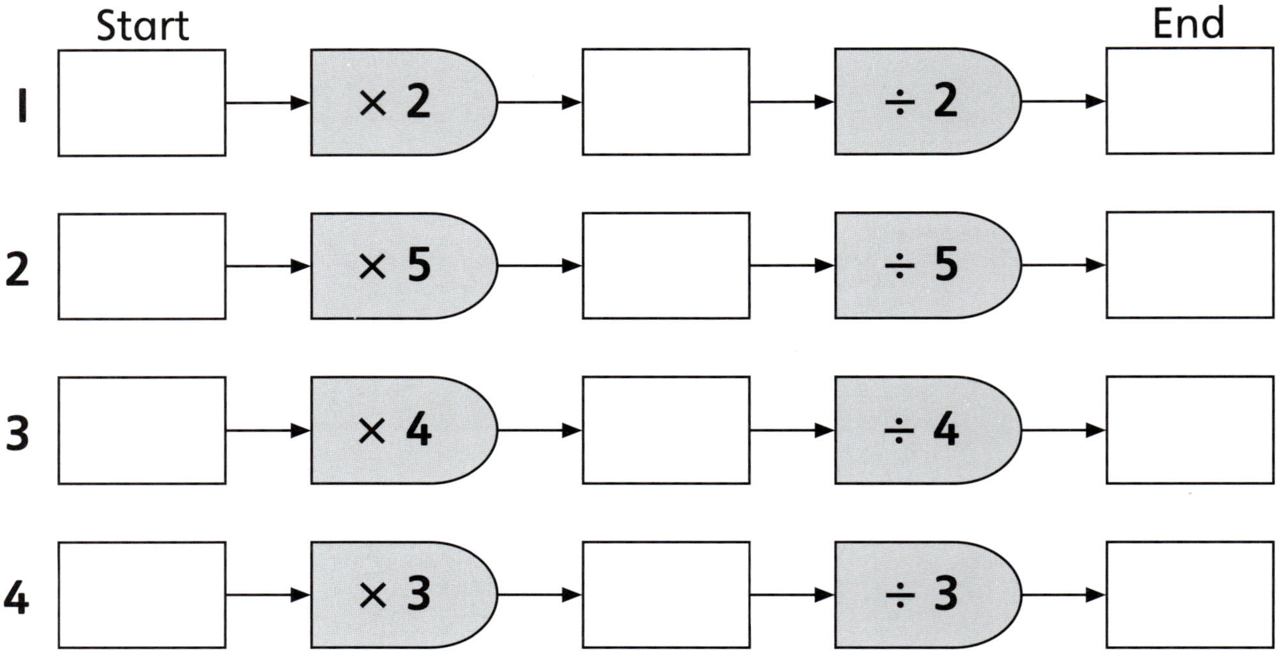

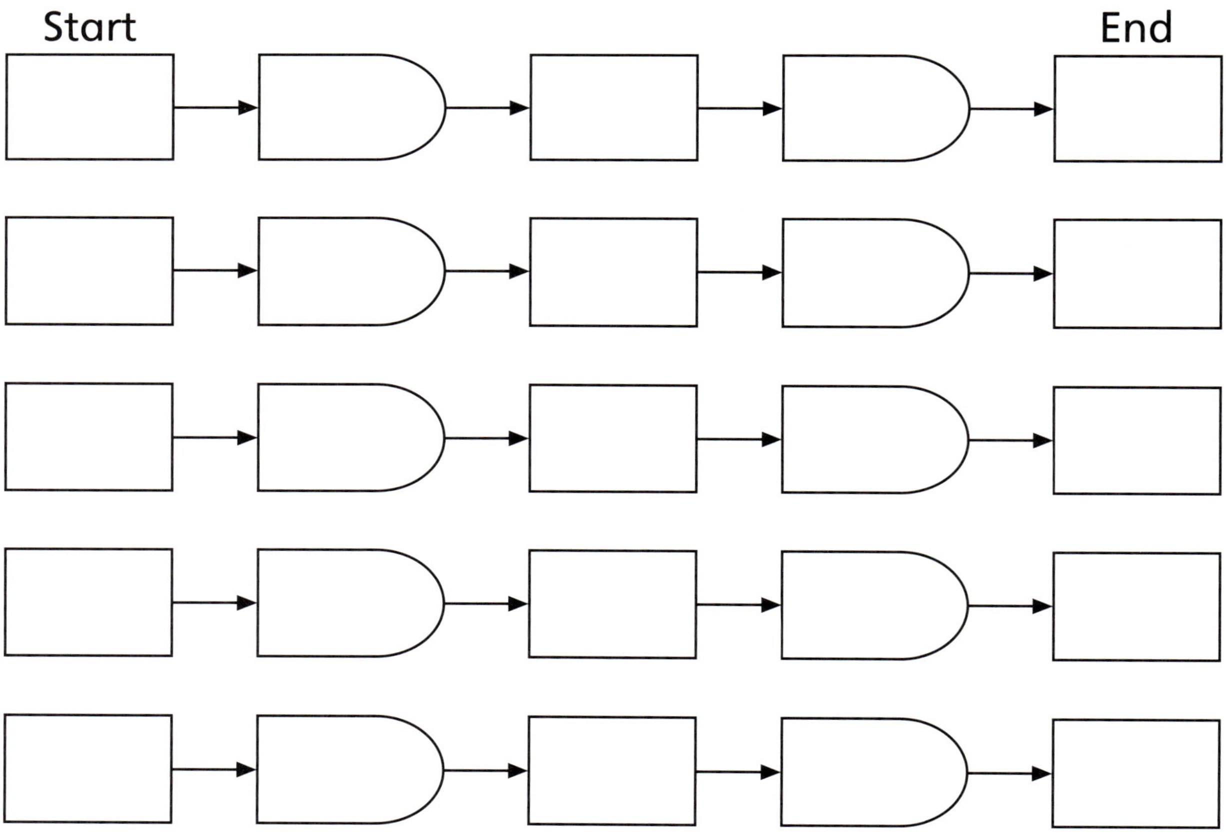

Multiplication and division arrays

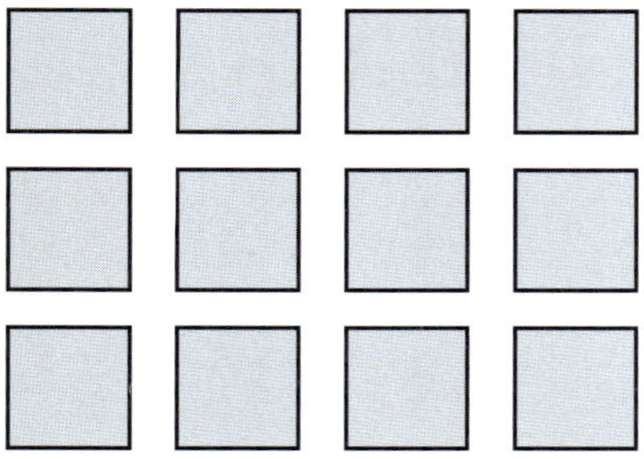

These 12 squares have been arranged into a 3 by 4 array.

There are 3 rows of 4 squares.

$$4 + 4 + 4 = 12$$
$$3 \times 4 = 12$$
$$12 \div 4 = 3$$

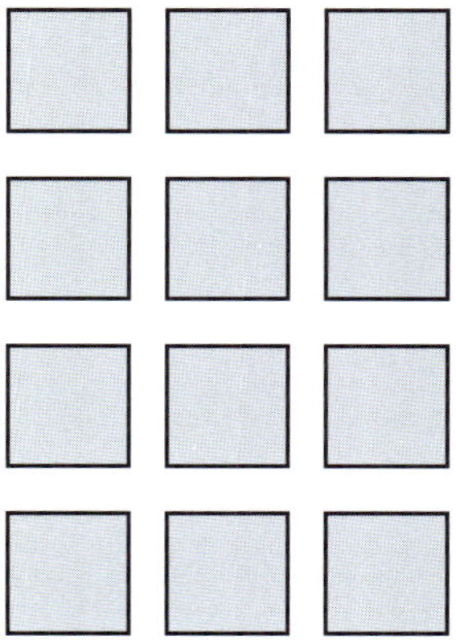

These 12 squares have been arranged into a 4 by 3 array.

There are 4 rows of 3 squares.

$$3 + 3 + 3 + 3 = 12$$
$$4 \times 3 = 12$$
$$12 \div 3 = 4$$

For each of these numbers, draw two arrays with that many squares.

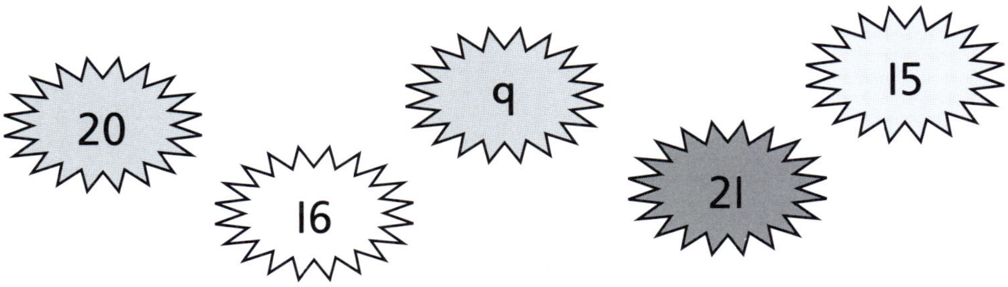

Write as many number sentences as you can to describe each array.

Shape fractions I

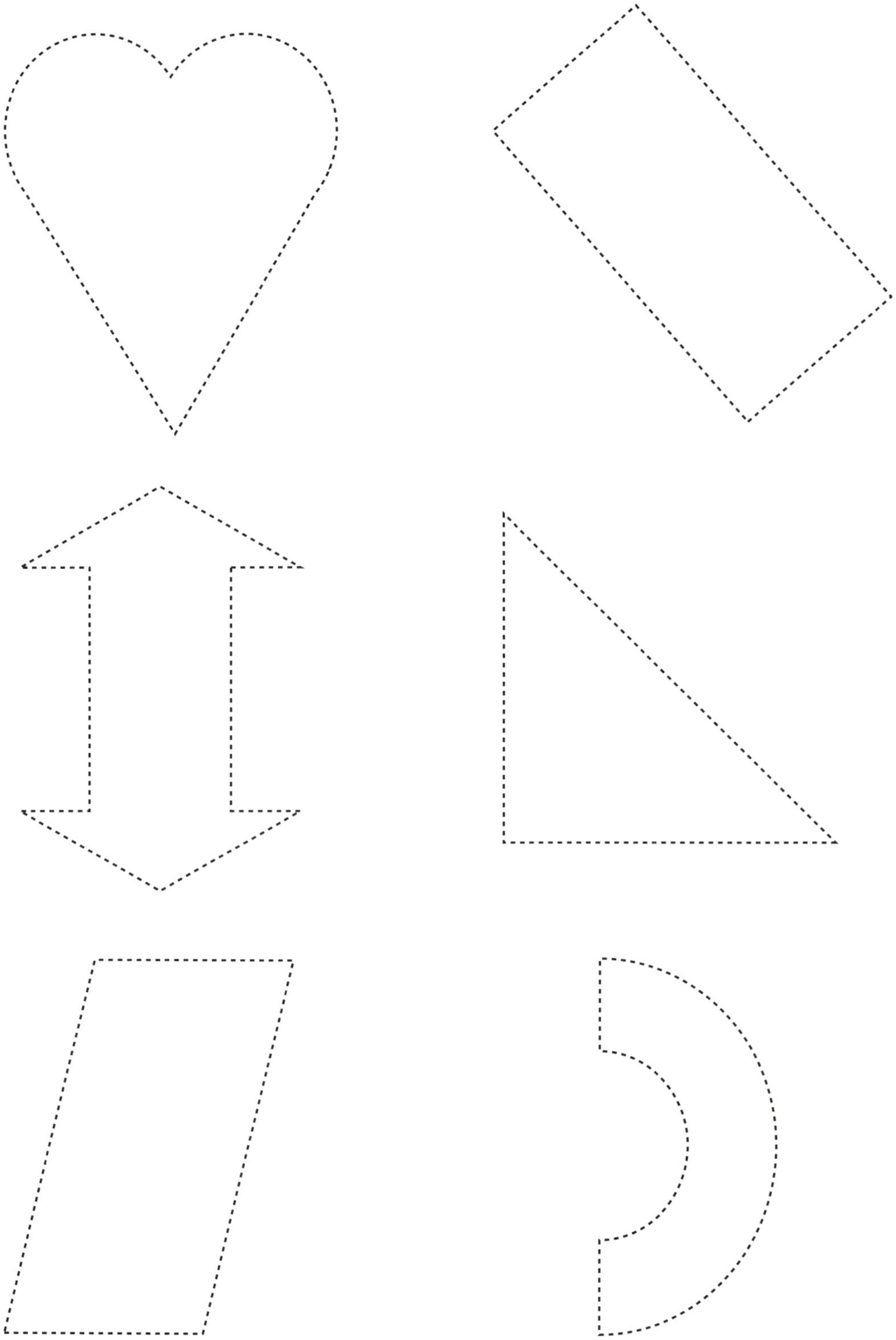

Shape fractions 2

Chomp the chocolate: spinner

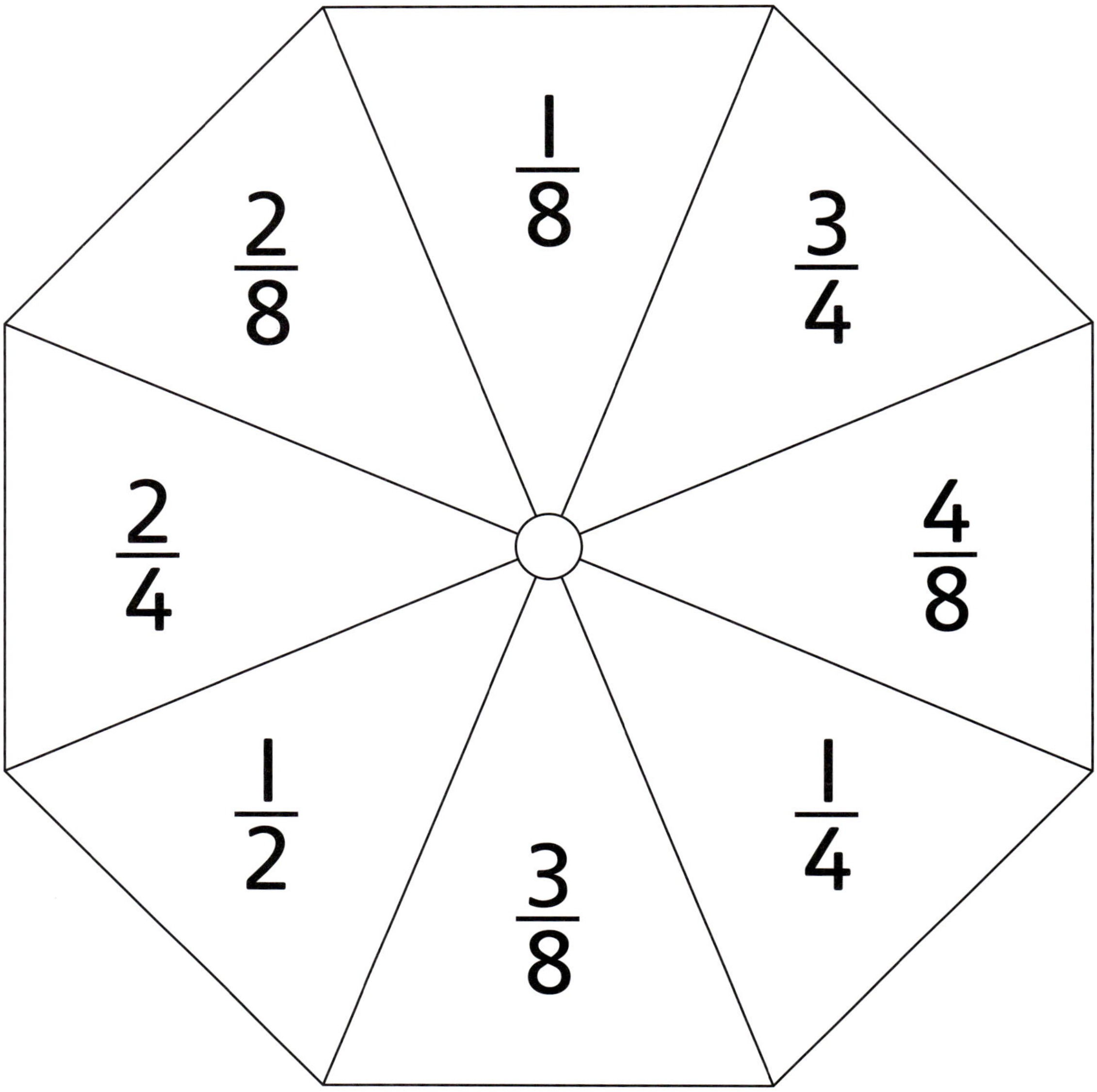

Chomp the chocolate: game boards

Ginn

Part of Pearson

Ginn is an imprint of Pearson Education Limited, a company incorporated in England and Wales, having its registered office at Edinburgh Gate, Harlow, Essex, CM20 2JE. Registered company number: 872828

www.pearsonschools.co.uk

Ginn is a registered trademark of Pearson Education Limited

First published 2009

13 12
10 9 8 7 6 5

British Library Cataloguing in Publication Data
A catalogue record for this book is available from the British Library

ISBN 978 0 602 57806 0

Typeset by Tech-Set Ltd, Gateshead
Cover photo/illustration © Per José Karlén
Printed in Britain by Ashford Colour Press

Acknowledgements
Every effort has been made to contact copyright holders of material reproduced in this book. Any omissions will be rectified in subsequent printings if notice is given to the publishers.

Authors

Gill Potter is an independent consultant with an international reputation for her research into empowering gifted and talented pupils online. She is a CAME (Cognitive Acceleration in Mathematics Education) tutor, and an experienced primary practitioner, specialising in developing thinking skills through mathematics.

Cherri Moseley is a teacher and mathematics subject leader at a primary school in Norwich. In her 'spare' time she is an author and independent consultant. She is actively involved with the Mathematical Association and the National Centre for Excellence in Teaching Mathematics.

Jane McNeill has worked in primary education since 1989. In addition to extensive experience as a class teacher and senior manager, she has supported numerous schools in developing their mathematics teaching and learning as a numeracy consultant. Currently working as a freelance mathematics consultant, Jane has been involved in writing many primary mathematics resources.